END TIMES

END TIMES

Elites, Counter-Elites,

and the Path of

Political Disintegration

PETER TURCHIN

PENGUIN PRESS

NEW YORK

2023

PENGUIN PRESS
An imprint of Penguin Random House LLC
penguinrandomhouse.com

LIBRARY OF CONGRESS CATALOGING-IN-PUBLICATION DATA
Names: Turchin, Peter, 1957– author.
Title: End times : elites, counter-elites, and the path of political disintegration / Peter Turchin.
Description: New York : Penguin Press, 2023. | Includes bibliographical references and index.
Identifiers: LCCN 2022044451 (print) | LCCN 2022044452 (ebook) |
ISBN 9780593490501 (hardcover) | ISBN 9780593490518 (ebook)
Subjects: LCSH: Political stability—United States. | Elite (Social sciences)—
Political activity—United States. | United States—Politics and government. |
United States—History. | Interdisciplinary approach in education.
Classification: LCC JK1726 .T87 2023 (print) | LCC JK1726 (ebook) |
DDC 320.01/10973—dc23/eng/20230307
LC record available at https://lccn.loc.gov/2022044451
LC ebook record available at https://lccn.loc.gov/2022044452

Printed in the United States of America
1st Printing

Book design by Daniel Lagin

CONTENTS

Part III
CRISIS AND AFTERMATH

APPENDIX

PREFACE

History is not "just one damn thing after another,"[1] British historian Arnold Toynbee once quipped in response to a critic. For a long time, Toynbee's opinion was in the minority. Historians and philosophers, including famous ones like Karl Popper, vehemently insisted that a science of history was impossible. Our societies are too complex, humans are too mercurial, scientific progress cannot be predicted, and culture is too variable in space and time. Kosovo is completely different from Vietnam, and antebellum America can tell us nothing about the America of the 2020s. This has been, and still largely is, the majority view. I hope that this book will convince you that this view is wrong. A science of history is not only possible but also useful: it helps us anticipate how the collective choices we make in the present can bring us a better future.

I began my academic career in the 1980s as an ecologist; I made my living studying the population dynamics of beetles, butterflies, mice, and deer. This was the time when animal ecology was revolutionized by the rapid growth in the processing power of computers. I had never been allergic to mathematics, so I embraced the turn of the field to complexity science, which mixes computer modeling with Big Data analytics to answer such questions as, for example, why many animal populations go through boom-and-bust cycles. By the late 1990s, however, I felt we'd answered most of the interesting questions I'd entered the field to work on. With some trepidation, I began to consider how the same complexity-science approach could be brought to the study of human societies, both in the past and today. A quarter of a century later, my colleagues in this endeavor and I have built out a flourishing field known as cliodynamics (from *Clio*, the name of the Greek mythological muse of history, and *dynamics*, the science of change). We discovered that there are important recurring patterns, which can be observed throughout the sweep of human history over the past ten thousand years. Remarkably, despite the myriad of differences, complex human societies, at base and on some abstract level, are organized according to the same general principles. For skeptics and those simply curious, I have included a more detailed general account of cliodynamics in an appendix at the end of this book.

From the beginning, my colleagues and I in this new field focused on cycles of political integration and disintegration, particularly on state formation and state collapse. This is the area where our field's findings are arguably the most robust—and arguably the most disturbing. It became clear to us through quantitative historical analysis that complex societies everywhere are affected by recurrent and, to a certain degree, predictable waves of political instability, brought about by the same basic set of forces, operating across the thousands of years of human history. It dawned on me some years ago that, assuming the pattern held, we were heading into the teeth of another storm. In 2010, the scientific journal *Nature* asked specialists from different fields to look ten years into the future, and I made this case in clear terms, positing that judging from the pattern of US history, we were due for another sharp instability spike by the early 2020s. Sadly, nothing about my model has been disproved in the intervening years. The book you're reading is my best effort to explain this model in accessible, which is to say nonmathematical, terms. It builds on an enormous amount of important work in a variety of different fields; I make no claims of radical originality. What I will say is that we should all take heart from the fact that societies have arrived at this same crossroads before, and though sometimes (even most of the time) the road has led to great loss of life and societal breakdown, sometimes it has led to a far happier resolution for most people involved.

What, then, is this model? To put it somewhat wonkily, when a state, such as the United States, has stagnating or declining real wages (wages in inflation-adjusted dollars), a growing gap between rich and poor, overproduction of young graduates with advanced degrees, declining public trust, and exploding public debt, these seemingly disparate social indicators are actually related to each other dynamically. Historically, such developments have served as leading indicators of looming political instability. In the United States, all of these factors started to take an ominous turn in the 1970s. The data pointed to the years around 2020 when the confluence of these trends was expected to trigger a spike in political instability. And here we are.

Certainly, there's little doubt that America is in crisis, though we fall out bitterly with each other when it comes to the explanation. Some people blame racists, white supremacists, and the rest of the "deplorables" who voted for Trump. Others blame antifa, the deep state, and "libtards." The truly paranoid fringes imagine that the agents of Communist China have penetrated the American government at all levels or, alternatively, see the invisible hand of Vladimir Putin jerking Trump's puppet strings. In the meantime, the deeper causes of our age of discord remain too little understood.

There are indeed "hidden forces" pushing America to the brink of civil war—and possibly beyond. But the truth lies not in conspiracies plotted by shadowy domestic groups or foreign agents. The explanation is both simpler and more complex. It is simpler because we don't need to build elaborate theoretical constructs that "connect the dots" and impute sinister motives to actors. In fact, the information we need to understand our predicament is openly available and not in dispute.

The bulk of what we need to know has nothing to do with the shenanigans of evil or corrupt individuals. Instead, we need to look to the widely agreed-upon Big Data about wages, taxes, gross domestic products, and sociological surveys churned out by government agencies and organizations like Gallup. These data feed into statistical analyses published by social scientists in academic journals. And herein lies the reason why the explanation that this book offers is also more complex. Not to put too fine a point on it, but we need complexity science to make sense of all the data and analyses.

Pundits and politicians often invoke "lessons of history." The problem is that the historical record is rich, and each pundit can easily find cases in it to support whichever side of a policy debate they favor. Clearly, inference from such "cherry-picked" examples is not the way to go.

Cliodynamics is different. It uses the methods of data science, treating the historical record, compiled by generations of historians, as Big Data. It employs mathematical models to trace the intricate web of interactions between the different "moving parts" of the complex social systems that are our societies. Most importantly, cliodynamics uses the scientific method, in which alternative theories are subject to empirical tests with data.

So what does cliodynamics tell us about our current time of troubles? It turns out that ever since the first complex societies organized as states appeared—roughly five thousand years ago—no matter how successful they might be for a while, eventually they all run into problems. All complex societies go through cycles of alternating stretches of internal peace and harmony periodically interrupted by outbreaks of internal warfare and discord.

My narrative is an effort to explain how impersonal social forces push societies to the brink of collapse and beyond. I will look across human history for examples, but my primary goal is to speak to how we have slid into our current age of discord, with the United States as my empirical focus. Because the crisis has deep historical roots, we'll need to travel back in time to the New Deal era, when an unwritten social contract became part of American political culture. This informal and implicit contract balanced the interests of workers, businesses, and the state in a way similar to the more formal, explicit tripartite agreements in Nordic countries. For two human generations, this implicit pact delivered unprecedented growth of broadly based well-being in America. At the same time, the "Great Compression" dramatically reduced economic inequality. Many people were left out of this implicit pact— Black Americans, in particular, a fact I will address in some detail. But overall, for roughly fifty years the interests of workers and the interests of owners were kept in balance in this country, such that overall income inequality remained remarkably low.

This social contract began to break down in the late 1970s. As a consequence, typical workers' wages, which had previously increased in tandem with overall economic growth, started to lag behind. Worse, real wages stagnated and at times even decreased. The result was a decline in many aspects of quality of life for most of the American population. The most striking trend was the stagnation and even decline of the average life expectancy (which started well before the COVID-19 pandemic). While the wages and incomes of workers stagnated, the fruits of economic growth were reaped by the elites. A perverse "wealth pump" came into being, taking from the poor and giving to the rich. The Great Compression reversed itself. In many ways, the past forty years resemble what happened in the United States between 1870 and 1900. If the postwar period was a true golden age of broadly based prosperity, after 1980 we indeed entered the "Second Gilded Age."

As our model predicts, the extra wealth flowing to the elites (to the proverbial "1 percent," but even more so to the top 0.01 percent) eventually created trouble for the wealth holders (and power holders) themselves. The social pyramid has grown top-heavy. We now have too many "elite aspirants" competing for a fixed number of positions in the upper echelons of politics and business. In our model, such conditions have a name: elite overproduction. Together with popular immiseration, elite overproduction, and the intraelite conflicts that it has engendered, has gradually undermined our civic cohesiveness, the sense of national cooperation without which states quickly rot from within. Growing social fragility has manifested itself in collapsing levels of trust in state institutions and unraveling social norms governing public discourse—and the functioning of democratic institutions.

This is, of course, a bare-bones summary. The meat of the book will unpack these ideas, relate them to the statistical trends for key economic and social indicators, and trace some archetypal human stories of people buffeted by these social forces. Although my focus here is primarily on America and Americans, the book will make forays into other parts of the world and into previous historical eras. Again, our crisis in America is not without precedent; we are in a position to learn from our past.

Ultimately, the central question of the book is about social power.

Who rules? How do ruling elites maintain their dominant position within society? Who are the challengers of the status quo, and what is the role of elite overproduction in generating such challengers? And why do ruling classes, both historically and today, sometimes suddenly lose their grip on power and get overthrown? Let us begin to answer these vital questions.

Part I

THE CLIODYNAMICS
OF POWER

CHAPTER 1

ELITES, ELITE OVERPRODUCTION, AND THE ROAD TO CRISIS

Who Are the Elites? Sources of Social Power

Who are the elites? You, reader, are you "elite"? If I were a betting man, I'd predict that 99 percent of my readers would answer "no!" So let's define what I mean by "elites." In sociology, elites are not those who are somehow better than the rest. They are not necessarily those who are more hardworking, or more intelligent, or more talented. They are simply those who have more social power—the ability to influence other people. A more descriptive term for elites is "power holders."

Because power is such an important part of the story to come, we will return to it in later chapters, where I discuss how sociologists define power and power holders in different societies, past and present. But for now, let's take a shortcut. In America, power is closely correlated with wealth. As a result, it is relatively straightforward to figure out who belongs to different ranks of power holders. (A more sophisticated answer to the question of who rules will have to wait until chapter 5.)

If you are an American and your net worth is in the $1–$2 million range, for example, then you are roughly in the top 10 percent, which puts you in the lower ranks of American elites.[1] Most people in this category are not particularly powerful in the sense of having a lot of other people to order around. But a few million dollars in wealth (and higher incomes that are typically associated with it) gives ten-percenters a lot of control—power—over their own lives. They can turn down jobs that are unpleasant, or don't pay enough, or are located in regions they don't care to move to. Or they can choose to retire from the rat race. They typically own houses and send their children to good colleges, and sudden medical emergencies will not wipe them out. They have certainly escaped "precarity."

The correlation between wealth and real power starts to become tighter for those whose net worth is counted in tens or, better, hundreds of millions. People in this class include owners of businesses and CEOs of large corporations, who wield their power over hundreds or thousands of employees. Many powerful politicians are also in this range. (There are about fifty members of Congress whose net worth is greater than $10 million.) The correlation between wealth and political power is not perfect. Nine American presidents didn't even make it into the $1 million or above territory (in today's dollars), including Harry Truman, Woodrow Wilson, and Abraham Lincoln. But more than half of them had enough wealth to put them into what today would be the top 1 percent.[2] And before 1850, all American presidents were one-percenters (at the least).

Another point to keep in mind is that poor people who become power holders in America don't stay poor for long. Bill Clinton grew up in a poor Arkansas family with an alcoholic and abusive stepfather, but now his wealth is estimated to be at least $120 million.[3] The close correlation between wealth and political power in America arises partly because many a politician, poor at the start of their career, joins the ranks of the wealthy after leaving public office. But an equally important reason is that people who are already very wealthy are much more likely to seek and gain public office than the rest of us. Think of the Roosevelt and Kennedy clans, Ross Perot, Michael Bloomberg, and—yes—Trump.

Still, the correlation between wealth and power, even in America, is not perfect. So let's talk about other sources of power. The hardest—and crudest—form of social power is coercion: force, or a threat of force. Americans specializing in coercion, such as army generals and police officers, are generally thoroughly subordinated to other forms of power. Exceptions, such as J. Edgar Hoover, who was the first and most powerful FBI director, are rare.

The second kind of power is wealth (or accumulated material resources, more generally). Wealthy people can hire people to do what they want (within limits).

The third and more subtle kind of power is bureaucratic or administrative. Modern human beings belong to a variety of organizations. We have a variety of "bosses" whose orders we generally follow. There is an element of coercion to these relationships, of course, because not following orders may get you fired, fined, or arrested. But most of the time we follow orders simply because of the power of social norms. The bosses at various levels of organizations all wield different amounts of power, which tends to increase the larger their organizations and the higher their positions within them.

The fourth and "softest" kind of power is ideological—the power of persuasion. Soft power, or persuasion, is an extremely potent force that can sway multitudes. It includes the realm of thought influencers, such as famous "public intellectuals," columnists at major newspapers, and, more recently, social media figures with millions of followers.

As we can see, this simple question—who are the elites?—doesn't

have a simple answer. Human societies are complex systems, and trying to characterize the flows of social power within them by way of
an overly simplistic scheme would be counterproductive. My job is to
make my theory as simple as possible, but not simpler.[4]

The Game of Aspirant Chairs

Once we start thinking about so-called elite behavior, we encounter
several layers of complexity. First, in terms of wealth, there is no hard
boundary between the elites and non-elites. Ten-percenters (roughly,
millionaires in today's dollars) have a lot of power over their own lives.
One-percenters (roughly, decamillionaires) have a lot of power over
other people's lives. Centimillionaires and billionaires wield even more
power. But there are no sharp boundaries between one-percenters and
ten-percenters—the distribution of incomes is a smooth curve. And there
is no huge difference in social attitudes between the one-percenters and
ten-percenters, or between the ten-percenters, the top income decile,
and the next decile. In chapter 3, we will see that another way of distin-
guishing social classes, in terms of the more educated (those with a four-
year college degree) and the less educated (those without one), is much
more salient if we want to understand the diversity of life trajectories
and social attitudes.[5]

Second, different elites tend to specialize in different kinds of
social power: generals, admirals, and police chiefs mete out coercion;
CEOs and wealth holders wield economic power; senators and secre-
taries of federal departments manage administrative power; and TV
anchors and influential podcasters deal in persuasion. Each kind of influence has its own power hierarchy. This is most clearly seen in mili-

tary chains of command, but softer kinds of power also have their pecking orders.

The third layer of complexity arises when we ask, how are elites made? In order to understand elite overproduction, we need to understand social reproduction of the elites—what happens with them over time.

Let's distinguish between people already in elite positions—established elites—and those who want to get into such positions—elite aspirants. Elite aspirants come in a variety of shapes and forms, depending on the kind of power they want and what level they aspire to. For example, most lieutenants want to become majors, and most majors want to become one-star generals, and one-star generals aim for additional stars to their insignia. Similarly, decamillionaires want to become centimillionaires, and those who have already made their first $100 million aim to get into the billionaire class.

Although not everybody has ambition to acquire more power, there are always more aspirants than power positions. Inevitably, there are those who try but fail to obtain a power position—frustrated elite aspirants. Elite overproduction develops when the demand for power positions by elite aspirants massively exceeds their supply. Let's focus for now on the nexus between wealth and politics and see how elite overproduction can develop in this sphere.

Starting in the 1980s, the number of superrich in America—those worth at least $10 million, or decamillionaires—started to grow rapidly.[6] In 1983, there were only 66,000 such households, and by 2019 (the last year for which data are available), their number increased more than tenfold to 693,000. This was not a result of dollar inflation; we adjusted the threshold to determine who is in this class (using constant 1995 dollars). During this period, the overall number of households grew by 53 percent, so in proportionate terms, decamillionaires swelled from 0.08 to 0.54 percent of the total population.

A similar upsurge in the fortunes of the wealthy also happened lower on the food chain. If the numbers of decamillionaires grew tenfold, the number of households worth $5 million or more increased sevenfold, and the number of mere millionaires expanded fourfold. Overall, the larger the level of the fortunes we look at, the more growth they have seen over the past forty years.

On the surface of it, an increase in the number of wealthy people doesn't sound like such a bad thing. Isn't it part of the American dream to get rich? But there are two downsides to this good news. First, the ballooning of the superwealthy class did not happen in isolation from the fortunes of the rest of the population. While the numbers of super-rich have multiplied, the income and wealth of the typical American family have actually declined. (The more precise term for "typical" wealth is "the median," which divides the wealth distribution into equal halves; the economic decline of American workers will be a major topic in chapter 3.) This divergence between the financial well-being of common Americans and the wealthy elite is what drove the rapid increase in economic inequality, which has been much discussed in recent years.

The second problem is much subtler and less widely understood.[7] When the social pyramid becomes top-heavy, this has dire consequences for the stability of our societies.

To understand why, consider a game. In the musical *Evita*, a group of Argentinian military officers plays a game of musical chairs. It goes like this. The music starts playing, and officers walk around a set of chairs. When the music stops, each must find a chair to sit on. However, there are more players than chairs, so one unlucky officer fails to occupy a chair and is eliminated. Then a chair is removed, and another round is played. At the end, there is one winner. In *Evita*, the winner is

Colonel Juan Perón, who later in the musical (as in real life) becomes president of Argentina and founder of the Peronist Party.

In the elite aspirant game, or the aspirant game, for short, instead of reducing the number of chairs each round, we increase the number of players. The game starts just as musical chairs, with ten chairs representing power positions (such as political offices). In the first round, eleven players (elite aspirants) play to get a chair. Ten become established elites, and the loser is a frustrated aspirant. In the following rounds, we increase the number of players, eventually doubling, then tripling, them (while keeping the same ten chairs). The number of winners stays the same, but the number of frustrated aspirants increases from the initial one to ten, then twenty. As the game progresses, just imagine the growing degree of chaos and conflict. (I would not suggest playing this game at a child's birthday party.) There is also a curious amplification effect: as we increase the number of aspirants by a factor of two, then three, the number of frustrated aspirants balloons tenfold, then twentyfold. (This is a generic feature of elite overproduction games.)

In game theory, a branch of mathematics that studies strategic interactions, the players must devise winning strategies within the given rules. But in real life, people bend rules all the time. Inevitably, as the number of aspirants per power position grows, some will decide to stretch the rules. For example, you can slow down by a chair or even stop and wait right next to it for the music to stop, while shoving away other contenders. Congratulations, you have just become a counter-elite—someone who is willing to break the rules to get ahead in the game. Unfortunately, others quickly catch on, and each chair soon acquires a jostling crowd, and before long you have the recipe for a free-for-all fistfight. This turns out to be a good model for understanding the consequences of elite overproduction in real life.

In real life, as we saw, over the past forty years the number of wealth holders at various levels has increased fourfold, sevenfold, or even ten-fold. Only a small proportion of them decide to spend a chunk of their fortune to run for political office. For example, they might aspire for a seat in the House of Representatives or the Senate. They might enter a race for state governor. The ultimate prize is, of course, the presidency. The number of these power positions has stayed the same over the past decades, but the number of aspirants for them has increased together with the overall number of wealth holders. Because of the amplification effect, the number of frustrated aspirants exploded even faster than the already impressive expansion in the number of wealth holders.

This conclusion is not just an abstract model. We can now make sense of several trends in the elections for public office in the United States, which have been documented by the Center for Responsive Politics.[8] One is that the number of self-funded candidates started increasing during the 1990s. In the congressional elections of 2000 (adding the House and the Senate seats), there were nineteen candidates who individually spent $1 million or more of their own money on their campaigns. In the next election round, there were twenty-two such wealthy aspirants for a seat in Congress. Twenty years later, their number had roughly doubled, with forty-one and thirty-six candidates individually spending $1 million or more in 2018 and 2020.

An even better metric for following the effect of overproduction of wealth holders on elections is the cost of running a successful campaign. After all, not all politically ambitious rich people run for office themselves. Many instead choose to fund professional politicians who can advance their policy agendas in Washington. According to the data collected by the Center for Responsive Politics, the average spending of the House winner increased from $400K in 1990 to $2.35 million in 2020, while the same statistic for the Senate started at $3.9 million (in 1990) and grew to $27 million in the last electoral round.

Over the past forty years, we've been playing the elite overproduction game once every two years. As the number of players grows, the chance of rules breaking down goes up. Is it any wonder that the rules of the game—social norms and institutions governing democratic elections—have been unraveling in real life?

But elite overproduction is only half of the story. The expansion of the wealth-holder class did not happen in isolation from the rest of society. It's time to bring the second factor into our model for the stability of our societies: popular immiseration.

Popular Immiseration

Our society collectively produces a lot of products and services, and economists have learned a great deal about how to estimate this total, the gross domestic product (GDP). Yes, there are still some pesky issues. (How should we include housework? What about criminal activities?) But to a very good degree of approximation, we can use the GDP statistics, as published by government agencies, to get an idea of the total amount of wealth generated in any particular country every year.

This total usually increases with time, thanks to economic growth, but is nevertheless finite. Thus, how it is divided up between different kinds of consumers becomes a very interesting question. In our theory, we represent the structure of society as consisting of three main parts: the state, the elites, and everyone else. This is a model that greatly simplifies the glorious complexity of our modern societies (and we saw that defining who the elites are is not straightforward). But as we'll see, it maps onto reality to an extent that is empirically meaningful and informative.

At whose expense did the wealth held by the elites swell in recent years? Wealth is accumulated income; in order for it to grow, it has to be fed by directing a portion of GDP to the elites. The proportion of GDP consumed by the government has not changed much over the past four decades.[9] The main loser has been the common American.

For two generations after the 1930s, real wages of American workers experienced steady growth, achieving a broad-based prosperity for America that was unprecedented in human history. But during the 1970s, real wages stopped growing. While the overall economy continued to grow, the share of economic growth going to average workers began to shrink. We can index the operation of this wealth pump by tracing the dynamics of relative wages—typical wages (for example, for unskilled workers or for manufacturing workers—it doesn't matter as long as we use the same group) divided by GDP per capita. Before the 1960s, the relative wage increased robustly, but after that decade it began declining, and by 2010 it had nearly halved.[10] This trend reversal in the share of economic growth going to workers also resulted in the change of the fortunes of the wealthy. It's the Matthew Effect: if you take from the poor and give to the rich, then the rich will get richer while the poor get poorer.

When America entered an era of wage stagnation and decline, it affected not only the economic measures of well-being but also biological and social ones. I'll talk more about it in chapter 3, but for now it is sufficient to note that life expectancies of large swaths of the American population started to decline years before the COVID-19 pandemic. "Deaths of despair" from suicide, alcoholism, and drug overdoses spiked among the noncollege-educated from 2000 to 2016, while remaining at the same, much lower level among those with at least a college degree.[11] This is what popular immiseration looks like.

And popular immiseration breeds discontent, which eventually turns to anger. Popular discontent coupled with a large pool of elite aspirants makes for a very combustible combination, as we have experienced in America since 2016.

Trump: An Unlikely President

Donald Trump was an unlikely president. He was the only US president to arrive in office without any history of previous public service of any kind.[12] In 2014, nobody, including perhaps even Trump himself, could imagine that he would become the ruler of the mightiest nation on earth. His dizzying ascent to the pinnacle of global power was so astonishing that half of the American population and the majority of the American ruling elites were convinced that he didn't win the presidency legitimately. Many chose to believe a conspiracy theory positing that the election of Donald Trump was the result of Russian machinations. To this day, pundits and columnists continue arguing about how and why Trump happened.

Our human brains are wired in such a way that we see "agency" behind any development, especially one that affects us in a strong way.[13] It is difficult for us to grasp that many consequential events happen not because they have been engineered by shadowy plotters but because they were driven by impersonal social forces. But to understand the ascent of Trump—and more broadly, why America is in crisis—we need not a conspiracy theory but a scientific theory.

To understand why Donald Trump became the forty-fifth president of the United States, we should also pay less attention to his personal qualities and maneuvers and more to the deep social forces that propelled him to the top. Trump was like a small boat caught on the crest of a mighty tidal wave. The two most important social forces that gave us the Trump presidency—and pushed America to the brink of state breakdown—are elite overproduction and popular immiseration.

It seems strange to speak of Donald Trump as an elite aspirant. After all, he was born rich and inherited (or was given by his father) hundreds of millions of dollars.[14] But he perfectly fits the definition I gave above. Trump is one among that rapidly expanding cohort of the superwealthy who aspire to political office. Although he was already quite rich (certainly a centimillionaire, perhaps a billionaire, as he claims) and famous, he wanted more.

Trump was not the first superrich person with no previous political experience to run for the US presidency. Steve Forbes (fortune estimated at $400 million) ran as a candidate in the Republican primaries in 1996 and 2000, but he didn't get very far. Billionaire Ross Perot ran as an independent in 1992 and 1996, receiving nearly 20 percent of the popular vote in his first run. Why was Trump successful when Forbes and Perot failed?

My answer has two parts. First, by 2016 popular immiseration had become much worse than in 1992, and Trump cleverly and ruthlessly exploited this social force in his presidential bid. In the end, a large proportion of Americans who felt left behind voted for an unlikely candidate—a billionaire. For many of them, this was not so much an endorsement of Trump as an expression of their discontent, shading into rage, against the ruling class. We'll talk more about the sources and consequences of popular discontent in chapter 3.

Second, by 2016, the elite overproduction game had reached a bifurcation point where the rules of conduct in political campaigns had been tossed to the wind. The 2016 Republican Party presidential primaries had the largest number of major candidates in history to that point. A total of seventeen contestants entered the race.[15] Members of the stunned American public became involuntary viewers in a bizarre spectacle of an elite aspirant game reaching its logical culmination. The candidates competed in saying the most outlandish things and tossing out wild quotes in order to win press attention and stay in the race, while "serious" candidates declined in the polls and were eliminated.[16]

In the end, there is no question that Trump piloted his boat better than his competitors (and he had other significant crew members, such as the self-proclaimed revolutionary strategist Steve Bannon). Nevertheless, it would be a mistake to give him (or Bannon) too much credit for succeeding where other billionaire aspirants before him failed. What gave him the presidency was a combination of conflict among the elites and Trump's ability to channel a strain of popular discontent that was more widespread and virulent than many people understood, or wanted to understand.

Our current predicament is not unique—this is one of the central themes of the book. Let's travel back in time to look at another elite aspirant whose life trajectory illustrates the operation of the twin forces of instability: elite overproduction and popular immiseration.

Lincoln: Another Unlikely President

Abraham Lincoln, the sixteenth president of the United States, is one of the most revered figures in American history. The statue of Lincoln, larger than life, sits serenely in his monument at the end of the Mall in Washington, DC. Yet the actual life of Lincoln was anything but serene. He lost many more elections than he won, had a nervous breakdown, and at one point in his life decided to give up his political career.

Of course, he won his most consequential election, the one in 1860. But during his presidency, he was abused from all sides. The historian Stephen Oates dryly notes:

> Northern Democrats castigated him as an abolitionist dictator, abolitionists as a dim-witted product of a slave state, and all manner of Republicans as an incompetent charlatan. In truth, Lincoln may have been one of the two or three most unpopular living Presidents in American history.[17]

Lincoln was another unlikely president whose rise to power was propelled by the twin social forces of elite overproduction and popular immiseration. Before the Civil War, the United States was ruled by an elite of aristocratic Southern slaveholders allied with Northeastern patricians—merchants, bankers, and lawyers.[18] The economic basis of this alliance was the agricultural commodities grown on Southern plantations with slave labor, first and foremost cotton. Trade in cotton was the most important business of New York's merchant elites, who exported Southern-grown commodities and imported European-manufactured goods. Another segment of the elites (especially in Massachusetts) used Southern cotton to produce textiles. This coalition, and especially its Southern slaveholding component, dominated the politics of antebellum America. The votes of Southern white men had a greater weight due to the infamous three-fifths compromise of 1787, which counted three-fifths of the slave population in apportioning representatives and presidential electors (without, of course, letting slaves vote). The Southern elites also controlled half of the Senate, although the free population of the North was almost twice that of the South. Two-thirds of the wealthiest people in the US lived in the South—4,500 out of 7,000 Americans with wealth greater than $100K (more than $2 million in today's dollars[19]). Wealthy aristocrats had the resources and leisure to pursue elected offices and careers in government, and to influence elections, and there were simply more of them in the South than in the North. Southern elites also controlled the top government offices; most presidents and vice presidents, cabinet ministers, top government officials, senators, and chief justices came from the South.

Lincoln, on the other hand, came from a very humble background. He was a self-educated lawyer and started his career as a politician in Illinois (at the time, a state on the country's northwestern frontier), far from the centers of power in Virginia and the Eastern Seaboard. He was very different from the wealthy aristocrats who dominated the early Republic. Lincoln's presidential ambitions were not taken seriously until very late in the game. In fact, he was better known for his prior failures than for his successes. How was this self-taught lawyer from the boondocks propelled to the presidency?

The America of the 1850s and the America of 2020, despite being very different countries, share a number of striking similarities. Between the 1820s and 1860s, the relative wage, the share of economic output paid out as worker wages, declined by nearly 50 percent—just as it did in the past five decades.[20] The effect on the well-being of common Americans was devastating. This trend is best captured by the biological measures of quality of life. Average life expectancy at age ten decreased by eight years! And the heights of native-born Americans, who in the eighteenth century were the tallest people on earth, started shrinking. Immiseration breeds discontent, and the signs of it were all over. One clear sign of building social pressures was the incidence of urban riots. Between 1820 and 1825, when times were good, there was only one lethal urban riot (that is, a violent riot in which at least one person was killed). But in the five years before the Civil War, 1855–1860, American cities were convulsed by no fewer than thirty-eight lethal riots. An additional sign of growing popular discontent was the rise of populist parties, such as the anti-immigration Know-Nothing Party.

Another related factor in Lincoln's rise, and the Civil War that his election triggered, was elite overproduction. After 1820, most of the gains from the growing economy went not to the workers but to the elites; elite numbers and wealth ballooned. Between 1800 and 1850, the number of millionaires (billionaires in today's dollars) increased from half a dozen to about one hundred. Of course, the country's population also grew (from five to twenty-three million), but the number of millionaires per one million of the population during this period quadrupled.[21] The size of the top fortune in 1790 was $1 million (held by Elias Derby) and increased to $3 million (held by William Bingham) by 1803. And then it went up as though there were no limit: $6 million (held by Stephen Girard) in 1830, $20 million (held by John J. Astor) in 1848, and $40 million (held by Cornelius Vanderbilt) in 1868.[22] A host of other statistics looking at different strata of the wealthy all show the same trend: as the poor were getting poorer, the rich were getting richer.

The new wealth was materially due to mining, railroads, and steel production rather than cotton and overseas trade. The new millionaires chafed under the rule of the Southern aristocracy, as their economic interests diverged from the established elites. The new elites, who made their money in manufacturing, favored high tariffs to protect budding American industries and state support for "internal improvements" (turnpike, canal, and railroad construction). The established elites, who grew and exported cotton, and imported manufactured goods from overseas, naturally favored low tariffs. They also were against using state funds for internal improvements, because they shipped their products by river and sea to the world markets. The new economic elites favored domestic industrialization, import substitution, and the export of agricultural commodities, such as wheat, produced by free labor. These businessmen began to argue that the stranglehold of the Southern slaveholders over the federal government prevented necessary reforms in the banking and transportation systems and thus threatened their own economic well-being.

Furthermore, the dramatic expansion of the elite numbers destroyed the equilibrium between the demand and supply of government posts. Some wealth holders ran for office themselves, while others threw their resources behind rival politicians. Additionally, the sons of merchant families often chose to go into professions—the law profession, in particular. Obtaining legal training was, and still is, the chief route to political office in the United States. Becoming a lawyer in that period was relatively easy because one didn't need a degree from a law school. The surging numbers of lawyers, including Lincoln, generated an increasing number of aspirants for political positions. At the same time, the supply of political offices stagnated. For example, the number of US representatives between 1789 and 1835 increased from 65 to 242 but thereafter stagnated.[23] As the number of elite aspirants exploded, competition for political power intensified.

Those were cruder times, and intraelite conflict took very violent forms. In Congress, incidences of violence and threatened violence increased, reaching a peak during the 1850s. The brutal caning that Representative Preston Brooks of South Carolina gave to Senator Charles Sumner of Massachusetts on the Senate floor in 1856 is the best-known episode of such violence, but it was not the only one. In 1842, after Representative Thomas Arnold of Tennessee "reprimanded a pro-slavery member of his own party, two Southern Democrats stalked toward him, at least one of whom was armed with a bowie knife—a 6- to 12-inch blade often worn strapped to the back. Calling Arnold a 'damned coward,' his angry colleagues threatened to cut his throat 'from ear to ear.'"[24] During a debate in 1850, Senator Henry Foote of Mississippi pulled a pistol on Senator Thomas Hart Benton of Missouri. In another bitter debate, a New York congressman inadvertently dropped a pistol— it fell out of his pocket—and almost precipitated a general shootout on the floor of Congress.[25] Lincoln was a part of this rough-and-tumble politics, especially in his early career. He often verbally abused his opponents and several times came near to blows with them, once nearly fighting in a duel.

Differences over economic policy and the competition for office generated powerful incentives to break the Southern domination of the federal government. History textbooks tell us that the American Civil War was fought over slavery, but this is not the whole story. A better way to characterize this conflict is to say that it was fought over "slavocracy." Indeed, although by 1860 the majority of Northerners felt that slavery was morally wrong, only a tiny minority, the Northern abolitionists, felt strongly enough to make this issue central to their political program. In the South, the "peculiar institution" was so lucrative for the great majority of white people (since most either owned slaves or aspired to own them) that they felt compelled to defend it. Most Northern white people were clearly not sufficiently motivated by the plight of enslaved Black people to fight and die over it. However, as slavery provided the economic basis for Southern dominance, a political attack on the slaveholders could be strengthened by an ideological attack on slavery. The majority of Northerners railed against the "slave power"—the wealthy and aristocratic Southerners—and their domination of national politics. Lincoln's political program reflected these sentiments. Initially, he did not intend to abolish slavery in the South, but he was strongly opposed to the extension of slavery (and the power of slavocracy) to new states.

The rest is history. The collapse of the Second Party System resulted in a fragmented political landscape during the 1850s. Four major candidates competed in the 1860 presidential elections. Lincoln got less than 40 percent of the vote but won in the Electoral College. The South seceded, triggering the American Civil War. The victory of the North in the war resulted in the overthrow of the antebellum ruling class and its replacement by the new economic elite that has dominated the American state since then. (We will discuss this at length in chapter 5.)

There are many similarities between the age of discord that we are living through now and the one that ended with the Civil War 160 years ago. Pundits today often comment that it feels like we are reliving the 1850s. And, indeed, even though antebellum America and the US today are two very different countries, they share many similarities. Let's now look at yet another elite aspirant who also lived in turbulent times and was propelled to the pinnacle of power. This time, we shift from the Western Hemisphere to China.

Hong: An Unlikely Emperor

Two hundred years ago, China's economy was by far the mightiest in the world, accounting for nearly one-third of the global GDP.[26] Today, China's GDP, figured in PPP (purchasing power parity) terms, is again the largest, beating that of the next largest national GDP (USA) by about 20 percent. Between these two periods of prosperity, however, China experienced a century from hell, or the Century of Humiliation, as the Chinese today refer to it. After 1820, China's total GDP began to shrink, and by 1870 it was less than half that of Western Europe. The country experienced a seemingly unending run of famines, rebellions, and humiliating defeats by external enemies. The worst catastrophe was the Taiping Rebellion (1850–1864), which has the sad distinction of being the bloodiest civil war in human history. How did China become the "Sick Man of East Asia," and what accounts for its miraculous recovery in the past fifty years?

Between 1644 and 1912, China was ruled by the Qing dynasty. Although this dynasty was established through conquest by Manchuria (which before the Qing was not part of China), the Manchu rapidly adopted the traditional Chinese forms of governance. In particular, the Qing Empire was ruled by a class of scholar-administrators, who could advance up the ranks only after successfully passing a series of increasingly difficult examinations. The majority of the population, more than 90 percent, was peasants. The remainder was a mixed bag of artisans, merchants, and soldiers. But the mandarins—the credentialed class— ruled all. Even the top command levels of Qing armies were usually occupied by scholar-bureaucrats, not warriors.

The first half of the dynasty was a period of robust economic growth and cultural brilliance. Improved agricultural techniques and broad adoption of new crops, such as corn and sweet potatoes, increased production of food. Early industrialization also helped to fuel robust population growth. But population growth did not stop, even after the beneficial effects of these innovations had been exhausted. By 1850, the Chinese population was four times greater than at the beginning of the Qing dynasty. The arable land per peasant shrank nearly threefold, real wages declined, and average heights (a reliable measure of biological well-being) decreased. The early Qing period had no massive famines; the last one, in 1630–1631 in northwest China, hit at the end of the previous dynasty, Ming, and contributed to its collapse. The next massive famine arrived in 1810 and was followed by a string of others: 1846–1849, 1850–1873, 1876–1879 (this one killing between nine and thirteen million people), 1896–1897, and 1911 (triggering the revolution that put the Qing dynasty out of its misery). Overall, it is clear that after 1800 the level of popular immiseration in China was very high.[27] What about elite overproduction?

During the Qing period, elites were mostly recruited through the civil examination system, which consisted of several levels of degrees, conferred to successful candidates in local, provincial, and court examinations. The system worked well for the first part of the Qing period. It ensured a high level of literacy and competence among the bureaucrats. The study of Confucian classics helped to create a common ethos—a shared sense of culture, morality, and community—within the ruling class. And its emphasis on promotion by merit buttressed state legitimacy.

Unfortunately, the civil service system proved to be highly vulnerable to the pressures of population growth. The number of official positions was primarily determined by the number of administrative units, ranging from provinces (at the highest level) to counties (at the local level). The number of power positions was thus relatively constant, while the number of aspirants grew throughout the Qing period, powered by the fourfold increase in the population of China. The number of elite aspirants increased not only because of the larger source population but also because there was a substantial growth in the wealthy merchant class, who supplied new aspirants aiming to join the ranks of the literati. Without meaning to do so, the Qing Empire set up a game of aspirant chairs. A vast pool of frustrated aspirants, who had no hope of obtaining an official position, formed in China toward 1850.

Hong Xiuquan (1814–1864), the leader of the Taiping Rebellion, was one of these frustrated aspirants. He was the third son from a well-to-do family that could afford to hire teachers to provide a formal education for him. He successfully passed the first-level civil service exam to become a xiucai, a licentiate (roughly, the level of a master's degree).

But beyond that, he hit a wall. Hong tried to pass one of the imperial examinations four times, failing each time.

After Hong failed to pass the examination for the third time, the gap between his ambition and reality proved to be too much for him. He had a nervous breakdown, fell ill, and nearly died. While he was sick, he had a series of religious visions. Later, reading Chinese-language pamphlets published by Christian missionaries, he combined what he learned from them about Christianity with his visions to form a new syncretistic religion, a major goal of which was to purge China of Confucianism, which was essentially the state religion in Qing China. While Hong thought of his new faith as a brand of Christianity, the established Christians, Western missionaries, most emphatically disagreed.

After failing the provincial imperial examination for the fourth time in 1843, Hong began preaching his new creed, first to his relatives and friends and then more broadly. Two of his first converts, Feng Yunshan and Hong Rengan, became his lieutenants. Both were also failed imperial examination candidates. The three frustrated elite aspirants thus made the conversion to counter-elites. The authorities took notice and sent troops to suppress the nascent Taiping movement, which Hong called the Society of God Worshippers. Ironically, *taiping* means "great peace," but what the Taipings brought to China was not peace but the bloodiest rebellion in world history.

During its first few years, the Taiping movement expanded slowly. In 1847 there were only two thousand followers of Hong's society, organized into many independent congregations. They were having fits and speaking in tongues. More ominously, from the point of view of the authorities, they started attacking Buddhist temples and smashing statues, or "idols." The society's numbers suddenly exploded during an 1850 epidemic, when word spread that sick people were healed by praying to the Taiping God.[28]

When Qing officials, worried about this new threat, sent soldiers to round up Hong Xiuquan and Feng Yunshan, a nearby congregation of God Worshippers, armed with swords and spears, attacked and easily defeated the imperials. After this victory, Hong called for his followers to gather together for the first time. The next year, 1851, Hong Xiuquan declared the founding of the Taiping Heavenly Kingdom, with himself as its Heavenly Emperor. Multitudes of his followers sold their possessions and flocked to his banner. Over the next two years, the Taiping army marched north through Guangxi Province as it fought the Qing forces attempting to put down the rebellion. Hong started with ten thousand troops, but the general conditions of popular misery, landlessness, and failure of order in the countryside that prevailed in China by this point ensured a massive supply of recruits. By 1853, the Taiping army numbered half a million.[29] Popular immiseration together with elite overproduction is an explosive combination. Immiserated masses generate raw energy, while a cadre of counter-elites provides an organization to channel that energy against the ruling class.

In March of 1853, the huge Taiping army conquered Nanjing, the southern capital of China. For more than a decade thereafter, Hong Xiuquan governed a kingdom with its capital in Nanjing, occupying a large chunk of southeastern China, with a population of thirty million at its peak. He nearly succeeded in bringing down the Qing dynasty, as other parts of China were also convulsed by major rebellions at the same time, but in the end he lost. After years of fighting, a Qing army led by General Zeng Guofan besieged Nanjing. Hong fell ill and died on June 1, 1864. A month later, Nanjing fell, and the Great Peace experiment was over.

As a young man, Hong had been persistent and, as his subsequent career proved, brilliant in his way. But there were too many aspirants for a fixed number of positions, and he ended up in the pool of frustrated ones. And he was not alone. His top lieutenants and more than half of the next level of leaders of the Taiping Rebellion were failed imperial examination candidates.[30]

Hong's nemesis, General Zeng Guofan, also came from a humble background.[31] Zeng was the eldest of five brothers born to a farming family. His father was relatively well-to-do and could afford education. Yet Zeng's father failed the district-level examination, the lowest-level examination, sixteen times—sixteen times!—before finally passing it. Zeng Guofan failed the same examination (only) six times and passed it when he was twenty-two. The next year, Zeng passed the provincial examination (the level at which Hong Xiuquan failed four times). Finally, after twice failing the highest-level examination, the imperial examination in the capital, he passed it on the third attempt with the highest honors. Eventually, he ended up in Hunan, a province on the western frontier of the growing Taiping Empire. Thus, it fell to Zeng to organize and lead the main Qing force that defeated the Taipings after a long struggle. In the Taiping Rebellion, which nearly brought down the Qing Empire, the opposing sides were led by a member of the established elites and a frustrated elite aspirant turned counter-elite.

The Road to Crisis

Donald Trump, Abraham Lincoln, and Hong Xiuquan were very different elite aspirants who lived in very different worlds. Yet, at some deep level, their personal trajectories share much in common. They all lived (or live) during an age of discord, when the social pressures for instability—immiseration and elite overproduction—crested high. All three were elite aspirants who achieved the pinnacle of power, if only for a short time. And they all ruled as their countries unraveled.

The magnitude of disasters that followed the ascent to power of these three aspirants varied hugely. Undoubtedly, the Taiping Rebellion was the worst, as it was arguably the bloodiest civil war in human history. It lasted for fourteen years and killed between thirty and seventy million people.

With six hundred thousand battle casualties, the American Civil War remains the bloodiest American conflict to date. This struggle also claimed Abraham Lincoln, who was assassinated by John Wilkes Booth, an actor and Confederate sympathizer.

The presidency of Donald Trump had the mildest consequences (at least so far). Still, he presided over an epidemic that killed more people than the Spanish flu, and a year from hell, 2020, when political unrest caused the deaths of twenty-five people,[32] more than ten thousand injuries,[33] and over $2 billion in damages.[34] His presidency was capped off by the storming of the Capitol, which delivered an enormous shock to the American political system. Of course, we don't yet know how our own age of discord is going to end. The history of the future hasn't been written yet. What we do know is that the twin forces pushing America into civil war—immiseration and elite overproduction—continue unabated as of 2022. What can history tell us about such crisis periods?

CHAPTER 2

STEPPING BACK:
LESSONS OF HISTORY

The Road Map

All complex human societies organized as states experience recurrent waves of political instability. The most common pattern is an alternation of integrative and disintegrative phases lasting for roughly a century. Integrative phases are characterized by internal peace, social stability, and relatively cooperative elites. Disintegrative phases are the opposite: social instability, breakdown of cooperation among the elites, and persistent outbreaks of political violence, such as rebellions, revolutions, and civil wars. There are variations on this common theme; later I'll talk about why some cycles are shorter and others longer. Also, the crisis severity is variable. Despite this variability, the time of troubles always comes. So far, we haven't seen an exception to this rule. No society that my team has studied had an integrative phase lasting more than around two hundred years.[1]

For a detailed account of the history and methodology of cliodynamics, especially as it relates to the model at the center of this book, please see appendix chapters A1 and A2. The gist of that story is that a large research network, which I have been coordinating over the past decade, has built a large database involving hundreds of historical and contemporary states, with a particular emphasis on how these societies slid into political crises—and then emerged from them, with variable degrees of success. Analysis of this crisis database (CrisisDB) yielded clear evidence that despite the many obvious (and not so obvious) differences between the cases, we see robust common threads.

Our analysis points to four structural drivers of instability: popular immiseration leading to mass mobilization potential; elite overproduction resulting in intraelite conflict; failing fiscal health and weakened legitimacy of the state; and geopolitical factors. The most important driver is intraelite competition and conflict, which is a reliable predictor of the looming crisis. Other factors are usually present, but they are not universal. For example, for large, powerful empires, geopolitical factors tend to be of reduced importance. Such states tend to be too big to be affected by what their neighbors do, and social breakdown within them is generated by internal forces. To borrow from Arnold Toynbee, great empires die not by murder but by suicide.[2]

I need to mention one additional complicating factor. When we look closely at the disintegrative phases, we discover that they are not uniformly grim. Instead, the level of collective violence tends to follow a rhythm. One generation fights an all-out civil war, but the next generation ("the sons"), scarred by this violence, keeps uneasy peace. The following generation ("the grandsons"), who grew up not being directly exposed to violence, repeats the mistakes of the grandfathers. This dynamic sets up a recurrent cycle of violence of roughly fifty years in length (that is, two human generations), which persists until the structural conditions are somehow resolved, leading to the next integrative phase.

Now let's make these theoretical ideas more concrete by tracking the dynamics of social instability and state breakdown in one particular region over a long period of time. I'll start my survey of instability cycles in medieval France, the wealthiest and most powerful kingdom of Western Europe in the High Middle Ages. Then we will move forward in time, tracing the successive waves of instability in France and, more broadly, Western Europe. I chose Europe here because we have a lot of quantitative data to call upon, telling us about the trends in popular immiseration, intraelite conflict, and other major drivers of instability. But make no mistake: the historical forces that bring about crises are not Eurocentric—all complex societies are vulnerable to them.

The Late Medieval Crisis in France

The thirteenth century was the golden age of medieval France. The territory controlled directly by the French crown tripled over the course of this century, and by 1300 France had come to dominate Western Europe militarily, politically, and culturally. The population of France was more than 20 million—every third inhabitant of Western Europe owed allegiance to the French king. The city of Paris, with its 230,000 people, was by far the largest and most splendid city of Latin Christendom. France during the High Middle Ages was not only the most powerful kingdom in Western Europe but also a cultural powerhouse. The Gothic style of architecture, known to contemporaries as the French style, developed in Île-de-France and spread from there to England, Germany, Spain, and northern Italy. During the thirteenth century, the University of Paris became the main center of learning and philosophy in Europe, attracting the best thinkers of the age. French became the most important international language of Europe, spoken by the nobilities of England, Flanders, Hungary, and the Kingdoms of Naples and Sicily.[3]

Toward 1300, however, the brilliance of the French kingdom began to tarnish. The golden age turned into a gilded age. While elite opulence continued unabated, the living conditions of common people deteriorated. The root cause of popular immiseration was the massive population boom in Western Europe in the two centuries before 1300. If in 1100 there were around six million people inhabiting the territory within the modern borders of France, two centuries later the population more than tripled, exceeding twenty million. Population explosion overwhelmed the capacity of the medieval economy to provide land for peasants, jobs for workers, and food for all. The majority of the population lived on the edge of starvation, and a series of crop failures and livestock epidemics between 1315 and 1322 tipped the system over the edge. By 1325, the population of France was 10–15 percent below the peak it reached in 1300. Then came the Black Death, killing between one-quarter and one-half of the population. By the end of the fourteenth century, the population of France collapsed to ten million—half of what it was in 1300.

As though millions of deaths were not enough, the demographic catastrophe had another, more subtle but nevertheless devastating effect on social stability by making the social pyramid unsustainably top-heavy. After 1250, the number of nobles increased even faster than that of the general population, because their economic position was better than that of the commoners. In fact, popular immiseration benefited the elites, who profited from high land rents, low wages, and high food prices. In other words, massive overpopulation during the thirteenth century created a wealth pump that enriched landowners at the expense of peasants.

As their incomes increased, many lower-rank nobles found that dividing their estates between two or more sons could allow all heirs to have enough income to maintain noble status. Wealthy magnates with far-flung possessions used some inconveniently located properties to set up younger sons as middle-rank nobles. There was also an increased rate of upward social mobility, with wealthy peasants and successful merchants ascending into nobility. When the famines and epidemics hit, the elites were better positioned to ride them out, suffering lower mortality than the commoners. All of these trends combined to increase the number of nobles in relation to the productive class, making the social pyramid top-heavy and, after a lag time, reversing the economic fortunes of the nobility. Whereas before 1300 the nobles enjoyed a favorable economic conjunction in which there were relatively few elites and cheap, plentiful labor, by the mid-fourteenth century the situation was completely reversed.

Lacking revenues to sustain their elite status, nobles responded by seeking employment with the state and by extracting a greater proportion of resources from the peasants. However, the state could not employ all impoverished nobles—there were too many of them, and the crown itself was sliding into financial insolvency. Inflation of prices, driven by the massive population growth, ate into state revenues, and attempts to respond to elite demands strained royal finances beyond the breaking point.

Extracting greater revenues from peasants meant that the landlords went beyond skimming the surplus and started cutting into the resources that peasants needed to survive. Landlord oppression undermined its own economic basis, as peasants responded by flight, starvation, or death in futile rebellions. As both of these strategies failed, the nobles turned to preying on each other. The elite overproduction game entered its final, violent phase, and intraelite conflicts popped up all over France.[4] In the 1350s, the breakdown of internal order reached the heart of the kingdom.

When the last Capetian king died in 1328 without leaving a male heir, the crown went to Philip VI, the first king of the Valois dynasty. But there were two other claimants who had an equally strong claim on the crown: Charles II of Navarre and Edward III of England. The three-way struggle among these powerful lords, coupled with the urban uprising in Paris led by Étienne Marcel and the rural insurrection, the Jacquerie, resulted in a complete state collapse by 1360.

This is not the place for a blow-by-blow account. Instead let's continue with our bird's-eye survey and see what happened next.

The collapse of the French state during the 1350s shocked the governing elites. At the Estates-General meeting in 1359, the different factions were able to bury their differences and agree on a common approach to saving the state. During the next two decades, the French conducted systematic, if unspectacular, military operations (avoiding grand battles that had previously been, for them, catastrophic). By 1380, the royal army had crushed the internal rebels and expelled the English from nearly all French territories. But this success turned out to be temporary, because the structural forces driving France into crisis—popular immiseration, elite overproduction, and state weakness—had not yet been properly addressed. Again, we find that cycles of collective violence tend to recur during the disintegrative phases, with a roughly fifty-year periodicity. The Late Medieval Crisis in France was not an exception.

As the new generation of leaders replaced the one that had first-hand experience of the state collapse in the 1350s, they repeated the mistakes of their elders. Two aristocratic factions, the Burgundians and the Orleanists, battled for the capital, massacring each other in turn, as the fortunes of civil war shifted. Another bloody urban uprising broke out in Paris in 1413, and in 1415 another English king, Henry V, entered the fray. History repeated itself with a catastrophic defeat of the French army at Agincourt, which was a close replay of the Battle of Crécy. It is eerie how closely the second collapse of the French state followed the trajectory of the first. Maybe history doesn't repeat itself, but it certainly rhymes.[5]

The second state collapse was even deeper than the first, and it took longer for the surviving French elites to pull themselves together. But they did, and they again expelled the English, with the last major city, Bordeaux, reconquered by the French in 1453.[6]

Following the end of the Hundred Years' War, France enjoyed a century-long integrative phase. Why was the century before 1450 so bleak and the one after so brilliant? The answer is that the forces pushing France into internal warfare ceased operating around 1450. Popular immiseration was "taken care of" by the famines, epidemics, and internal warfare, whose cumulative effect was to halve the French population. There was now plenty of land for peasants, and the dearth of labor more than doubled workers' real wages. Plunging land rents and increasing wages effectively shut down the wealth pump.

Most importantly, the hecatombs of Crécy, Poitiers, Agincourt, and a host of lesser-known battles removed tens of thousands of "surplus" nobility. Add to that the massacres during the factional infighting. (As an eyewitness described in his diary in May 1418, the streets of the capital were littered with the corpses of the defeated faction, which were "piled up like pigs in the mud.") While the overall population was halved between 1300 and 1450, the number of nobles in the same period declined by a factor of four.[7] The social pyramid ceased to be top-heavy, regaining a much more stable configuration, with a broad base and a narrow top. In the absence of elite overproduction, intraelite competition and conflict subsided. At the same time, the memory of the dark period of social breakdown and the external pressure from the English forged a new feeling of national unity among the elites. In this new climate of intraelite cooperation, it proved to be possible to reform state finances and provide France with a solid fiscal foundation for generations ahead.

The main internal pressures for instability—immiseration and elite overproduction—receded. What about the external factors? Many history books portray the Hundred Years' War as a dynastic conflict between the French and English kings. But this is a very shallow take on an exceedingly complex series of multisided conflicts. As the famous French historian Fernand Braudel wrote, a better name for this period is the "Hundred Years of Hostility."[8] The root causes of both state collapses in the fourteenth and fifteenth centuries were internal, with the English essentially playing the role of a jackal feeding on the body of the dead lion (with apologies to my English readers). With medieval England possessing less than a third of the population and resources of France, these two kingdoms were simply in different weight categories (a situation that would change a few centuries later). The spectacular victories at Crécy, Poitiers, and Agincourt, in which the English kids take justifiable pride, yielded no lasting gains for the English crown in the end. In fact, they ultimately aided the French by helping with their elite overproduction problem and by forging a sense of national unity that was so important to achieving an elite consensus on how to put the state on a solid financial foundation.

This is not to say that the role of the English in the Hundred Years of Hostility was negligible, but that the Anglo-French conflict was not a root cause of the two state collapses. After all, England and France were at war almost continually from the eleventh to the nineteenth centuries.[9] There was nothing special about the period 1338–1453 from this point of view.

Ages of Discord

Historians have long noted that there is a rhythm in history. "Golden ages" of internal order, cultural brilliance, and social optimism are followed by "times of troubles" of recurrent internecine fighting, declining high culture, and social gloom. Historians of Europe gave each of these periods a name. Thus, the High Middle Ages were followed by the Late Medieval Crisis. The Renaissance was followed by the General Crisis of the seventeenth century. The last complete cycle before our own—the Enlightenment, or the Age of Reason—was followed by the Age of Revolutions.

Historians of China see a similar pattern, which they call the dynastic cycles. Between 221 BC and 1912, from the Qin dynasty to the Qing dynasty, China was repeatedly unified (and reunified) and governed effectively for a while. Then moral corruption set in, bringing decline and fragmentation. As the Chinese historical novel *Romance of the Three Kingdoms* says, "The empire, long divided, must unite; long united, must divide. Thus it has ever been." Historians of ancient Egypt also divide its history into the Old Kingdom, the Middle Kingdom, and the New Kingdom, each followed by the First, Second, and Third Intermediate Periods.

Statistical analysis of CrisisDB confirms this historical intuition, but this macrohistorical pattern is not simple, mathematically precise cycles. First, the length of the overall integrative-disintegrative sequence varies depending on the characteristics of the society. Second, during the disintegrative periods, collective violence tends to recur with roughly fifty-year periodicity.

In France, the integrative phase of the High Middle Ages started during the reign of the great unifier, Philip II, also known as Philip Augustus (1180–1223), and ended in 1350. After the late medieval disintegrative phase (from 1350 to 1450), the next integrative phase, the Renaissance, lasted for just over a century (1450–1560). The next disintegrative phase (1560–1660) started with the outbreak of the French Wars of Religion (1562–1598), followed by the second wave of instability, which began in the 1620s with magnate rebellions, Huguenot insurrections, and peasant uprisings and culminated in the Fronde of 1648–1653. In the last complete cycle in France, the integrative phase, the Enlightenment, extended from 1660 to the outbreak of the French Revolution in 1789. The disintegrative phase, the Age of Revolutions, includes the Napoleonic period, the Revolutions of 1830 and 1848, and the aftershock of the Paris Commune in 1871 (although the last was precipitated by the catastrophic defeat in the Franco-Prussian War). Each phase thus lasted about a century, give or take a few decades, and the overall cycle lengths were roughly 250, 210, and 210 years.[10]

The Real Game of Thrones

For an instructive comparison with France, let's trace the cycles in England. Here the medieval cycle was bracketed by two periods of prolonged civil wars, the Anarchy during the reign of King Stephen (1138–1153) and the Wars of the Roses (1455–1485). Although the integrative period was relatively peaceful (compared to what was to come), it was interrupted by baronial rebellions, recurring at roughly fifty-year intervals.[11] Like France, England was hit by a double whammy of the Great Famine of 1315–1317 and the Black Death but, unlike France, it didn't immediately go into a tailspin. Why? The cliodynamic theory of the integrative-disintegrative cycles does not imagine some strict periodicity driving cycles of fixed length. It is a dynamic model, following how internal forces develop within each society. Again, the most important driver for looming instability is elite overproduction. What should happen if it is suddenly somehow abated? The crisis will be delayed into the future. And that's what happened in late medieval England.

When France broke down in the 1350s, all the English surplus elites—and there were huge numbers of them in England, just as in France—followed their king across the Channel. Some of them were killed in the fighting, but the majority found that the French wars were an exceedingly lucrative business. The victories at Poitiers and Crécy (and smaller battles that followed) yielded a few huge ransoms and a lot of smaller ones from the thousands of captured French nobles. The French countryside was still rich and yielded an enormous amount of loot, which was gathered during the so-called chevauchées (lightly disguised plundering expeditions). And there were castles and land in the conquered territories to dole out to the trusty retainers of the king and the magnates. In other words, England exported its surplus elites—and instability—to France.

But no good times last forever. Beginning in 1360, the French got their act together and by 1380 had kicked the English out. And that's when England went into its own tailspin. Suddenly, all those surplus elites were back, battle-hardened after incessant wars in France; inured to murder, torture, and extortion; and impoverished and embittered by their defeat. As is usual during such periods, social breakdown was manifested in several ways simultaneously. Peasants, who were more oppressed the more the elites themselves fell on hard times, finally had enough. The Peasants' Revolt, led by Wat Tyler in 1381, was bloodily suppressed, but it frightened the elites and forced them to lighten the burden they placed on the productive classes. In the west, there was a separatist rebellion in Wales led by Owain Glyn Dŵr. In the center, the struggle of the king, Richard II, and his faction against the group of nobles known as the Lords Appellant swung back and forth, but it eventually culminated in the deposition of Richard II in 1399, resulting in a change of dynasty from the Plantagenets to the Lancasters. If this all sounds like *Game of Thrones*, it's because George R. R. Martin modeled his fictional Lannisters on the historical Lancasters.[12]

When France broke down again in the early fifteenth century and another English king entered the fray in 1415, the hordes of impoverished elites flowed back across the Channel after him. Earlier, I remarked on how eerily the successive crises tend to resemble the previous ones. It's like societies have a cultural stencil plate for state collapse— the French way or the English way, as the case may be. England's trajectory after 1415 was another example of this curious pattern. As before, things went well for the English—for a while. Instability was successfully exported to France, and there were no significant disturbances in England between 1415 and 1448. However, as the French successfully reconquered their country around 1450, increasing numbers of English surplus elites had to return home. The current king, Henry VI, was unfit to rule, and the Royal Council governed in his name. The leadership of the Lancastrian faction fell to Margaret of Anjou. A contemporary wrote about her: "This woman excelled all other, as well in beauty and favour, as in wit and policy, and was of stomach and courage, more like to a man, than a woman."[13] (Martin clearly modeled Cersei Lannister after her.)

Elite factions and royal favorites encouraged the rise of disorder. The great nobles maintained growing private armies of armed retainers, with which they fought one another, terrorized their neighbors, paralyzed the courts, and attempted to dominate the government. There was another great peasant rebellion in 1450, this one led by Jack Cade. And in 1455, the Wars of the Roses broke out, and they would drag on until 1485.

It is said that Martin, when he watched the first season of *Game of Thrones*, was shocked by the graphic brutality, betrayal, and murder that the characters he created inflicted on each other. But the historical Wars of the Roses were just as brutal. Three kings were deposed and killed, and numerous magnates were executed, often without trial. Lords who ended up on the losing side of a battle were made to kneel in the mud and beheaded on the spot. Furthermore, the battles between the Lancastrians and the Yorkists were just the tip of an iceberg. In parallel with this dynastic conflict over the throne, there were numerous private wars between rival elites at the regional and local levels. In *The End of the House of Lancaster*, British historian R. L. Storey describes at least eight such conflicts plaguing the west, the north, and the east of England. Common people suffered greatly from this intraelite infighting because each faction often targeted the tenants of the opposing faction for extortion, robbery, and murder.

It's important to remember that, although medieval England was generally a much more violent country than the UK is today, the levels of violence characterizing the Wars of the Roses were way above the norm. During the integrative phase, every other generation saw a baronial rebellion against the crown, but compared to the Wars of the Roses, those rebellions were more like armed demonstrations intended to impress baronial demands on the king. The rebellion of 1215–1217, for example, was resolved by the king signing the Magna Carta to satisfy the mutinous elites. In the Wars of the Roses, the goal of each side was the extermination of the enemy.

Viewers of *Game of Thrones* sometimes complain that the characters they come to like are eliminated from the story with depressing regularity. But that's how things went in real life. After all, the prime mover of the Wars of the Roses was the horrible degree of elite overproduction in England circa 1450. Until it was somehow resolved, the conflict couldn't stop, except due to sheer exhaustion. But then it would simply be replayed again when a new generation, not immunized against violence, took over. For a disintegrative phase to end, the structural conditions that brought it about need to be reversed.

Of course, death in battle or through execution was not the only mechanism reducing elite overproduction. It seems to be the main one at the magnate level, but lower down the social ladder, the main role was played by downward social mobility. Most gentry were not killed in civil or private wars; they simply accepted, after a while, that their incomes did not allow them to maintain their elite status, and they quietly slipped down into the yeomanry. Civil wars, and the overall high level of violence, were still an important, if indirect, motivator for acquiescing to the loss of gentry status. After years and decades of violence and insecurity, the most violent were killed off, while the rest realized the futility of prolonging the struggles and settled down to peaceful, if not glamorous, lives. The numbers of English elites at all levels, from the magnates to the country gentry, declined severalfold during the Late Medieval Crisis.

In England we have a useful quantitative proxy to trace this trend, because drinking wine (rather than ale) was one marker of elite status. At the peak of their fortunes, English elites imported and consumed twenty thousand tuns of wine from Gascony. By the end of the Wars of the Roses, fewer than five thousand tuns were imported, and wine imports did not start recovering until after 1490. The implied fourfold decline in English elite numbers parallels the estimated fourfold decrease in the French nobility by the end of their own age of discord.[14]

Although the most intense period of internal warfare ended in 1485, there were a few aftershocks; we know of three quickly suppressed minor rebellions between 1489 and 1497. After that, England did not have another rebellion for two generations, which was quite a feat, given the general violence in early modern England. The next integrative phase finally set in.

The next two cycles in England had lengths similar to the French cycles. But because England emerged from the Late Medieval Crisis well after France, the two countries stayed out of sync. The General Crisis of the seventeenth century started in England with the Scottish rebellion, known as the Bishops' Wars, in 1639, immediately followed by the English Civil War, which ended in 1651. After a usual short spell of uneasy peace, England had to endure another outbreak of internal war, the Glorious Revolution (1688–1689), which brought its seventeenth-century disintegrative phase to an end (again, lagging a few decades behind France). And the Age of Revolutions arrived in England in 1830, while in France, of course, it was kicked off by the Storming of the Bastille in 1789. In short, France and England behaved like two dangling weights, swinging back and forth within the same period but one lagging behind the other.

Another difference between the two kingdoms during the Age of Revolutions was that while France was repeatedly hit by one revolution after another (1789, 1830, 1848 . . .), England entered a "revolutionary situation" in 1830 but then somehow managed to avoid state breakdown. Why this happened is an extremely interesting topic because it may provide us with some hints on how to repeat this feat ourselves. I will return to this question in chapter 9.

The Elite Polygamy Effect

Despite fighting nearly constantly between 1100 and 1815,[15] or maybe because of it, England and France had a very similar social makeup. Thus, it is not surprising that their cycle lengths were so similar (if out of sync). But such dynamic similarity is not necessarily the case for any complex human society. Depending on their constitution, some societies go through integrative-disintegrative cycles more swiftly and others more slowly.

Because the most important driver of social and political instability is elite overproduction, let's give some thought to how the details of elite reproduction (and overproduction) can affect the social pace—how fast a society gets into and out of crises. In preindustrial societies, in which gaining an elite status was difficult, although far from impossible, for a commoner, the speed with which the elite ranks could grow, and thus elite overproduction could develop, was strongly influenced by the biological reproduction of the elites—more specifically, by the reproduction rate of elite men. (Whether we like it or not, men dominated the upper reaches of power in those societies.) In humans, the greatest influence on male reproductive success is simply the number of mates men have access to.

In Western European kingdoms, such as France and England, Christianity restricted how many legal mates men could have. Of course, powerful men could, and often did, enter relationships with mistresses outside their marriages with lawful wives. And the offspring of such unions had a chance to enter the ranks of nobility. But this "bastard effect" did not significantly increase the rate of elite aspirant production in medieval and early modern European societies.

In Islamic societies, conversely, a man could have four legal wives and as many concubines as he could support. There was no stigma associated with being a concubine's son. Extensive polygamy, the practice of marrying many spouses, was also the rule for steppe pastoralists, such as the Mongols. As a result, these societies churned out elite aspirants at a frightening rate. The faster the pace at which elite overproduction develops, the shorter the integrative phases.

The theory thus tells us that there should be a significant difference in cycle lengths between societies with monogamous ruling classes and those with polygamous ones. According to my calculations, the typical length of cycles in monogamous societies should be around two hundred up to three hundred years, but in societies with polygamous elites, it should be only about a century, or even less.[16] We saw that the cycles in France and England (and according to CrisisDB, in other European societies as well) conform to this theoretical prediction. What about polygamous societies?

It turns out that this question was answered many centuries ago by a remarkable Islamic historian and philosopher, Abu Zayd Abd ar-Rahman ibn Muhammad ibn Khaldun al-Hadrami, born in Tunis in 1332. Ibn Khaldun noticed that political dynamics in his native Maghreb (North Africa, west of Egypt), as well as in the rest of the Muslim world, tend to move in cycles. After a new dynasty is established, it lasts for about four generations before falling and being replaced by a new dynasty. And then the cycle is repeated.[17] Some dynasties last for only three generations, others five, but on average, the length of Ibn Khaldun's cycles is four generations, which corresponds to about one hundred years. This is much shorter than the European cycles, as the theory predicts. But let's see whether Ibn Khaldun's cycles can also be observed in other polygamous societies, such as the nomadic herding societies of Central Eurasia.

A good point of comparison is the Mongol conquests led by Chinggis

Khan and his immediate successors. The huge territory conquered by the Mongols during the first half of the thirteenth century contained four large "cultural areas" inhabited by farming people. Working our way from east to west, they were China, Transoxania, Persia (including Mesopotamia), and Eastern Europe. From the middle of the thirteenth century, each of these four regions was ruled by a Chinggisid dynasty.[18] According to our theory, these four dynasties should be subject to Ibn Khaldun's cycles of around a century. This is indeed what happened. In all four regions, Chinggisid dynasties collapsed by the middle of the fourteenth century.[19] A more formal statistical analysis of CrisisDB confirms that rise-and-fall cycles in societies with polygamous elites are substantially shorter than such cycles in monogamous societies.

Contagion and Dynamic Entrainment

Scientists studying complex systems must navigate a middle course between the Scylla of overcomplication and the Charybdis of oversimplification. On the one hand, history is not just one damn thing after another. But on the other hand, it's not a simple repetition of mathematically precise cycles.

Our discussion of Ibn Khaldun's cycles showed that the time scales at which societies go through boom-and-bust cycles depend on their cultural characteristics, such as the degree of polygamy among the elites. A comparison between the two "dear enemies," England and France, suggested another complicating factor—that the geopolitical environment can extend or shorten cycles. By exporting instability to France during the Late Medieval Crisis, England was able to delay entering its own time of troubles. This is why the framework of nonlinear dynamics, and complexity science more generally, is so fruitful for understanding history—it gives us tools for studying how different factors interact with each other to generate systemic dynamics. A relatively small set of mechanisms can generate exceedingly complex dynamics. This is the essence of complexity science: complex dynamics do not have to have complex causes.

What other insights does complexity science yield? One productive idea is dynamic entrainment. If you put several metronomes on the same board and start them swinging randomly (out of sync), after a while they will all start swinging together in perfect synchrony.[20] The Dutch physicist Christiaan Huygens, who first observed this phenomenon in 1665, called it "odd sympathy."

Entrainment can help us understand why waves of instability often hit many societies at the same time. Take the General Crisis of the seventeenth century, which was Eurasia-wide. Why did the English Civil War, the Time of Troubles in Russia, and the collapse of the Ming dynasty in China happen at roughly the same time? And why was the eighteenth century a time of internal peace and imperial expansion in all three countries?

One possible reason for such synchrony is external forcing. Earlier in the chapter, we saw how a series of years of poor weather and bad harvests inflicted the Great Famine on Western Europe between 1315 and 1317. The Great Famine coincided with a trough in solar activity known as the Wolf Minimum (1280–1350). Most climatologists agree that lower solar activity produces cooler global temperatures. The primary cause of crop failures in Europe north of the Alps is cool and wet weather, which delays the ripening of crops and increases the chance that they will rot before being harvested. Other periods of low solar activity, including the Spörer Minimum (1460–1550) and the Maunder Minimum (1645–1715), are also correlated with cooler-than-average temperatures and incidences of crop failure.

Correlating societal collapse with climatic perturbations is a favorite pastime of collapsologists. But drawing a direct causal arrow from worsening climate to social breakdown doesn't work very well. The troughs of solar activity during the past millennium only sometimes coincide with disintegrative phases. It is possible that the poor climate during the Wolf Minimum was a cause of the Great Famine, which in turn undermined the stability of late medieval European societies. The later Maunder Minimum had its own great famine, which affected northern Europe, from France to Scandinavia to Russia. In France, two million people starved to death between 1694 and 1703. During the same period, Russia might have lost up to 10 percent of its population to famine. But both empires—one ruled by Louis the Great, the other by Peter the Great—had a lot of resilience (as the royal nicknames suggest). These famines caused massive human suffering and put an enormous strain on both monarchies, but they did not push them beyond the breaking point.

In my view, external forcing due to climate fluctuations is not a direct cause of social breakdown. Its effect is more subtle. Here's where metronomes swinging in odd sympathy can help. Think of empires as metronomes swinging between integrative and disintegrative phases. Now suppose that two empires in different regions of Eurasia start out of sync. Both are, however, affected by the same fluctuations of global climate. If one empire is "ahead" in its cycle, a period of good climate will allow it to last a little longer before it spins into crisis. A stretch of bad climate, to the contrary, will push an empire that is behind into crisis earlier. As the effects of such climatic "nudges" accumulate, the two empires will become increasingly synchronized, just as two metronomes on the same board do. Of course, imperial boom-bust cycles are much more complex than swinging metronome arms. But the general principle operates in both kinds of "oscillators" in a similar way. The external force need not even be periodic. Nudges can come at completely random times—their role is to synchronize cyclic tendencies, not to cause cycles themselves, which are driven by mechanisms internal to each empire.

The second synchronizing force, contagion, is even more potent than external forcing. Cliodynamic analysis indicates that major epidemics and pandemics are often associated with periods of major sociopolitical instability. We observe this pattern for at least the last two thousand years, going back to the Antonine Plague (second century CE) and the Plague of Justinian (sixth century). The spread of the Black Death through Afro-Eurasia (fourteenth century) was an integral part of the Late Medieval Crisis; a major resurgence of the plague coincided with the General Crisis of the seventeenth century. And the most devastating cholera pandemics (nineteenth century) occurred during the Age of Revolutions. The causality underlying this correlation is complex, with feedback loops going in both directions.[21] Let's unpack these causal relations a bit by tracing how the phase of the secular cycle affects the probability of a major epidemic.

As we saw earlier in this book, each secular cycle comprises an integrative trend followed by a disintegrative one. In the beginning of the cycle, the population grows from the minimum and is still far from the ceiling of the carrying capacity (the total number of people that the territory can feed, depending on both the amount of arable land and the current agricultural technology). As a result, real wages are high, and labor productivity is also high because land is still plentiful. In addition, most of the agricultural surplus is consumed by the producers themselves, making this period a golden age of the peasantry.

However, population growth eventually runs up against the Malthusian limit. With growing popular immiseration, the golden age of the peasantry ends, and the society enters a golden age of the elites, who profit from low wages and the high prices of products from land they own. The increasing purchasing power of the elites creates employment opportunities for artisans and merchants. Rural unemployment coupled with urban demand for labor (in crafts and trades but also as servants for the wealthy) generates a population flow toward the cities, which grow much faster than the general population during this period. The elite demand for luxury goods drives long-distance trade.

These trends make the appearance of new diseases and the spread of existing ones more likely. First, population growth results in the crossing of the "epidemiological threshold"—the population density above which a new disease is able to spread. Second, declining living standards due to popular immiseration lead to malnutrition and the weakening of the body's defenses against infection. Third, urbanization means that an increasing proportion of the population is crammed into cities, which were notoriously unhealthy places in preindustrial times. Fourth, increased migration and vagrancy result in thicker interaction networks, through which disease can spread more easily. Fifth, long-distance trade connects far-flung regions and promotes disease spread at the continental level.

As a result, societies that are approaching a crisis are very likely to be hit by an epidemic. But the causality also flows in the opposite direction. A major epidemic undermines societal stability. Because the poor suffer greater mortality than the elites, the social pyramids become top-heavy. Lethal epidemics also undermine social cooperation by delegitimizing governments. In old times, such major calamities were taken as a sign that God had turned away from the ruler, or that Heaven had withdrawn its Mandate. Today, we tend to think in more materialistic terms, blaming the government for dysfunction and failure to take effective steps to stop the epidemic. The end result has the same negative consequences: the collapse of trust in the state's institutions undermines its ability to keep internal peace and order. Major demographic disasters, such as epidemics and famines, often become triggers that tip societies into crisis, because they lead to a spike in popular immiseration (and mass mobilization potential) and a plunge in the state's legitimacy (and its ability to suppress internal violence).

Contagion is thus an important mechanism driving instability waves that swamp many societies continent-wide or even worldwide. The agent of contagion, however, doesn't have to be a virus or a microbe. Ideas can also be contagious.

Remember the Arab Spring?[22] It started in Tunisia on December 18, 2010, the day after the fruit vendor Mohamed Bouazizi immolated himself to protest police corruption and ill treatment. From there it spread to Algeria (December 29, 2010), Jordan (January 14, 2011), Oman (January 17, 2011), Saudi Arabia (January 21, 2011), Egypt (January 25, 2011), Syria (January 26, 2011), Yemen (January 27, 2011), and Sudan (January 30, 2011). By the end of February, it had spread to the rest of the Arab countries (including Iraq, Libya, Kuwait, Morocco, and Lebanon). Bouazizi's self-immolation was not the root cause of the Arab Spring. It was a trigger—a single spark that started a prairie fire.[23] The structural conditions that were required for the conflagration had developed slowly over the years and decades preceding the Arab Spring.[24] But the nearly simultaneous breakout of rebellions and revolutions in the Arab world was due to contagion—of ideas.

Many political commentators blame newfangled social media as the cause of the Arab Spring. But those who think that it was an unprecedented event in human history simply don't know history. Before the Arab Spring of 2010, there was the Springtime of Nations in 1848. It started in Italy in January but was little noticed at the time. The most influential event was the February Revolution in France, which inspired uprisings in Germany, Denmark, and Sweden in March. In the Hapsburg

Empire, there were also multiple rebellions in March, with the most notable occurring in Hungary and Galicia. In June, the 1848 revolutions spread to Romania; in July, to Ireland.[25]

There was no internet in the Europe of 1848, but the news spread swiftly by means of newspapers. The trigger was France, where the revolution began on February 22, 1848. By the end of March, most of the European continent was in turmoil.

Summing Up: The Story So Far

In part I, our inquiry into the causes of recurrent instability waves that afflict human societies began in present-day America and then expanded by moving back in time and to other parts of the world. In part II, I circle back to the United States and delve more deeply into the "subterranean" processes that have been shaping our current age of discord. On a methodological note, my approach so far has been to illustrate the lessons we learned from cliodynamic analysis with specific examples of past societies sliding into crises and then somehow dealing with them. But cliodynamics is much more than a collection of historical examples. To extract truly useful lessons from history that can equip us with the knowledge needed to navigate the troubled waters ahead, we need to translate our verbal ideas about how societies work into mathematical models. Then we need to integrate our theories with data while avoiding the pitfalls of cherry-picked examples. This means that we have to construct and statistically analyze historical databases. To those readers who wish to learn more about how cliodynamics works in practice, I suggest that you now read the appendix chapters before tackling chapter 3. For those who prefer to jump right into the thick of it, continue with the main sequence.

Part II

THE DRIVERS
OF INSTABILITY

CHAPTER 3

"THE PEASANTS ARE REVOLTING"

Now armed with comparative context regarding the structure and dynamics of our social systems, let's return to our inquiry of the USA. We'll start with the largest interest group: the working class. It may be surprising in a work built up from analysis of large data sets about human behavior in aggregate, but I will open this chapter, and several that follow, with a short story, an archetypal example, if you will. Other than my fear that it is easy to lose sight of real human beings when modeling impersonal social forces, my only defense is that every material fact embedded in these stories has ample real-world precedent.

Steve

"So, you are voting for Trump in November?" I asked Steve in the summer of 2016. "But he is a billionaire. What does he know—or care—about common people? And he is such a clown."

Steve shook out a cigarette from a pack of Marlboros and lit it.

"It's not Trump I am going to vote for. The problem is the liberal elites who have been driving this great country into the ground. That woman only cares about bankers keeping their wealth. She says that 'deplorables' like me are the problem. Me and 'white privilege'? What a sick joke. The real white supremacy is the CEOs of Fortune 500 companies, ninety percent of whom happen to be white men. But somehow the corporate media doesn't see that elephant in the room. No, I don't buy what the Democrats and the liberal media tell us. At least Trump is saying out loud what we all think."

Steve grew up in upstate New York in a lower-middle-class family. His father worked as a machinist at a factory that manufactured highway infrastructure products. This job brought in a modest but steady income that allowed Steve's family to maintain their middle-class status. Steve's mother didn't work, and the family owned their own house and could afford to send Steve's older sister to a local college.

Steve himself decided that he was not interested in college. His high school grades were not that stellar. Additionally, when his sister graduated with a degree in liberal arts and sciences, her diploma had no visible effect on the kind of job she was offered or the wage she got. Two years after finishing college, she and her husband moved away to North Carolina, where the taxes and the cost of living were lower and where her husband's employment prospects were better.

Instead of college, Steve signed up for the army, which sent him to Germany. But he completed only one tour of duty. At that time, the United States was just about to embark on a series of foreign wars in places like Afghanistan and Iraq. Steve didn't see the point of risking his life in wars in which he didn't have much of a stake. In a sad development, his father suddenly passed away from a heart attack at a relatively young age, and Steve wanted to support his mother during this difficult time. When he returned home, Steve found that, unlike his father's generation, he could not count on holding a steady job. For a while he worked in construction, but he eventually trained himself as a car mechanic.

Although not suited to any managerial role, he is a good worker with his hands, and his skill at fixing cars is valued by his bosses. Despite that, the level of his salary in real terms is much lower than what his father earned. Additionally, he has no job security. Something always happens—the repair shop goes out of business, or it has to downsize the workforce due to lack of demand, or the owner demands extra work while refusing to pay overtime.

The upshot is that Steve cannot hold a job for more than a year or two and periodically has to rely on unemployment benefits. Applying for benefits is a demeaning process that takes time, and Steve often goes for weeks without any income. A downside of receiving benefits is that there is a lot of pressure to accept low-wage jobs, even if they don't fit his skills. He knows that he is a good worker, and in previous jobs he earned as much as twenty-five dollars per hour. Why should he accept a job that pays minimum wage? And after taking out taxes, he is actually going to earn less than the unemployment benefits he is currently getting. Steve wants to work—he enjoys fixing cars and is good at it. But he resents being called lazy because he is reluctant to take low-paying temporary jobs. Although he doesn't know the word, he is part of the "precariat."[1]

It helps that his mother got a job at the local Walmart. Dealing with rude customers is unpleasant, and the job pays a low wage. On the upside, the commute is short. Also, Steve and his mom consider themselves lucky that they own their house. Real estate taxes in their town are high—more than $5,000 a year. Still, living in your own home beats renting an apartment. Another stroke of luck is that, as a veteran, Steve gets free health insurance through the Veterans Health Administration.

It also must be admitted that Steve has proven unable to save any of his income for a rainy day. Even when he does well, money somehow always disappears before the next payday.

Steve wants to have a family and kids. But although he has had several girlfriends, none of his relationships grew into long-term ones. He doesn't know what the problem is, but now that he has started his fifth decade, he feels that he may have to resign himself to a child-free life.

Steve has two passions: cars and guns. The first helps to bring money in, and the second is one of the reasons why he has no savings. He has quite a collection of firearms and regularly shoots them at the firing range. His buddies are mostly veterans and, like him, gun nuts. The most sacred part of the US Constitution for them is the Second Amendment: "the right of the people to keep and bear Arms." Through his friends, Steve learned about the Oath Keepers. As a veteran, he was welcome to join, and he has participated in several demonstrations in favor of the Second Amendment, but more recently, he has drifted away from the organization.

Steve's political views have been shaped by personal experience and his social environment. Overall, it is clear to him that his country is moving in the wrong direction. His grandparents grew up during the Great Depression and World War II. Life was hard for a while, but then it got visibly better as the country entered the postwar era. The next generation, that of his baby boomer parents, had it even better. America was a great country in which the quality of life for the common people had been noticeably improving for each generation. But not for Steve and his friends. Somehow, the age of prosperity for the common people has ended and been replaced by an age of precarity. It is not right that children should be worse off than their parents.

What's even worse, according to Steve, is that the "cosmopolitan elites," who control the American state, have essentially declared war

on people like him—white heterosexual males without college educations. They are "deplorables," as Hillary Clinton famously described
them in 2016—"racist, sexist, homophobic, xenophobic, Islamopho-
bic." Especially when he is between jobs, Steve feels like one of the least
powerful people in America. He and his buddies believe that the elites
can't wait to get rid of them. Liberal pundits and politicians count the
years before people like Steve are finally outnumbered by the "correct"
voters. As he hears from right-wing commentators, the elites actively
work to bring that day closer by encouraging immigration.

While his father was a staunch Democrat, Steve didn't bother to
vote before 2016. No mainstream politicians appealed to him. It all
changed in 2016 with the stratospheric rise of Donald Trump, who unexpectedly gained the Republican nomination. Steve didn't completely
buy Trump, but at least he was expressing in words what Steve and his
friends felt. He promised to drain the swamp and to build the wall. This
message resonated, even though Steve was skeptical that Trump would
be allowed to do any of it. But it didn't matter. Steve welcomed Trump's
candidacy as a battering ram against the Washington elites. It was a de-
light to watch the elites squirm under Trump's onslaught.

Steve is not a revolutionary. He doesn't want to break the state and
reshape society. Instead, he wants things to return to what they were for
his parents and grandparents. This is how he understands the Trump
slogan, "Make America Great Again."

As much as he loathes mainstream politicians, Steve despises the
mainstream media even more. The only mainstream media program
that he watches is *Tucker Carlson Tonight* on Fox News. But his main
sources of information and ideas are bloggers and YouTubers who are
veterans like himself. He laughs when the corporate media call his news
sources "fake news"—in his view, it's channels like CNN that peddle
fake news. One particular topic of fake news, according to Steve, is the

current epidemic of shooting rampages. Most of them are engineered by gun control advocates with the goal of swaying public opinion against the Second Amendment. This is one thing that he feels strongly about; his line in the sand will be crossed when the state comes to take his guns away. He is willing to use arms to defend his right to bear arms. As his pal Brad likes to repeat, "If they treat us like this when we are armed, what will they do to us after they take our arms away?"

Kathryn

About a year or two after Donald Trump astounded the world by getting himself elected, when our political elites were still trying to process this shocking turn of events, I had an interesting conversation with one of them. Kathryn, a one-percenter herself, lives in Washington, DC, and has extensive connections among both wealthy philanthropists and established as well as aspiring politicians. She often acts as an intermediary between the two groups. She had heard somewhere that years ago I had published a forecast predicting the coming instability in the US, and she wanted to know what this forecast was based on. More specifically, she was looking for insights into why so many people voted for Trump in 2016.

I started to give her my usual spiel about the drivers of social and political instability, but I didn't get beyond the first one, popular immiseration. "What immiseration?" countered Kathryn. "Life has never been better than today!" She then advised me to read *Enlightenment Now*, a then just published book by Steven Pinker. She also suggested that I take a look at the graphs on Max Roser's website, Our World in Data. Channeling both, she urged me to rethink my take: "Just follow the data. Life, health, prosperity, safety, peace, knowledge, and happiness are on the rise."[2] Global poverty is declining; child mortality is declining; violence is declining. Everybody, even in the poorest African country, has a smartphone, which contains a level of technology that is miraculous compared to what previous generations had.

Kathryn is right, as far as it goes. According to Max Roser,[3] if in 1820 more than three-quarters of people in the world lived in extreme poverty, today only one-tenth suffer this condition. Decade by decade for the last two centuries, global poverty has declined, with the rate of decline particularly impressive after 1970.

But Steve doesn't care what has happened to global poverty since 1820, or even 1970. Most of the poverty decline since 1970 was, in any case, due to the massive economic growth of China. Of what possible relevance is that to him? Why does it matter that he is wealthier than most people in sub-Saharan Africa? He compares himself not to a sorghum farmer in Chad but to his father. He knows full well that his generation is economically worse off than the generation of his father.

When Kathryn says that life has never been better, it's based not only on what happens globally—there is also a personal angle. She and the people she talks to (predominantly other one-percenters, with a few ten-percenters mixed in) have done fabulously well in the past few decades. Her own experience is in agreement with the optimistic statistics cited by Pinker and Roser. But that's not the personal experience of Steve and those in his social milieu. No wonder these two groups disagree about the direction in which the country is going.

In Kathryn's view, Steve's problems are mostly his fault. In today's knowledge-based economy, a high school degree is not enough—to flourish he needs a college education. He also needs to practice financial discipline. Instead of spending his extra money on guns and ammo, he should be putting it into an individual retirement account.

So who is right? How typical is Steve's experience, and is he justified in thinking that America is heading in the wrong direction? Such questions can only be answered with statistics.

Plumbing the Numbers

Kathryn acknowledges that growing inequality is a problem. In her view, however, though rising inequality is real, it is somewhat overstated as a problem that needs urgent action. Although the living standards of poorer people are not improving fast enough, they are still improving. The economic system based on capitalism and free markets is delivering. The best solution for inequality is simply more economic growth.[4]

Are the living standards of the US population improving? The usual way to answer this question is to look at what has been happening with household incomes. Since our aim is to understand why Trump won in 2016, let's look at how incomes changed during the forty-year period preceding this date. The year 1976 is a good starting point for this comparison because this was a year when Steve's young father already had a steady job. He and his wife had moved into their new home, and they were expecting their first child, Steve's sister. Life was good and getting better.

According to the US Census Bureau,[5] the average real household income (expressed in inflation-adjusted 2020 dollars) increased from $61,896 in 1976 to $89,683 in 2016. This is an increase of 45 percent, which looks quite good. However, the average income is not the best number for us to look at, because the average is calculated over both a poor family, in which a single breadwinner earning close to the minimum wage brings home $20,000, and a rich family, in which a CEO of a large company earns, on average, $16.6 million.[6] What we want to know is what happened to typical families, not the extremes of the distribution. For this we need to look at the median income: the level dividing the distribution of incomes precisely in half. The US Census Bureau helpfully provides data on the median income. Between 1976 and 2016, it grew from $52,621 (in 2020 dollars) to $63,683, a change of 21 percent. Not as good as 45 percent but still a decent increase, right?

However, let's compare these family income statistics to what happened with wages. After all, although the combined income of Steve and his mom in 2016 was greater than what his dad earned back in 1976, this was due to both members of the household working. Steve's mom works at Walmart not because she enjoys the experience but simply because they wouldn't be able to pay the bills without her earnings. The increase in their household income was not accompanied by an increase in her quality of life. It merely enabled them to not fall behind.

When we look at wages, the supposed improvement in economic conditions is diluted even more. The median real wage between 1976 and 2016 increased from $17.11 to $18.90 per hour—that is, by 10 percent.[7] When we break down the numbers by race, we see that the improvement for Black workers was slightly better—12 percent. But because they started from a lower level in 1976, their median wage in 2016 was only $16.06. The improvement for Hispanic workers, in contrast, was only 6 percent. At the lower end of the wage distribution, we also see that the first decile (the 10 percent of lowest-paid workers) also improved by only 6 percent.

As we delve into the numbers, the rosy picture of how economic growth has supposedly delivered for the majority of the US population gets less rosy. Ten percent spread over forty years is not really that impressive. And keep in mind that this overall change was by no means continual. During the 1990s, for example, typical workers were losing ground—they actually earned less than in the 1970s.

Tracing how real wages changed in the different parts of the wage distribution is a useful approach but not the only one, and perhaps not even the best one. There are no sharp breaks between the different deciles—the distribution is smooth. An alternative approach is to look at how wages changed for different classes of workers. Recently, social scientists started paying attention to how educational attainment affects economic well-being.[8]

Statisticians sort Americans into five classes reflecting their educational achievement: less than high school (9 percent of the population in 2016), high school (26 percent in 2016), some college (29 percent in 2016), bachelor's degree (23 percent in 2016), and advanced degree (13 percent in 2016).[9] The big break, in terms of economic fortunes, is between the first three classes (less educated), which all lost ground, and the last two (more educated), which pulled ahead. The average real wage of workers with bachelor's degrees increased from $27.83 to $34.27 per hour. (As before, I am comparing 1976 to 2016 using inflation-adjusted dollars.) Americans with advanced degrees did even better, going from $33.18 to $43.92. But workers with just high school degrees saw their wages decrease from $19.25 to $18.57. For workers who did not complete high school, wages shrank from $15.50 to $13.66. Looking at different demographic categories, we see some variation around this overall pattern: men fared worse than women, and Black people fared worse than white or Hispanic people.[10] But for all categories, the gap between the less and more educated has deepened over time.

The startling conclusion from these data is that Americans without a four-year college degree—64 percent of the total population—have been losing ground in absolute terms; their real wages shrank over the forty years before 2016. But we are not done yet. So far, we've been focusing entirely on inflation-adjusted wages, or "real wages." But what makes them real? Adjusting wages for inflation is not quite as straightforward as it may seem. Over the past decades, some goods became cheaper: TVs, for example, and many toys. The cost of other things, such as new cars, hasn't changed much in current dollars, which means that new cars became cheaper in inflation-adjusted dollars. But the cost of other items and products increased much faster than the official inflation rate. To estimate this rate, government economists must define a basket of consumables and then calculate how its cost changes from year to year. There are several problems with this approach. First, the baskets of Steve and Kathryn are utterly different. In other words, each experiences a different rate of inflation. Second, the basket of consumables changes dramatically over time. For example, people didn't have smartphones in 1976, and now everybody uses them. How do we factor this in?

The process by which government economists construct and adjust the basket of consumables is somewhat opaque and, as some critics claim, vulnerable to manipulation. After all, when government agencies report economic growth, there is a strong incentive to underestimate the inflation rate, because it makes the government look better. GDP is calculated as the sum of all goods and services produced in the United States. It is then divided by the US population, giving us GDP per capita. Finally, it is adjusted by the cost of the basket, yielding real GDP per capita. Underestimating inflation inflates real GDP per capita, which makes the government look better. Several critics have come up with their own approaches to estimating inflation, although mainstream economists typically dismiss them as spurious. Whoever is right, the main point here is that adjusting wages for inflation is not a straightforward business and can introduce large errors into the statistics we use. Different government agencies use different price indexes: the consumer price index (CPI) and the personal consumption expenditures price index (PCE). The average difference between them is 0.5 percent.[11] This may not look like a lot, but keep in mind that a 10 percent change over forty years (which is how much the real median wage increased) translates into a 0.25 percent change per year, or half of the difference between the CPI and PCE indexes.

Nevertheless, it is clear that the dollar earned in 2016 is different than the dollar earned in 1976, and we need to adjust for this change somehow. The usual way to do it is to use government statistics. As we have seen, according to this calculation, the real median wage has grown by 10 percent over forty years, or by 0.25 percent per year. Even this looks quite anemic. Another approach is to disaggregate the basket and look at different types of goods and services separately. For example, what are the most important big items that define the quality of life for the American middle class? One is clearly higher education. Another one is owning a home. Another is keeping yourself healthy. Curiously, the cost of all three of these major expenses has increased much faster than official inflation.

To bring this message home, let's forget about real dollars (which turn out to be not quite real) and do a calculation using just nominal (current) dollars, thus skipping the step of adjusting for inflation. In 1976, the average cost of studying at a public university was $617 per year. That sounds almost unreal. A worker earning the median wage in 1976 needed to work 150 hours to earn one year of college. In 2016, the average annual cost of public university tuition and fees was $8,804. A median-wage worker needed to work 500 hours to pay for it—that's more than three times longer. The challenge of affording a median house tells a similar story: a median worker must work 40 percent longer to earn it in 2016 compared to 1976. That 10 percent increase in real median wage starts to look even punier than before.

Even worse, if we do the same calculation but instead of the median wage use the average wage of a high school graduate—remember, it decreased in absolute terms between 1976 and 2016—the increase in the hours worked to pay for college is nearly fourfold (3.85, to be precise). In 2016, "working-class" (less educated) parents had to work four times as long to pay for college for their children compared to 1976. This means that the ability to move from the less educated to the more educated class has dramatically eroded in just a few decades.

Biological Well-Being

So far in this investigation of the changing fortunes of the American working class, we have only looked at the economic dimensions of well-being. But well-being and its opposite, immiseration, have other dimensions: biological and social. The first of these, broadly having to do with health, is in many ways a better and more honest indicator of quality of life. What can we say about health?

One of the most sensitive indicators of biological well-being is the average height of a population.[12] Physical stature is shaped by the balance between nutritional intakes and demands made on the organism by the environment during the first twenty years of its life. The most important aspect of nutrition is energy intake, but diet quality (availability of fresh vegetables, for example) also affects height. Environmental pressures that can stunt growth include high prevalence of disease, as fighting off infection costs energy, and heavy labor, if it is required from children and adolescents. Many factors determining stature are thus affected by the economic status of the family. Greater income translates into greater quantity and quality of food. Wealth also buys better medical services and frees children from the need to work in factories. Beach vacations allow growing organisms to replenish their stocks of vitamin D. Thus, the average height of a population provides a highly useful corrective to purely economic measures, such as the real wage. It is possible to get reliable estimates of height from human bones, enabling us to track population well-being in prehistoric populations.

In the eighteenth century, America had the tallest people in the world.[13] The average height of US-born Americans continued to increase until the cohort born in 1830. During the next seventy years, it declined by more than four centimeters. After another turning point, in 1900, and for about seventy more years, the trend was again highly positive. During this period, the average height increased by a whopping nine centimeters. Then something happened. Beginning with children born in the 1960s, gains in height stopped. This trend change only affected the US. In other high-income democracies, average statures continued to increase, and today the tallest people on earth live in countries such as the Netherlands, Sweden, and Germany. But not in the United States. What's going on?

Adult heights are reached when adolescents between fifteen and twenty years old go through their growth spurts. Once we reach our early twenties, we stop growing (and eventually begin shrinking, although very slowly). The heights of children born in 1960 were thus partially set by the environmental conditions they experienced between 1975 and 1980. And these conditions were largely determined by the wages of the parent generation. As a result, when the real wages of typical Americans stopped growing in the late 1970s, so did the average height of their children.[14]

Another highly useful indicator of biological well-being is life expectancy. This one is harder to estimate for populations living in the distant past. Nevertheless, thanks to research conducted by the Nobel Prize laureate Robert Fogel and other economic historians, we are fortunate to have the data for the entire history of the United States.[15] During these two centuries, changes in life expectancy closely mirrored the dynamics of the stature data.[16] This is not surprising, because at the individual level there is a strong positive correlation between life expectancy and stature, except at extreme heights. In other words, these two measures provide complementary views of biological well-being. When they both decline, the case that something is wrong with the population is strengthened.

Today we dispose of very detailed data that allow social scientists to reconstruct the trends in life expectancy or, alternatively, death rates for different population strata within the society. When a person dies in the United States, for example, they are issued a death certificate, which provides all kinds of data on the deceased, including their educational attainment. The distinguished economists Anne Case and Angus Deaton recently used these statistics to discover a highly troubling trend in this measure of well-being. They found that life expectancy at birth for white Americans fell by one-tenth of a year between 2013 and 2014. In the next three years, life expectancy fell for the US population as a whole. Mortality at all ages rose, but the most rapid increase happened to white Americans in midlife. "Any decline in life expectancy is extremely uncommon. With a three-year decline, we are in unfamiliar territory; American life expectancy has *never* fallen for three years in a row since states' vital registration coverage was completed in 1933," Case and Deaton write.[17] The decline in the life expectancy of Americans began several years before the COVID-19 pandemic, but the pandemic delivered a major punch. By 2020, life expectancy at birth lost 1.6 years, as compared to 2014.[18]

The story that the Case and Deaton book tells is mostly that of white working-class Americans. Non-Hispanic white Americans make up 62 percent of the working-age population, and tracking their well-being is very important for understanding where America is going as a country. But it would be a mistake to limit the implications of Case and Deaton's research to just "angry white men," as is sometimes done in the press. The economic and social forces that have been harming labor have affected all working-class Americans, regardless of gender, race, or ethnicity. The timing of when their lives were impacted by these forces, however, can be markedly different.

The current wave of globalization, which got going around 1980, hit Black Americans, especially those living in inner cities, particularly hard. Better-educated Black Americans left for safer neighborhoods and the suburbs. In the urban core, marriage rates fell; crime rates and mortality from violence rose; and the twin epidemics of crack cocaine and AIDS had a disproportionate effect on Black Americans. What happened to working-class Black Americans during the 1980s could thus serve as a preview of similar developments that affected white Americans thirty years later. Black mortality rates have always been above those of white Americans, and in the early 1990s, they were more than twice those of white Americans. But after 2000, as white mortality rates rose, Black mortality rates rapidly fell, closing the gap between them to 20 percent. Unfortunately, the improvements in Black life expectancy ceased by 2013. A major factor in this trend reversal was the rise in "deaths of despair" among less educated Black Americans after 2013.[19]

Deaths of Despair

Earlier in the chapter, we saw that the economic fortunes of the "credentialed class" (Americans holding a bachelor's or an advanced degree) and the "working class" (less educated) have diverged in absolute terms over the past four decades. The wages of the more educated grew; those of the less educated shrank. What happened to other dimensions of well-being? Thanks to the massive research carried out by Case and

Deaton, we know the answer, and it is not good. Death rates for the credentialed continued their secular decline. For the working class, however, death rates increased, and life expectancies declined.

The first population group in which Case and Deaton documented growing death rates was working-class white men between forty-five and fifty-five years old. The trend reversal for this group came in the late 1990s.[20] The rise in mortality rates was driven by a combination of causes, which Case and Deaton refer to in aggregate as "deaths of despair." Deaths of despair are caused by suicide, alcoholism, and drug abuse—all ways of escaping physical and psychological pain. Suicide is the fastest way out, but deaths from drug overdoses and alcoholic cirrhosis are equally self-inflicted; they simply take longer. What was particularly striking was that whereas deaths of despair increased fourfold for less educated men, they hardly budged for more educated men.[21]

Deaths of despair do not solely afflict men, however. Case and Deaton write:

Early media coverage of our work often carried headlines about "angry" white *men* dying, which we think stemmed from an inability to imagine that women could kill themselves in these ways. Historically, they did not. But that has changed. Women are less likely to kill themselves—this appears to be true everywhere in the world where we have data, even in China, which used to be an exception—and they are less likely to die from alcoholic liver disease or from drug overdoses. Yet the graph shows that the epidemic is affecting men and women in almost equal numbers. This is true for each component—suicide, drug overdose, and alcoholic liver disease—examined separately. . . . This plague has not discriminated by sex.

In the early 1990s, both less and more educated white women were at low risk of dying from alcohol abuse, suicide, or drug overdoses. From that point on, however, education-specific trajectories diverged for women, just as they did for men.

Then, in 2005, deaths of despair started to increase before middle age. The death rates of Americans in their thirties and forties grew faster than the death rates of their parents, even though we usually observe the opposite, due to the effects of aging. A paradoxical situation arose in which an older generation had a lower mortality rate than a younger generation. As Case and Deaton write, "Parents should not have to watch their grown children die. It is a reversal of the normal order of things; children are supposed to bury their parents, not the reverse."

Back in 2010, when I gave talks about my forecast for the Turbulent Twenties, I pointed to the declining relative wages, shrinking heights (especially for disadvantaged segments of the population), and worsening social dimensions of well-being (more on this below). But American life expectancy continued to increase, even though it was lagging behind improvements observed in other wealthy democracies. At the time, I explained it by saying, "We live in a post-Malthusian world in which we should hardly expect that immiseration would result in an absolute decline of life expectancies." I was wrong. When I first encountered the work of Case and Deaton in 2015, I was truly shocked.

The Trend Reversal of the Reagan Era

How can we understand this? Economic trends, such as growing inequality, play an important role, but it would be too crude to draw a direct causal arrow from inequality to immiseration. Here's how I reconstruct the constellation of causes that resulted in shrinking American life expectancy—and declining well-being more generally. My explanation is consistent with that of Case and Deaton, and of economists such as John Komlos.[22] But I reach further back into the past and put it within the general framework of cliodynamics.[23]

The United States, like any other complex society, has gone through alternating integrative and disintegrative phases. The first disintegrative phase began circa 1830 and ended circa 1930.[24] Within that period, there were two spikes of collective violence, separated by roughly fifty years: the Civil War (and its violent aftermath) and the instability peak around 1920. At the end of the first age of discord in the US, the governing elites, frightened by the levels of political violence that it wrought, managed to pull together and agree on a set of reforms that brought the first age of discord to an end. These reforms were initiated during the Progressive Era, starting around 1900, and finalized during the New Deal of the 1930s. One of the most important outcomes was an unwritten social contract between businesses, workers, and the state that gave workers the right to organize and collectively bargain, and ensured that they would more fully participate in sharing the gains of economic growth. This agreement was broader than just economics; it enshrined the idea of social cooperation between the different parts of society (in cliodynamic terms, the commoners, the elites, and the state). Although initially there was fierce resistance against the contract by certain segments of the elites,[25] the success of the country in dealing with the aftermath of the Great Depression and then World War II convinced all, except for a relatively small fringe, that this contract was a good thing.

We shouldn't forget that the working class who entered this compact were the white working class; Black Americans were left out in the cold. (I will return to this important point in chapter 6.) And, ironically, the opposite end of the wealth spectrum—the superrich—were also among the losers, because the tripartite agreement shut down and indeed reversed the wealth pump. Nearly half of the millionaires who thrived during the Roaring Twenties were wiped out by the Great Depression and the following decades, when worker wages grew faster than GDP per capita. The size of the top fortune in the USA lost ground between 1929 and 1982, both in real terms and when measured as multiples of median worker salaries.[26] The big winners were the middle classes.

But it didn't last. In the 1970s, a new generation of elites began replacing the "great civic generation."[27] The new elites, who didn't experience the turbulence of the previous age of discord, forgot its lessons and started to gradually dismantle the pillars on which the postwar prosperity era was based. The ideas of neoclassical economics, previously held by fringe economists, now became mainstream.[28] The Reagan presidency of the 1980s was the turning point when the idea of cooperation between workers and businesses was abandoned. Instead, we entered the age of "greed is good."

At the same time, worker wages came under pressure from diverse forces that shifted the balance of the supply and demand for labor. The supply of labor was inflated by the large baby boomer generation seeking jobs, by increased participation of women in the workforce, and by greatly increased immigration. The demand for labor was diminished as businesses moved production overseas in response to globalization and, more recently, increasing automation and robotization of production. As a result, oversupply of labor in relation to demand for it put downward pressure on worker wages. As institutions protecting workers were becoming weaker, wages were unable to resist this downward pressure. Real wages declined, especially for less educated workers, whose skills were less in demand in the new economy, and who experienced stronger competition from immigrants, automation, and off-shoring than college-educated workers did.[29]

While the balance of labor supply and demand clearly had a strong effect, purely economic factors are not sufficient to explain why the relative wages of typical workers had been in decline since the 1970s. A statistical analysis of wage data shows that an additional, and key, factor was shifting cultural and political attitudes about what is the appropriate level of pay for non-elite labor. A good proxy for this "extra-economic" factor is the real minimum wage.[30] From the New Deal to the Great Society, these nonmarket forces pushed the minimum wage up faster than inflation. During the 1970s, however, an opposing trend gained the upper hand, allowing the real minimum wage to decay as a result of inflation. What is important here, however, is not the direct effect of the minimum wage on overall wages, which is likely to be slight because it affects a small proportion of the American labor force. Furthermore, many states set their minimum wages above the federal level. The primary value of this variable is as a proxy for the complex of nonmarket forces, which also includes elite attitudes toward collective bargaining.[31]

Recent new papers by economists provide strong evidence for the importance of nonmarket forces in explaining the wage declines of American workers. A 2020 analysis by Anna Stansbury and Lawrence H. Summers presented a variety of evidence that declining worker power is a more important factor than increases in firms' power in the product market ("monopoly"), firms' power in labor markets ("monopsony"), or technological developments.[32] A 2021 article by Lawrence Mishel and Josh Bivens provides further evidence that wage suppression between 1979 and 2017 was due to a shifting balance of power, not to automation and technological changes. Mishel and Bivens identify the following factors that together accounted for three-fourths of the divergence between productivity and median hourly compensation growth:

1. Austerity macroeconomics, including facilitating unemployment higher than it needed to be to keep inflation in check, and responding to recessions with insufficient force;
2. Corporate-driven globalization, resulting from policy choices, largely at the behest of multinational corporations, that undercut wages and job security of noncollege-educated workers while protecting profits and the pay of business managers and professionals;
3. Purposely eroded collective bargaining, resulting from judicial decisions, and policy choices that invited ever more aggressive anti-union business practices;
4. Weaker labor standards, including a declining minimum wage, eroded overtime protections, nonenforcement against instances of "wage theft," or discrimination based on gender, race, and/or ethnicity;
5. New employer-imposed contract terms, such as agreements not to compete after leaving employment and to submit to forced private and individualized arbitration of grievances; and
6. Shifts in corporate structures, resulting from fissuring (or domestic outsourcing), industry deregulation, privatization, buyer dominance affecting entire supply chains, and increases in the concentration of employers.[33]

There is a growing consensus among center-left economists that unequal power played a more important role than technological changes in suppressing pay increases for non-elite workers from the 1970s on.[34]

Social and Psychological Well-Being

Diminished economic conditions for the less educated were accompanied by a decline in the social institutions that nurtured their social life and cooperation. These institutions include the family, the church, the labor union, the public schools and their parent-teacher associations, and various voluntary neighborhood associations. All of these institutions declined, and so did the overall degree of cooperation and social embeddedness.[35] As Case and Deaton show, the deaths-of-despair epidemic is only partially explained by declining economic conditions. Also vitally important is the progressive breakdown of social connectedness.

Worsening economic and social conditions have a direct effect on personal happiness and its reverse—misery. Social psychologists have discovered that it is possible to measure the level of happiness in a population simply by systematically asking people how they feel. Despite its simplicity, this approach yields reliable measures of "subjective well-being," with different approaches giving similar (strongly correlated) answers. Several recent studies, inspired by the work of Case and Deaton, have shown that the level of subjective well-being of Americans has decreased over the past two decades. For example, David Blanchflower and Andrew Oswald used the surveys conducted monthly by the Centers for Disease Control and Prevention to measure the level of "extreme distress."[36] They found that the proportion of Americans in extreme distress nearly doubled—from 3.6 percent in 1993 to 6.4 percent in 2019. The strongest effect, consistent with previous findings by Case and Deaton, was observed in white working-class Americans. In this group, extreme distress—despair—increased from less than 5 percent to more than 11 percent over the same period. Another study showed that an increasing degree of unhappiness has a strong predictive effect on political behavior. Using a different data set (from the Gallup daily poll, aggregated by county), George Ward and coauthors showed that low subjective well-being is a powerful marker of discontent and is highly correlated with anti-incumbent voting. In 2016, in particular, it was the strongest predictor of county-level voting for Trump.[37]

In this account, as we see, social, cultural, and psychological factors play a very important role. These noneconomic influences include corrosive ideologies, such as Ayn Rand's Objectivism and the new mainstream economics, which extolled economic efficiency and market fundamentalism at the expense of improving broadly based well-being. Another development, with somewhat unexpected consequences, was the rise of meritocracy. The philosopher Michael Sandel put it best:

> Winners are encouraged to consider their success their own doing, a measure of their virtue—and to look down upon those less fortunate than themselves. Those who lose out may complain that the system is rigged, that the winners have cheated and manipulated their way to the top. Or they may harbor the demoralizing thought that their failure is their own doing, that they simply lack the talent and drive to succeed.[38]

By 2016, then, the American population had sorted itself out into two social classes: the educated and the "immiserated"—à la Les Misérables. These are not classes, according to Marx, because they are not defined by their relations to the means of production. And neither of them is a cohesive actor in the political arena. The less educated "miserables," in particular, are deeply divided by race. (We will talk about the divisions within the educated class in the next chapter.) Instead, the two groups are sharply distinguished by a whole host of characteristics:

psychological (higher versus lower levels of "extreme distress"), social (lower versus higher marriage rates), political (tendency to vote Republican versus Democratic), economic (declining versus increasing economic prospects), and, perhaps most tragically, biological (decreasing versus increasing life expectancies). The divide between the classes has become harder to cross due to the runaway growth of college costs.

Although neither class is internally cohesive, each tends to perceive the other as more monolithic than it really is. Each also tends to blame the other for America getting on the wrong track.

The Wealth Pump, Again

In chapter 1, I introduced relative wages (wages divided by GDP per capita). Cutting out the step of inflation adjustment results in a less error-prone way of tracking the economic well-being of common Americans.

When we consider the dynamics of relative wages in the United States from the beginning of the Republic to the present, the data show a remarkable pattern of two waves. Between 1780 and 1830, the relative wage nearly doubled. After the peak of 1830, however, it lost most of its gains by 1860. It fluctuated at this low level until 1910, when there was another sustained period of growth that lasted until 1960 and again nearly doubled the relative wage. Starting in 1970, the relative wage declined, and continues to decline as I write this chapter. Between 1976 and 2016, the relative wage lost nearly 30 percent of its value.

What do the relative wage dynamics tell us about our society and, especially, about its resilience to external and internal shocks? A lot. Suppose that the relative wages of all deciles of American workers, from the lower 10 percent through the median to the top 10 percent, hold steady over an extended period of time. This means that wages for all workers are growing together with the overall economy. As John F. Kennedy said in 1963 (when the relative wage was at a peak), a rising tide lifts all boats. But in the past forty years, relative wages have been declining. The yachts of the top earners have been soaring, while the boats of everybody else have been sinking, with those of the lowest ten-percent plunging into an abyss. Relative wages have not declined in such a sustained manner since the three decades between 1830 and 1860. Together with relative wages, biological indicators of well-being, such as stature and life expectancy, have gone through the same two great cycles.

Basic considerations of fairness and equity suggest that declining relative wages do not make for a happy state of affairs. Why should most workers be excluded from equitably sharing in the fruits of economic growth? People in low-paying jobs perform critical tasks for society. It doesn't seem right that their wages do not go up as society grows more affluent. American society was by no means radically egalitarian, much less socialist, during the Kennedy era. The US was a capitalist country with substantial gaps in wealth between the rich and the poor. But the levels of trust in the institutions and state legitimacy were high, partly because even poor people saw how their lives were visibly improving from one generation to the next. Between 1910 and 1960, the relative wage nearly doubled. This means that the boats of the common people were actually lifted faster than the overall economy. It was the wealthy who were losing ground. But strangely, the wealthy and powerful were not unhappy about it. They became unhappy during the 1970s. We'll talk about the revolt of the elites later.

But perhaps, reader, your heart does not bleed for the plight of the poor. There are many perfectly fine human beings who believe that meritocracy should be the chief organizing principle of our society. Those who contribute a lot should be rewarded commensurably; CEOs who generate billions in revenue for their companies should become billionaires. Those falling behind need to get their acts together—obtain the right skills or work harder and smarter. As the ironic Russian saying goes, "Rescuing drowning people is the business of the drowning people themselves."[39]

Additionally, you may not feel sympathy for many in the less educated class—the gun-toting racists, white supremacists, sexists, homophobes, transphobes, and xenophobes. According to Hillary Clinton's famous estimate, about half of those who voted for Trump are such deplorables. In most complex human societies, the upper classes feel a measure of disdain for the lower classes. "The peasants are revolting."

But then you should consider another and very serious reason why the declining well-being of the working class is a bad thing—because it fundamentally undermines the stability of our society. Most obviously, when large swaths of the population experience falling living standards, this undermines the legitimacy of our institutions and thus weakens the state. Popular immiseration increases mass mobilization potential. In the past, peasants revolted when their misery could not be borne anymore. The Peasants' Revolt in England and the Jacquerie in France were such eruptions during the Late Medieval Crisis. Forward-looking 0.01-percenters, such as Nick Hanauer, have been warning us that the pitchforks are coming if we don't do something to fix glaring inequities.[40]

That much is fairly obvious. Less obvious is the fact that declining relative wages turn on the so-called wealth pump. The fruits of economic growth have to go somewhere. If the state's revenues are a relatively constant proportion of GDP, while the wages of common workers claim a decreasing proportion, the fruits of economic growth will be reaped by the economic elites that include the top earners (e.g., CEOs, corporate lawyers) and owners of capital. It takes time, but eventually the wealth pumped from the common people to the elites results in elite overproduction, intraelite conflict, and, if not checked in time, state collapse and social breakdown. The rich are perhaps even more vulnerable than common people during such periods of social and political turbulence, as outcomes of social revolutions suggest.

Another non-obvious insight from cliodynamics is that the general worsening of the well-being of the working class creates powerful incentives for its members to escape into the credentialed class. Getting education is, of course, a standard remedy for the problems we've discussed in this chapter. In nineteenth-century America, the advice to the immiserated masses on the East Coast was "Go west, young man!" Today it is "Go to college or, better, get a professional degree." And at the individual level, for those who want to escape precarity, this is good advice. But what happens at the collective level, when massive numbers of aspirants seek to enter the ranks of the elite?

Our database, CrisisDB, shows that while popular immiseration is a big contributor to social and political turbulence, elite overproduction is even more dangerous. Delving into the microdynamics of elite overproduction is the focus of the next chapter.

CHAPTER 4

THE REVOLUTIONARY TROOPS

Jane

The cops rushed a group of Occupy Wall Street protesters next to Jane, beating them with clubs and pepper-spraying them at point-blank range. Screaming bodies were convulsing on the ground as the police handcuffed them and started hauling them away. She had never faced such violence before in her life. It was horrifying to see.

Jane grew up in an affluent Manhattan family. Her father was a senior partner at a corporate law firm in New York. Her mother, a photographer and patron of the arts, served as a MoMA trustee. They lived in a large, two-level apartment on the Upper East Side and in the summer shifted to their Hamptons retreat.

Jane's parents sent her to one of the most exclusive private schools in the city. It was a harrowing time for her. In fact, she considers the last year before she graduated the worst time of her life. Egged on by their "tiger" moms and dads, students strived to get the highest grades and build up extracurricular portfolios that would improve their odds of getting into the top Ivy League colleges. When one of the students got an A- in French, the teacher had to endure a forty-minute harangue from his irate mother. Not surprisingly, the student graduated with a perfect grade point average. The pressure to match such performances was tremendous. For months, Jane felt so anxious, stressed out, and exhausted that she found herself unable to sleep. Her doctor prescribed sleeping pills.

Nevertheless, Jane did well and was admitted to Columbia. But having successfully passed the hurdle of getting into an Ivy League school, she now felt that she was on the wrong track. What did she have to look forward to? The next four years of college and then three years of law school—her father wanted her to follow in his footsteps—would be more of the same: a grueling rat race. Then she would have to endure years working seventy-hour weeks as a junior associate at a law firm, with unclear prospects of becoming partner. What was the point? The work her father did for big international companies didn't seem worth such a tremendous effort. Most of the time it was mind-bogglingly boring and occasionally evil, as when he helped a mining concern defend a case against Indonesian villagers whose water supply was poisoned by its operations. A life as the wife of a wealthy lawyer or CEO equally lacked appeal. She wasn't even sure she liked abstract art.

She decided to major in history and became fascinated by the history and politics of Latin America. Much of it was a depressing story of the US messing up Latin America's economies, imposing crushing debt burdens on populations, and supporting or even installing fascist regimes. But there were bright spots of successful anti-imperialist resistance. She read about the Sandinistas in Nicaragua; Chavez socialists in Venezuela; the Zapatistas and Subcomandante Marcos in Chiapas, Mexico; and, above all, Cuba. A small country that, despite decades of crushing American embargoes, managed to achieve a better life expectancy for its people than a much wealthier and more powerful United States.

To improve her speaking Spanish, she signed up for a language school in rural Guatemala, where she lived for three months with a local family. This was an eye-opening experience. Her hosts were very poor. Their diet was almost entirely based on corn and beans, with a little bit of chicken or pork consumed once or twice a week. Yet they were generally happy, warm, and welcoming, and they freely shared what little they had with her. It was a remarkable contrast with her other world, the elite private schools populated by stressed-out, self-centered superachievers. A world of solidarity and cooperation, where everybody had time to stop and chat, against the world of frenzied competition and limitless vanity.

After coming back from Guatemala, she joined a radical student group at Columbia. Other students came from a variety of ideological backgrounds: anarchists and Trotskyists, pro-Palestinian activists and Iraq War protesters. They talked about the myth of democracy and the reality of living in a divided country, where Black people were oppressed and where millions of the poor were in debt peonage to finance capital. Despite being surrounded by middle-class privilege, she became aware of the injustices and inequities surrounding her. She wanted to effect change; stop state brutality and oppression; and build a just, peaceful world.

She became active in the Occupy Wall Street movement, camping in a tent in Zuccotti Park in October of 2011. The attack she experienced came after days of demonstrations in New York and other American cities from Atlanta to Portland, during which the police used tear gas, stun grenades, and rubber bullets on peaceful protesters. In Oakland, a cop shot Iraq War veteran Scott Olsen in the face with a beanbag round, fracturing his skull. Olsen was lucky to survive, but he was maimed for life. More police brutality followed, and the coercive apparatus of the state eventually suppressed the Occupy movement and evicted Jane and others from Zuccotti Park. This was a life-changing experience. Before, her revolutionary ideals were rather theoretical and abstract. Now it felt personal.

She became deeply concerned about the explosive growth of violent racist and white supremacist groups. The surging alt-right movement and the election of Trump brought home the need to fight against the authoritarian tide. Jane became active in the anti-fascist movement's fight against the resurgent far right.

She came to accept that the authoritarians had to be stopped by any means, violent if need be. However, she was not a frontline fighter punching the fascists, burning cars, or breaking shop windows. Instead, her role was to organize and to mind the logistics.

Although she dislikes ideological labels, her current views can be described as anarchist. She works with Trotskyist comrades, but she thinks that classical Marxism is now somewhat outdated. She doesn't feel much solidarity with the working classes. Too many of them are racists and homophobes. They are too willing to support a fascist, having voted for Trump. The Marxists explaining working-class support for authoritarianism by invoking their "false consciousness" sound lame to her. Those in the violent far right often work with the police to suppress the progressives.

Then her trajectory took a sharp turn. I ran into Jane in the fall of 2020 and was surprised to learn that she was already in her second year of Yale Law School.

"Your father must be happy!" I needled her.

She laughed. "I am not going to become a corporate lawyer, however." Jane told me that she had become somewhat disillusioned with antifa activism. The state is the enemy, but scuffling with racists, throwing bricks at the police, and breaking shop windows didn't seem to lead anywhere. Also, Trump was now out of Washington, but the same old established elites were back in charge. "We don't want Biden, we want revolution" became a new slogan for the far left.

The law degree is the springboard for going into politics. Once she graduates, Jane plans to run for office in a liberal, left-leaning area—perhaps as a DA, perhaps as a member of a city council. As an elected official, she will have real power to advance her life's ambition. The ultimate goal is still to build a world without police, prisons, and states. But to get there, she first needs to work within the existing power structures.

Mao famously said that political power grows out of the barrel of a gun. But in the twenty-first century, Jane thinks, revolution may grow out of a ballot box. She intends to find out, at least.

Overproduction of Degrees

In chapter 3, we contrasted the diverging fortunes of the less educated with the more educated. The well-being of the first group has declined over the past few decades, while that of the second group has increased. But a major problem with this narrative is that it treats the second group as if it were monolithic. Yes, the credentialed class did well on average, but this doesn't mean that all degree holders are winners. That was true back in the 1950s and '60s but not today. Far from it. To see what changed, let's play the aspirant game again.

Let's say that the goal of the game is to become a ten-percenter. (But keep in mind that the same game can be played for other stakes: to get into the 1 percent or 0.1 percent; to become a billionaire or a US senator.) The ten chairs represent this prize. To play the game, you need to buy a ticket. You pay tuition and invest four years of your time to obtain a bachelor's degree.

When the game was played in the early '50s, fewer than 15 percent of people between eighteen and twenty-four years old went to college.[1] Thus, you had to contend with thirteen or fourteen other aspirants. Of course, one or two chairs could be grabbed by particularly bright and energetic working-class people who didn't buy tickets. Luckily, quite a few of your direct competitors would drop out of college or screw up in other ways, so all you needed to do was stay on course; get good grades and the degree; and conform to the expectations of your professors and bosses. If you followed these rules, you were virtually guaranteed a chair. And even if you were very unlucky and missed getting into the top wealth decile, you would have had to screw up in a major way indeed to miss getting into the second decile, which still guaranteed a very decent level of well-being. So far, so good.

But as the years go by, the game gets tougher. If you enter the contest fifteen years later, in 1966, you will be playing against thirty other aspirants. By 1990, more than half of your cohort is in the game—fifty players, still ten chairs. And today, two-thirds of youth between eighteen and twenty-four years old enter college.[2]

What can you do? Let's go back to 1966, when 30 percent of youth went to college. To get ahead of the competition, you'd need to up your game and buy a more expensive ticket. So after college you'd go to law school, or medical school, or some other graduate school. Now you and two or three other advanced degree holders each get your chair easily, with the rest going to mere bachelor's degree holders.

Things are great for a while, but others quickly catch on. Between 1960 and 1970, the number of doctorate degrees granted at US universities more than tripled—from less than ten thousand to thirty thousand. Soon enough, we are back in elite overproduction territory; only, the cost of a ticket got higher.

We've been playing this game in which the number of chairs is fixed. In the real world, of course, the number of elite positions changes all the time. In the 1960s and 1970s, there was a huge demand for PhD holders by universities who needed to hire professors to teach the baby boomer generation. One of my professors once confided to me that universities at that time were scraping the bottom and willing to hire anybody who had the degree. "I would never get hired today," he said in 1985, as I was finishing my own PhD. When I started looking for an academic job, I thought the market for newly minted PhDs was tough at the time, but it is much, much worse today.

Other professions requiring advanced degrees also experienced growth in the post–World War II period. Sputnik shocked American elites and, along with a host of additional factors, spurred a great increase in funding for scientific research, which absorbed huge numbers of PhDs. At the same time, the United States' economic reach had become global, and international corporations needed armies of lawyers. (That's how Jane's father got his golden ticket.) But eventually, all these surges of demand for advanced degrees subsided, whereas supply continued soaring. Between 1955 and 1975, the number of students enrolled in law schools, for example, tripled.

What determines whether we have a problem of elite overproduction is the balance of the supply of youth with advanced degrees and the demand for them—the number of jobs that require their skills. By the 2000s, unfortunately, as is well known, the numbers of degree holders were greatly outnumbering the positions for them.

The imbalance is large in the social sciences and even larger in the humanities. But the United States hugely overproduces even degrees in STEM (science, technology, engineering, and mathematics). Writing for Bloomberg Opinion in January of 2021, the popular blogger and columnist Noah Smith acknowledged that an overproduction of PhDs has been a problem for years in the US. On the one hand, a more educated populace is generally a good thing. But on the other hand, once PhD students graduate, they find that the academic jobs they've trained for have been drying up. "Do a quick Google search for trends in any academic field—history, anthropology, English—and you're likely to find scary numbers showing a decline in tenure-track faculty openings," Smith writes. He goes on:

> This condemns many would-be scholars to a bleak existence of low-wage, contingent work. Like waiters hanging around Hollywood hoping for their big break, many stick around year after year, forgoing health insurance or living in shabby apartments while their qualifications for jobs outside academia decay.
>
> But even as that coveted professor life drifted further out of reach, the country kept producing more Ph.D.s.[3]

Winners and Losers

When we look more closely at the supposedly well-off educated class, we find that things are not as peachy for them as we had assumed they would be. The title of a popular Mexican telenovela says it all: *Los ricos también lloran* (*The Rich Also Cry*). Today an advanced degree is not a perfect, or even reasonably effective, defense against precarity. In fact, Guy Standing, who injected the term *precariat* into the public consciousness, sees degree holders as one of the precariat factions. Of this group (the "progressives"), he writes:

It consists of people who go to college, promised by their parents, teachers and politicians that this will grant them a career. They soon realize they were sold a lottery ticket and come out without a future and with plenty of debt. This faction is dangerous in a more positive way. They are unlikely to support populists. But they also reject old conservative or social democratic political parties. Intuitively, they are looking for a new *politics of paradise*, which they do not see in the old political spectrum or in such bodies as trade unions.[4]

History (and CrisisDB) tells us that the credentialed precariat (or, in the jargon of cliodynamics, the frustrated elite aspirant class) is the most dangerous class for societal stability. Overproduction of youth with advanced degrees has been the most significant factor in driving societal upheavals, from the Revolutions of 1848 to the Arab Spring of 2011. Interestingly, different professions have different propensities for producing revolutionary leaders. You might not think of a teacher as a likely revolutionary, but Hong, the leader of the Taiping Rebellion, whom we encountered in chapter 1, was a village teacher before he became an insurgent. So was Mao.

The most dangerous occupation, however, appears to be the legal profession. Robespierre, Lenin, and Castro were lawyers. So were Lincoln and Gandhi. In the US, a law degree offers one of the best routes to public office, so most politically ambitious aspirants go to law school. Let's take a closer look at what's happened to law school graduates in the last few decades.[5]

For many years, the National Association for Law Placement, NALP, has been collecting data on starting salaries obtained by law school graduates. In 1991, this distribution was not particularly remarkable. There was a peak at $30K reflecting the most common salary. The left "tail" of the distribution was short, with no salaries less than $20K. The right tail was longer, with a cutoff at $90K. As was first noted by Vilfredo Pareto, it is quite typical for income distributions to have long right tails, indicating that as salaries become larger, such high earners become rarer.

In 1996, the right tail bulged a little, but there was no qualitative change in the shape of the distribution. The curve still had a single hump. The big break came in 2000. Suddenly, a second peak budded off to the right of the main peak. The main peak shifted a bit to the right, but it was centered at $40K. The new peak, in contrast, moved far to the right and was centered at $125K. Ten years later, the left peak shifted a bit more to the right and was then centered at $50K, but the right peak ran away to $160K. For the class of 2020, the left bulge flattened a bit, with most reported salaries between $45K and $75K, accounting for 50 percent of reported salaries. But the right-hand peak was now at $190K, with just over 20 percent of the distribution. There were very few salaries between the two peaks. The average salary was $100K, but this number is meaningless, as less than 2 percent of law graduates fell into that category.

This is what the aspirant game looks like when pushed to its extremes. The 20 percent in the right peak, with their $190K salaries, are well on their way to joining the established elites. Those who are in the lump on the left, earning between $45K and $75K, are in trouble. Considering that half of law school graduates in 2020 amassed debts of $160K or more (with one in four owing $200K), few of these individuals will manage to enter the ranks of the elites. Instead, most of them will be crushed by the debt and its relentlessly accumulating interest. It's strange to think of most law school graduates in America as members of the precariat, but that's what they are.

Perhaps our fictional heroine, Jane, was wise to refuse to play this game.

How to Thread a Needle

In *The Cheating Culture: Why More Americans Are Doing Wrong to Get Ahead*, a prescient book published in 2004, David Callahan analyzes the consequences of the cultural shift that, starting in the 1980s, unleashed unfettered competition, exploding inequality, and a winner-takes-all mentality. He writes about corporate scandals, doping athletes, plagiarizing journalists, and students cheating on exams. Cheating had become pervasive, a profound moral crisis. His argument that "an increase in cheating reflects deep anxiety and insecurity in America nowadays, desperation even, as well as arrogance among the rich and cynicism among ordinary people" resonates with a number of threads with which this chapter has engaged. On the corrosive effects of elite overproduction, in particular, Callahan writes:

> As the ranks of the affluent have swelled over the past two decades, so have the number of kids who receive every advantage in their education. The growing competition, in turn, has compelled more parents to spend more money and cut more corners in an effort to give their children an extra edge. Nothing less than an academic arms race is unfolding within the upper tiers of U.S. society. Yet even the most heroic—or sleazy—efforts don't guarantee a superior edge.[6]

Since 2004, things have become even more dire. For her article "Private Schools Have Become Truly Obscene," published in *The Atlantic* in April of 2021, Caitlin Flanagan interviewed Robert Evans, a psychologist who studies the relationship between private schools and their students' parents. "What's changed in the last few years is the *relentlessness* of parents," Evans told her. "For the most part, they're not abusive; it's that they just won't let up. Many of them cannot let go of their fears that somehow their child is being left behind." By the time their kids get to the upper grades, parents want teachers, coaches, and counselors entirely focused on helping them create a transcript that Harvard can't resist. "This kind of parent has an idea of the outcome they want; in their work life they can get it," Evans told Flanagan. "They're surrounded by employees; they can delegate things to their staff." Of the economic anxiety underpinning these parents' actions, Flanagan writes:

> Why do these parents need so much reassurance? They "are finding that it's harder and harder to get their children through the eye of the needle"—admitted into the best programs, all the way from kindergarten to college. But it's more than that. The parents have a sense that their kids will be emerging into a bleaker landscape than they did. The brutal, winner-take-all economy won't come for them—they've been grandfathered in. But they fear that it's coming for their children, and that even a good education might not secure them a professional-class career.

In 2019, the college admissions bribery scandal engulfed top universities, including Stanford, Georgetown, and Yale.[7]

The basic dynamic here is completely generic to what happens in aspirant games as they progress to their late stages. Unlike its milder versions, extreme competition does not lead to the selection of the best candidates, the candidates most suited for the positions. Rather, it corrodes the rules of the game, the social norms and institutions that govern how society works in a functional way. It destroys cooperation. It brings out the dark side of meritocracy. It creates a few winners and masses of losers. And some of those failed elite aspirants convert into radicalized counter-elites who are motivated to destroy the unjust social order that has bred them. And this brings us to the topic of radicalization.

The Fragmentation of the Ideological Landscape

Up until this point, I have been focusing on "structural-demographic" forces for social instability, with an emphasis on popular immiseration and elite overproduction. These are structural factors because they relate to societal structures, such as the distinctions between commoners and elites (or between less educated and more educated) and between different segments of elites. They are demographic because we track the changes in numbers and in the well-being of different population groups. The structural-demographic theory is an important part of cliodynamics because it helps us understand rebellions, revolutions, and civil wars. This theory was first formulated by the historical sociologist Jack Goldstone and later developed and articulated by Andrey Korotayev, me, and other colleagues.[8]

Structural studies of revolution and state breakdown, however, have often been criticized for their neglect of ideological and cultural factors.[9] The goal of cliodynamics, in contrast, is to integrate all important forces of history, whether they are demographic, economic, social, cultural, or ideological. We saw, for example, that such basic characteristics of society as the social norms regulating marriage (polygamy versus monogamy) have a fundamental effect on the characteristic lengths of boom-and-bust cycles (chapter 2).

The problem is that in today's climate, when ideology has been "weaponized" by rival elite factions, any discussion of it is like entering a minefield. A more conceptual difficulty in studying the role of ideology in societal breakdown is that the cognitive content of ideologies espoused by rival elite factions is highly variable over time and between different parts of the world. During the European civil wars of the sixteenth and seventeenth centuries, the defining feature of ideological battles was religion, as, for example, Huguenots versus Catholics in the French Wars of Religion. The great Chinese peasant rebellions were also often inspired by religious movements, such as the Taiping faith (chapter 1), which syncretized elements of Christianity and Chinese folk religion. From the Age of Revolutions on, the radical ideologies, at least in Europe, were secular, not religious.

Furthermore, the ideological content of many revolutionary movements, if they last long enough, tends to evolve. In his seminal contribution to the study of revolutions and rebellions, Jack Goldstone points out that one difficulty in describing the role of ideology is that it tends to be highly fluid. As Goldstone writes, ideology fails to provide "a clear guide to the intentions and actions of revolutionary leaders," for "in practice revolutionaries frequently shifted their positions in response to changing circumstances. And on many occasions, the twists and turns of the revolutionary struggle produced unforeseen results. English Puritans sought to create a community of saints, but England became a community dominated by soldiers when the civil wars ceased."[10] Another scholar of revolution, Theda Skocpol, similarly concludes that "it cannot be argued . . . that the cognitive content of the ideologies in any sense provides a predictive key to . . . the outcomes of the Revolutions."[11]

Following Goldstone, we can distinguish three phases of ideological evolution as societies slide into, and then out of, crises. During the first phase, or precrisis phase, the period leading up to state breakdown, the state is struggling to maintain control in the face of a multitude of ideological challenges coming from different elite factions. In the second phase, when the old regime has completely lost legitimacy (which often results in the state's collapse), numerous contenders who seek to establish a new monopoly of authority struggle among themselves for primacy. In the final phase, when one group gains the upper hand over its opponents and moves to stabilize its authority over the state, it focuses on gaining routine acceptance of the reconstructed political, religious, and social institutions.

A nearly universal feature of precrisis periods is thus the fragmentation of the ideological landscape and the breakdown of elite ideological consensus that underlies routine acceptance of state institutions. Some creeds that gain adherents are radical, in that they aim to remake the society in a new, better way. Others are traditionalist, looking back in time to restore an imagined golden age. However, such a "conservative" diagnosis can easily prompt radical action.[12] Because there is a general perception that the country is going in the wrong direction and that society has become vastly unjust and hugely unequal (not only between commoners and elites but also between the winners and losers among the elites), appeals to set things right by restoring "social justice" gain a lot of traction. Another general feature is that divisive—sectarian and identitarian—ideologies gain an upper hand over unifying ones, giving us ages of discord.

The process of ideological fragmentation and political polarization is thus challenging to study with quantitative methods. Helpfully, political scientists have found some very useful approaches.[13] Keith Poole and Howard Rosenthal, later joined by Nolan McCarty, collected a huge data set on the political leanings of all members of Congress from the beginning of the American Republic. They assigned each member of Congress to a position on a spectrum, occupied by conservatives at one end and liberals at the other, with the space between filled by moderates. A measure of political polarization is the distance between the average scores of the two major parties (the Republicans and the Democrats of today, as well as the Democrats and the Whigs of the nineteenth century), calculated for each Congress (that is, every two years).

When we plot the results of this analysis,[14] we observe that the long-term dynamics of political polarization in the US have gone through two great cycles. First, political polarization declined from moderately high levels around 1800 to very low levels in the 1820s. This decline in partisan acrimony is known as the Era of Good Feelings, roughly coinciding with the presidency of James Monroe (1817–1825). After 1830, polarization increased, and the period between circa 1850 and 1920 was characterized by a very high degree of fragmentation among the political elites. During the 1920s and 1930s, however, the political elites pulled together, and polarization again rapidly declined. Following the New Deal and World War II, the degree of polarization reached another minimum. The three postwar decades were thus characterized by relatively consolidated elites. During this period there was a broad degree of overlap between the liberal-conservative scores of Democrats and Republicans in Congress. The 1950s marked the height of ideological consensus in the US. This consensus included a firm commitment to capitalism but "with a human face," characterized by cooperation between labor, capital, and the state. General support for free market economics and democratic governance was solidified by the Cold War conflict with the Soviet Union. The country was ruled by a culturally homogeneous WASPHNM elite. (WASPHNM is my neologistic acronym, standing for "white Anglo-Saxon Protestant heteronormative male.") However, during the 1970s, the overlap shrank, and polarization surged. By the early 2000s, a large gap had opened up between the Republican and Democratic distributions. To be clear, such ideological uniformity can feel stifling, and many people were cruelly left out of this WASPHNM-dominated consensus. Further, stability and consensus are not necessarily virtues, if what is being held stable is an unjust regime. It would be cruel not to feel empathy for identity groups who were left out in the cold during this period, and it would be wrong not to acknowledge the progress on many important fronts that has been made over the past fifty years. By the same token, the low polarization period of the 1820s was no comfort if you were a laborer held against your will in a slave labor camp in the fertile lands of the American South that had recently been cleared of their previous inhabitants. However, the main point here is not to pass a value judgment on this trend but simply take note of it.

The Breakdown of the Postwar Ideological Consensus

McCarty, Poole, and Rosenthal's method places all US politicians on a single conservative-liberal spectrum. But as the process of ideological fragmentation became more extreme during the 2010s, this one-dimensional classification no longer sufficed. The election of Trump in 2016 split the Republican Party into two factions, with the anti-Trump faction led by the old guard (who have been unironically labeled "Republicans in name only," or RINOs). Similarly, there is a huge and growing fault line within the Democratic Party between the "centrists" and the "leftists."

Ideological fragmentation has now progressed so far that no classification scheme seems to be useful. The variety of ideas motivating political factions and proposals for action is simply too large. Ideas are combined and recombined promiscuously. New movements—the new New Right, the alt-right, the alt-lite—rise, gain brief prominence, and then fade.

Furthermore, we have entered a new era dominated by radical ideologies. The term *radical politics*, by popular definition, denotes the intent to transform or replace the fundamental principles of a society or political system, often through social change, structural change, revolution, or radical reform.[15] To understand the ideological landscape of today, it is useful to start with its opposite, the Era of Good Feelings II, during which there was remarkable consensus among the elites governing America. I'll refer to this ideological accord as the Postwar Consensus. It lasted for roughly thirty years, from 1937, when the New Deal was cemented, through World War II and the 1950s (the peak), and into the early 1960s.

On the cultural side, we can identify the following elements of the Postwar Consensus:

- The normative family was one consisting of a man and a woman, whose union was typically consecrated in church or another religious establishment, plus their children. People living "alternative lifestyles" were largely forced to do so in the shadows.
- Gender roles were clearly defined: men as breadwinners, women as homemakers.
- The Postwar Consensus frowned on nearly all attempts to change the "natural body" artificially. Most forms of body modification, from mild ones, such as tattooing and body piercing, to more severe ones, such as foot-binding and castration (to create eunuchs), were considered things that only "uncivilized" foreigners did. (There was one major exception to this rule, as male genital mutilation—

circumcision—was not only allowed but also normative.) Abortion was heavily discouraged and illegal in most states.

- Institutionalized racism, including the Jim Crow laws in the Southern states, fundamentally rendered Black Americans second-class citizens, denying them most of the fruits of the Postwar Consensus.

- Although the WASPHNM elite were predominantly Protestant, there was no state religion in the US. However, belonging to a church, a synagogue, a mosque, or another religious denomination was normative. Divorce was deeply problematic for elected officials; atheism was disqualifying.

- The secular ideology of the Postwar Consensus is sometimes referred to as the American Creed. The main elements of this ideology were democracy (whose principles are enshrined in the Constitution), laissez-faire economics, and American patriotism.

On the economic side, although the US was an avowed capitalist country (and repressed the Communist Party), in practice it was a social democratic or even socialist country along the lines of the Nordic model. The Postwar Consensus included the following economic elements:

- Support for strong labor unions.
- A commitment to increasing the minimum wage faster than inflation.
- Extremely progressive taxation, with taxes of over 90 percent on top incomes.
- Support for the welfare system, which included universal retirement pensions (Social Security), unemployment insurance, and welfare benefits for disabled or needy children.
- A low-immigration regime that favored workers and promoted

cultural homogeneity. (In this category, economic and cultural issues overlap.)

Casting an eye over this list, it is astounding how much the ideological landscape has changed. The cultural certainties started to break down as a result of the anti-war and civil rights movements of the 1960s. The economic pillars crumbled under the onslaught of neoliberal economics starting in the 1970s. (I will come back to this in the next chapter.) But as of 2020, the Postwar Consensus hasn't been replaced by anything similarly coherent that would be accepted by the overwhelming majority of the elites and the population. By using sociological data that polls American attitudes on a variety of questions, we can define a middle point on the ideological spectrum—the median position—but there is a huge degree of variance around it.

Furthermore, there is no single "radical creed" that challenges whatever passes for the ideological median today. Rather, there is a dynamic multitude of radical ideas, and there are huge differences between ideas accepted by different ideological factions within the more educated youth.

On the far left are committed revolutionaries, anti-fascists, anarchists, and a few old-style communists. Numerically, this is a small group, but there is no sharp boundary between the extremists and the next, much larger category. These are activists who stay away from the violence of urban riots but support the goals of the extremists, to a greater or lesser degree, or support some, though not all, of the progressive-left causes. They come to large anti-government demonstrations and donate to far-left causes, such as bailing out antifa who have been arrested by the police. This group, in turn, fades into the next category, who are not particularly motivated, or not at all motivated, by left causes but are unwilling to admit it and therefore support them in public.

Judging by the results of the 2020 presidential election, more than 80 percent of college students voted for Biden,[16] which gives us a rough estimate of the proportion of them who are leftist or left-leaning. Of the remainder, most do not appear to be particularly political and tend to keep their heads down when on campus. The final, small group comprises right-wing radicals in various college Republican clubs who are vocally opposed to left causes.

This spectrum is a rough approximation (at best) of the variety of ideological positions on cultural issues among the more educated youth. The left-wing radicals want to push society even further away from the Postwar Consensus than it has moved so far. The traditionalists and conservatives on the right want to return to it, which, in the case of many issues, is a more radical proposition than anything the left is agitating for. Also keep in mind that both the left and the right are extremely fragmented, and there are culture wars within each wing that may exceed the left/right conflicts in intensity.

The situation is further complicated by the different alignments on economic issues. Our fictional character Jane wants a revolution that will sweep away the oppressive and unjust US regime. Steve Bannon, who for a while was the chief ideologist in the Trump camp, also considers himself a revolutionary: "I want to bring everything crashing down, and destroy all of today's establishment."[17] Senator Bernie Sanders, who is no revolutionary, accuses the Democratic Party establishment of turning its back on the working class, and he calls on Democrats to make "a major course correction" that focuses on fighting for America's working class and standing up to "powerful corporate interests."[18] Such a convergence between (some of) the far right and (some of) the far left on economic issues is not unique to the US. In France, Marine Le Pen and Jean-Luc Mélenchon use remarkably similar language when talking about the working classes.

Counter-Elites as Political Entrepreneurs

Right-wing activists tend to be at a disadvantage on campus because they are heavily outnumbered by left-wing radicals and the majority of students, who at least passively support leftist causes. But those on the right gain a signal advantage once they graduate. This advantage is their capacity to mobilize support among the working-class (less educated) voters. A common situation during crisis periods is that of elite political entrepreneurs who use the high mass mobilization potential of the non-elite population to advance their ideological agendas and political careers. A great historical example is Tiberius and Gaius Gracchus, who founded the populist party (populares in Latin) in late republican Rome. Donald Trump, of course, used the populist strategy to propel himself to the presidency in 2016. In 2022, the most vivid example is Marjorie Taylor Greene, the US representative from Georgia. MTG, as she is widely known, has clearly internalized the lessons from Trump's 2016 strategy. Apparently, there is no far-right conspiracy theory that she fails to support, no matter how outlandish. She was removed from all committee roles by the vote of the House representatives, and her personal Twitter account was shut down.[19] But she appears to thrive on such attempts to "cancel" her, and she is clearly setting her sights on a loftier goal than Congress.

Our fictional character with whom this chapter started, Jane, is not a "typical" member of America's more educated youth. Ideologically and "professionally" (because she is a committed revolutionary, even as she is studying for a law degree), she is located on the far left. Nevertheless, her life trajectory was shaped by the same social forces that continue to shape the rest of the credentialed youth (even, and especially, the right-wing activists). Her life trajectory is also interesting because she is following in the footsteps of many famous revolutionaries and radicals of the past and other countries. Her immediate predecessors were the members of the Weather Underground, such as Bernardine Dohrn, Kathy Boudin, and Susan Rosenberg.[20] But the American radicals of the 1970s failed at triggering the revolution that they so desired because the structural conditions for revolution were not there. Rosenberg acknowledges as much in her memoir.

Other famous counter-elite revolutionaries—Robespierre, Hong, Lenin, Rosa Luxemburg, Mao, Castro—succeeded in bringing on revolutions. Perhaps they were simply lucky to be in the right places at the right times, living in countries in which structural drivers of instability ran full throttle. After all, for every Lenin, there had to be a Bolshevik Party. And the Bolsheviks were part of an ecosystem populated by other radical groups—the anarchists, the Mensheviks, the Bund, the Socialist Revolutionaries, etc. Most importantly, all those radical groups, like fish in water, swam in supportive social milieus. After the Russian anarchist Vera Zasulich[21] shot the governor of St. Petersburg in 1878, she became a hero to the progressive intelligentsia. A sympathetic jury acquitted her. The Weather Underground did not have such public support fifty years ago. But structural conditions in the US are very different today—much closer to other prerevolutionary societies, such as late-nineteenth-century Russia, than to the US of the 1970s.

The Revolution Devours Its Children

Although most visible battles, including actual street fighting, are between right and left extremists, there is so much division and infighting within both the left and the right that such broad groupings cannot be taken as cohesive parties. In any case, cognitive content of the creeds is of little significance. What's important is division and conflict.

As of 2022, we are clearly in transition from the precrisis phase, when the state is still struggling to maintain control of the ideological landscape in the face of a multitude of counter-elite challengers, to the next phase, when numerous contenders struggle among themselves for primacy. Politicians who still cling to old-regime values, which emphasize moderation and intraelite cooperation, have been retiring, or losing elections to challengers with more extreme views. The ideological center today resembles a country road in Texas, almost deserted save for the yellow stripe and dead armadillos. As a result of the center's collapse, ideological infighting is shifting from the struggle against the old regime (or in defense of it) to the struggle between different elite factions. Ideological differences are now used as a weapon in intraelite conflicts, both to pull down members of the established elites and to draw ahead of rival aspirants.

Many observers were taken aback by the intensity of the "cancel culture" that appeared seemingly out of nowhere. But such vicious ideological struggles are a common phase in any revolution. Jacques Mallet du Pan, who had the misfortune of living through not one but two revolutions (in his native Geneva in 1782 and then in France in 1789), formulated this observation as a dictum: "Like Saturn, the Revolution devours its children." This is a necessary corollary, essentially a mathematical certainty, following from elite overproduction as the most important driver of rebellions, revolutions, and civil wars. In order for stability to return, elite overproduction somehow needs to be taken care of—historically and typically by eliminating the surplus elites through massacre, imprisonment, emigration, or forced or voluntary downward social mobility. In America today, the losers are treated in milder ways, at least so far.

The legitimacy of the old regime ruled by the WASPHNM elites has been greatly diminished. The social logic of phase two of ideological battles, into which we seem to be transitioning, drives further radicalization. In the struggle between rival factions, the ones willing to escalate accusations win over the moderate ones. As the losers get sidelined, the battleground shifts. An idea that looked radical a few years ago becomes the ground for further ideological battles. The same logic works on both the left and the right ends of the ideological spectrum.

The Communist Manifesto proclaims, "The proletarians have nothing to lose but their chains." But old Marx turned out to be wrong. Immiserated proletarians are not the ones who run successful revolutions. The truly dangerous revolutionaries are frustrated elite aspirants, who have the privileges, training, and connections to enable them to wield influence at scale. Even the minority of newly credentialed youth who get into elite positions right away, like the 20 percent of law school graduates with $190K salaries, are not happy campers, because they feel the general insecurity. The growing proportion of credentialed youth who are doomed to become the educated precariat are the ones who have nothing to lose but their precarity.

CHAPTER 5

THE RULING CLASS

Andy and Clara

Clara met Andy when she interviewed him for a tech magazine. This was when he was a young entrepreneur, years before he made his first billion. They dated, then moved in together and eventually married. Andy's mathematical and engineering brilliance and Clara's social skills and judgment made them a great team.

Clara's parents came to America as poor migrants from Central America. They worked hard to start a restaurant and grow it into a success. When she was young, Clara often helped in the kitchen or with waiting tables. After high school, she went to UCLA, where she studied journalism.

Andy grew up in Central Europe. Both his parents were scientists, his father a physicist and his mother a biologist. From an early age, he showed great aptitude for mathematics. When the time came to go to college, he set his sights high and sent applications to several top

American schools, including MIT, Caltech, and Stanford. He chose to go to Stanford because they gave him a scholarship, and because he was eager to leave gloomy winters behind.

He decided not to follow in the footsteps of his parents, and he chose to become an entrepreneur. His first start-up, co-organized with two fellow Stanford students, was up and running even before he graduated summa cum laude. Other start-ups followed, interspersed with time Andy spent serving as chief technology officer of two Silicon Valley companies that did very well and made him a great deal of money. He is now the CEO of one of his start-ups, which has grown into a large corporation.

With wealth comes responsibility. Some years ago, Clara and Andy launched a charitable foundation, to which they give generously. Their foundation supports a variety of progressive causes. One that they both feel passionate about is immigration. Clara's parents and Andy came to the US in search of the American dream, and it worked very well for them. They want others who dream big and work hard to succeed. There is also a bit of a selfish motive here. Andy's firm needs a constant supply of bright, well-educated workers. In Andy's view, Americans mostly don't cut the mustard. To put it bluntly, they are mostly ignorant and lazy, and they want to be paid too much for the kind of work they produce. Of course, it's not the fault of young people that the American education system has fallen so far behind those of Europe and China. But that's the reality, and so Andy's company hires a lot of workers coming from East Asia, India, and Eastern Europe. They are well trained, willing to work long hours, and satisfied with reasonable salaries.

Clara also has an ulterior motive, or at least an influence on her thinking. Coming from a bohemian LA milieu, to which the overwhelming majority of her old friends belong, she knows that for most of them, maintaining their standard of living would not be possible in the absence of cheap immigrant labor. Salaries are not that great, and dry spells can hit at any time. What allows her fellow intelligentsia to live like the gentry are the affordable house cleaners, nannies, Uber drivers, and food deliverers. Such factors are not what she or Andy would necessarily admit to a stranger. And anyway, humans are complex, and there is a confluence of idealistic and materialistic motives underlying their support for loose immigration laws.

Andy and Clara also contribute generously to political campaigns. Their giving is strategic and not limited to their home state. The main client of Andy's corporation is the US government, as nearly 90 percent of his revenues come from federal contracts. He needs sympathetic congressmen in Washington to help ensure that lucrative contracts go to his company rather than to his competition. They give about equally to Democrats and Republicans. They like the Democrats' progressive agenda, but they also appreciate the Republicans' economics, especially their stance on lowering taxes. This is one thing about which they both feel strongly. They came to this country penniless and achieved their American dream entirely through their own efforts. Why should the government lay its greedy hands on their money? Most of their taxes, in any case, will be wasted as a result of corruption. They prefer to give directly to deserving causes through their foundation, rather than have their money wasted by corrupt and dysfunctional bureaucrats. As repellant as Trump is to them, they reluctantly give him credit for the Tax Cuts and Jobs Act, passed in 2017. It noticeably reduced their taxes. Still, it's a relief that Trump is out of the White House. Joe Biden represents a return to normal politics, and he wouldn't raise taxes on them, no matter what he might have said during the election campaign. He knows which side his bread is buttered on. And if the left wing of his party manages to get a tax-the-rich bill on the floor, they can trust the Republicans to filibuster it to death.

Ruling Classes in History and Today

Although neither Andy nor Clara has ever held a public office, they are nevertheless members of the American ruling class. This is not what they teach you in a high school civics class. I'm afraid, though, that on the evidence, it's more than fair to call the USA a plutocracy, or a society ruled by the wealthy. This is not a conspiracy theory but an accurate statement broadly accepted by social scientists who study the flows of power.[1] Before diving into the inner workings of power in the USA, however, let's first take a step back and talk about social power in general.

Let's start with a general principle. All large-scale, complex human societies have ruling classes. It doesn't matter whether a state is governed as a democracy or as an autocracy; there is always a small proportion of the population with a disproportionate share of social power concentrated in their hands. But, as we saw in chapter 1, there is a lot of variability between different countries, past and present, when it comes to what source of power is emphasized by the governing elites, and how the elites are "reproduced," which includes not only biological reproduction but also recruitment from the commoners.

Early states were usually governed by militocracies, whose main source of social power was simply force. This was a consequence of one of the most important principles of social evolution, namely that "war made the state, and states made war."[2] Early states did not simply grow through population growth or by peacefully accreting territory. They arose in environments of intense warfare, and they expanded either by conquest or by a military alliance becoming increasingly cohesive and centralized and eventually transforming itself into a state.[3]

Naked force, however, is not a terribly efficient way of governing a country, especially during times of peace. Remember a saying about a gun and a kind word, widely (but inaccurately) attributed to Al Capone? Well, the actual experience of historical states suggests that we need to invert it: "You can get more with a kind word and a gun than with just a gun." Legitimate force works better than force alone—if you can persuade the people to do what you want, you will not have to pay them or force them to do it.

Understanding this, early warrior elites sought to control ideological power by appointing themselves as priests, or by thoroughly controlling religion specialists. Many early states were ruled by priest-kings, or even by god-kings. Egyptian pharaohs, for example, were worshipped as gods. The rulers of early states also added economic power to the mix. Because the main means of production in preindustrial societies was land—for growing food and fiber and for raising livestock—they set themselves up as landowners and used peasants, serfs, or slaves to work it. Finally, as their domains became larger and more populous, they ran into the limitations of direct rule and reluctantly had to share power with administration specialists, the bureaucrats. Our analysis of a worldwide sample of historical societies has determined that polities with populations of up to a few hundred thousand could be ruled by chiefs and their retinues without full-time administrators.[4] But once you have a million or more subjects, you either acquire a civil service or suffer from such inefficiencies that your polity sooner or later collapses. Or loses in competition with bureaucratic empires. As a result, what started as a warrior aristocracy always evolved into a ruling class that might have continued to emphasize military prowess but in reality controlled all sources of power. Those elites who failed to diversify were overthrown, either by internal or external enemies.

Egypt, a Militocracy

A contemporary example of a militocracy (a state governed by military elites) is the Arab Republic of Egypt. Egypt is a military dictatorship, although it runs elections for cosmetic purposes. The roots of this form of governance go back many centuries. Let's take a short historical detour to trace the development of the institutional frameworks that eventually resulted in the current ruler of Egypt as of this writing: Abdel Fattah al-Sisi. There is a remarkable cultural inertia that informs what kinds of institutional arrangements different regions of the world return to even after serious perturbations, such as revolutions and state collapse. Culture is persistent.

Consider Saladin, or more formally Al-Nasir Salah al-Din Yusuf ibn Ayyub (1137–1193), probably the most famous Kurd in world history. Saladin fought against the Crusaders in Palestine, and his crowning achievement was their expulsion from Jerusalem. By the end of his reign, he built an extensive empire encompassing Egypt, Syria, Palestine, and the western fringes of the Arabian Peninsula. His successors, however, gradually ceded the control of military power to their Mamluk generals. Mamluks were a caste of warriors who were purchased on the slave markets and then trained as soldiers. In 1250, they overthrew the last heir of the Ayyubid dynasty (named after Saladin's father) and began their long reign of Egypt. The Ayyubids lasted for less than a century. (As we have seen, such short political cycles are typical of societies with polygamous elites, because they overproduce elite aspirants much faster than societies with monogamous elites.)

Remarkably, the Mamluks maintained their grip on Egypt for nearly three centuries. They accomplished this feat by forbidding the sons of Mamluks to inherit their fathers' positions. Instead, they continued to purchase boys originating from Central Asia and the Caucasus on the slave market and train them as soldiers, officers, and ultimately rulers. Whether intentionally or not, avoiding elite overproduction made the Mamluk regime particularly stable. To give you an idea of how effective the Mamluks were, consider that they were the only military force that managed to stop the Mongols (at the Battle of Ayn Jalut in 1260).

Unfortunately for the Mamluks, they failed to modernize their army. Their cavalry was excellent, but they lagged in adopting gunpowder weapons. As a result, in 1517, Egypt was conquered by the nearest "gunpowder empire"—the Ottomans. Nevertheless, the Mamluks continued to rule Egypt as vassals of Istanbul. Their power was finally broken three centuries later by another general, Muhammad Ali, an Albanian military commander sent by the Ottoman Empire to recover Egypt in 1805, after the withdrawal of the French expeditionary forces under Napoleon. Muhammad Ali practiced a rather extreme approach to undoing elite overproduction. He invited the Mamluk leaders to a celebration and then simply massacred them, thus gaining absolute power over Egypt. Under the dynasty he established, Egypt became, first de facto and then de jure, independent from the Ottoman Empire (although it also became a British protectorate during part of its history). The Muhammad Ali dynasty lasted for nearly 150 years. His last successor, King Farouk, was overthrown by a military coup d'état in 1952.

I think you can see the general pattern. From the twelfth century, Egypt was ruled by a succession of military elites. As soon as the ruling elite lost its control of military power, it was replaced by another set of warriors. How does this help us understand Egypt today? After the revolution of 1952, Egypt was ruled by a succession of generals: Mohamed Naguib, Gamal Abdel Nasser, Anwar Sadat, and Hosni Mubarak. This was the reversion to the Mamluk rule, except the military recruited from among the Egyptian population instead of purchasing recruits on the slave markets.

Then came the Arab Spring. You might reasonably think that the Egyptian revolution in 2011 was a result of massive popular protests against police brutality; lack of civil liberty and freedom of speech; corruption; high unemployment; food-price inflation; and low wages.[5] That's true as far as it goes, but a structural-demographic analysis of the Egyptian revolution by the Russian Arabist and cliodynamicist Andrey Korotayev gives us additional insights into the deep social forces acting below the surface of events.[6]

Before the 1990s, only a small proportion of Egyptian youth joined the credentialed class.[7] Then the Mubarak regime, intent on modernizing the country, greatly expanded access to university education. As a result, during the 1990s, the proportion of the population enrolled in colleges and universities more than doubled. This expansion of university education coincided with a "youth bulge." Between 1995 and 2010, the number of people in their twenties grew by 60 percent. At the same time, the number of positions for these degree-holding youth barely budged. The result was a rapidly developing acute problem of elite overproduction. It was these university graduates without jobs who provided the revolutionary troops for massive anti-regime demonstrations.

Equally important was the split within the ruling elites. Mubarak gained power in the usual manner: by first working his way through the military ranks and then becoming the heir apparent of his predecessor, Anwar Sadat. However, once in power, he broke the rules of succession by starting to groom his son, Gamal Mubarak, as successor. Gamal did not work his way to power through the army ranks; instead, he earned an MBA and became a leader of the new economic elites in Egypt. Had Gamal succeeded his father as ruler of Egypt, it would have amounted to a social revolution in which the old military elites were replaced by the new economic elites. The army officers were clearly not enthused about losing power. According to Korotayev's reconstruction of the intraelite conflicts underlying the revolution (followed by the counter-revolution), when massive protests erupted in 2011, the army stood aside and allowed the Mubarak regime to fall. The coalition that drove Mubarak from power, however, was very heterogeneous. The two main groups within it were liberal secular revolutionaries, coming from the urbanized credentialed class, and the Islamist Muslim Brotherhood, with support mainly in the rural areas. As soon as they overthrew Mubarak, these two groups, with opposite visions of where Egypt needed to go, immediately fell out. The Brotherhood won at the polls, as a result of which its leader, Mohamed Morsi, became president. Now liberal protesters went back to Tahrir Square to protest the government by Islamists. Even more consequentially, the business elites (whose conflict with the military was at the root of the revolution) became thoroughly frightened by the illiberal direction in which Egypt now headed. When the army overthrew Morsi, the economic elites returned to the army-business coalition as a junior partner. The end result of the 2011–2014 crisis was that Egypt returned to a traditional—for it, at least—power configuration, which has been in place for at least a millennium. The military elites are back in charge.

What does this excursion into Egyptian history tell us? For one thing, in order to understand the forces for instability, including the role of elite overproduction, we have to place them within the institutional frameworks of the country we are interested in. These institutional frameworks and the political cultures sustaining them can vary a lot from region to region. But for each country, they show a lot of resilience over time, often reconstituting themselves, even after very strong shocks.

Consider another example—China. Unlike Egypt (and the USA), for more than two millennia, China has been governed by elites for whom the primary source of power is administrative. In other words, by bureaucracies. China's ruling class was recruited through an elaborate system of local and imperial examinations. To succeed, the recruits had to undergo intense training in the Chinese classics. As a result, Chinese officials were also Confucian scholars, thus combining administrative with ideological power. The military and economic elites were closely controlled and not allowed much of a say in the affairs of state. The latest shock to this system was the Communist revolution. And where is China today? Pretty much where it has been for the past two thousand years. It is governed by a ruling class of bureaucrats. The acronym CPC, which stands for the Communist Party of China, might as well stand for the Confucian Party of China. From the theory of dynastic cycles' point of view, today China is governed by a successor of the Qing dynasty, which we might as well call the "Red dynasty." One of the cultural tasks each dynasty must complete is writing a definitive history of the previous dynasty. In 2002, the People's Republic of China announced that it would complete the *History of Qing*, thus making its dynastic status official.

Throughout Chinese imperial history, the mandarins kept the merchant class on a short leash, and the same is true for the Red dynasty. On August 17, 2021, the current ruler of China, Xi Jinping, gave a major speech in which he called for common prosperity and emphasized the need to regulate excessively high-income groups, which was interpreted by the Western press as an attack on the rich.[8] But there is nothing new here, merely the mandarins (again) reminding the billionaires who is in charge in China.

China is the archetypal example of a bureaucratic empire and has been one for the past two millennia. But the switch from militarized ruling classes to administrative ruling classes is a general rule in history, at least for the largest states. What about elites whose primary source of power is ideological or economic? Such states are found in history, but they have been relatively rare. An example of a historical theocracy is the Papal States. Today the best example of a theocracy is the Islamic Republic of Iran, in which the ultimate authority is vested in the supreme leader, a Shia Islamic cleric who is selected by an assembly of elders.

Plutocracies have also been rare in history. Well-known historical examples include such Italian merchant republics as Venice and Genoa, as well as the Dutch Republic. Today the best example of a plutocracy is the United States of America.

The Formation of the American Ruling Class

We cannot understand a society at any given point in time without knowing where it came from. For this reason, my account of the American ruling class needs to go back to its origins. Fortunately, we need not travel back very far in time, merely to the aftermath of the Civil War.

As we have seen, before the Civil War, the United States was ruled by a coalition of Southern slaveholders and Northeastern merchant patricians. The defeat of the South in the Civil War destroyed this ruling class.[9] A quarter of Southern men of military age were killed on the battlefield. More lastingly, Southern wealth, the greater portion of which was invested in enslaved human beings, was destroyed by their emancipation. Additionally, wartime damage to Southerners' properties and the repudiation of all war debts and obligations of the Confederacy wiped out much of what remained. In the political arena, the defeat of the Confederacy introduced a long era of dominance of the Republican Party. Between 1860 and 1932, the Democrats (for a long time the party of the white-supremacist South) were able to capture the presidency only three times: in 1884, 1892, and 1912.

An influential school of historical thought views the Civil War and its aftermath, Reconstruction, as the Second American Revolution, albeit an unfinished one. Although the Civil War freed the slaves, it utterly failed to produce racial equality. The main effect was thus the revolution at the top: the turnover of the elites. After the power of the Southern slaveholding elites over the federal government was decisively broken, they were replaced by a new ruling class dominated by Northern businessmen.

As Kevin Phillips wrote in *Wealth and Democracy: A Political History of the American Rich*, at the same time that the Civil War destroyed Southern wealth, it immensely enriched Northern capitalists. Holding Union debt was extremely lucrative. Supplying the Union war effort was even more profitable. "A surprising number of the commercial and financial giants of the late nineteenth century—J. P. Morgan, John D. Rockefeller, Andrew Carnegie, Jay Gould, Marshall Field, Philip Armour, Collis Huntington, and several other railroad grandees—were young Northerners who avoided military service, usually by buying substitutes, and used the war to take major steps up future fortune's ladder," Phillips wrote.[10] In just ten years, from 1860 to 1870, the number of American millionaires exploded, from 41 to 545.

The rise of the new ruling class brought about a marked shift in the nation's politico-economic relations. We can see this economic transformation reflected in the makeup of the Lincoln administration. This aspect of Lincoln's career is not widely emphasized, but he practiced a lot of corporate law, working with several railroads in the Midwest, especially the Illinois Central. Many members of his administration had strong railroad or financial ties. It should come as no surprise that large amounts of land were granted, as promotional measures, to railroad concerns that operated in western states. The political influence of the railroad barons also extended to the selection of Supreme Court justices. As a result, "by 1876 the railroad industry had clearly emerged as the dominant politico-economic force in the nation."[11]

Other legislation initiated by the Lincoln administration also reflected the dominance of Northern business interests. Northern industries were protected with high tariffs, and a national banking system was established. The Pacific Railway Acts authorized government bonds and extensive land grants to railroad companies, reversing the previous policy that did not favor such internal improvements. Although the bulk of legislation during the Lincoln presidency was motivated by the needs of the new economic elite, Lincoln also rewarded other constituencies that were instrumental in bringing him to power in 1860. The radical abolitionists got the Emancipation Proclamation of 1863, which was followed by the Thirteenth Amendment two years later. Emancipation also benefited Northern capitalists, if indirectly, by impoverishing Southern elites and reducing their power to influence policy at the federal level.

The Homestead Act of 1862, in contrast, was the payoff to the free farmers. It enabled the movement of surplus labor to unclaimed land, abundant stocks of which could be found in the West. Its secondary effect was to reduce the supply of labor in the East and drive its price up. To counteract this undesirable consequence (for the business interests, of course; workers welcomed higher wages), the Republican-dominated

Congress passed the Immigration Act of 1864, whose purpose was self-admittedly to ensure an adequate supply of labor, and created a bureau of immigration that facilitated the importation of laborers from Europe. The 1864 Republican platform explained the importance of such steps as follows: "[F]oreign immigration, which in the past has added so much to the wealth, the development of resources, and the increase of power to this nation—the asylum of the oppressed of all nations—should be fostered and encouraged by a liberal and just policy."[12]

We shouldn't exaggerate the degree of unity of post–Civil War elites. Once the old ruling class was "gone with the wind," intraelite conflicts immediately broke out among the new ruling class. The period between 1870 and 1900, known as the Gilded Age, was an extremely chaotic and contentious one in American history. Furthermore, in 1870 the new ruling class still lacked the institutions that would later forge a sense of shared identity and help coordinate collective action by the elites, transforming it into "a class for itself," if I may borrow from Marxist terminology.

One set of upper-class institutions that evolved during the Gilded Age had the dual function of enhancing communication among the elites and simultaneously creating a clear boundary that separated elites from commoners. The Social Register, which listed the members of so-called high society, became a kind of patent of nobility. Elite social clubs and exclusive summer resorts served a similar purpose. Scions of elite families were socialized into their class by going to prestigious boarding schools, most of which were founded during this period, and then to Ivy League colleges.

Parallel developments were taking place on the political economy side. Toward the end of the Gilded Age, the idea that unrestricted competition was injurious to all players became expressed more and more frequently by business leaders, including such titans as John D. Rockefeller and J. P. Morgan.[13] Their dislike of the resulting disorder and their pursuit of predictability resulted in the Great Merger Movement of 1895–1904. In most cases, these turn-of-the-century combinations were economically less efficient than the new rivals that appeared almost immediately. Their main benefits, however, were not in increasing economic efficiency but in increasing the political power of business. Following the consolidation of iron and steel manufactories in 1901, the editors of *The Bankers' Magazine* commented on it with unusual candor:

> When business men were single units, each working out his own success regardless of others in desperate competition, the men who controlled the political organization were supreme. They dictated laws and employed the proceeds of taxation in building up the power of their organization. But as the business of the country has learned the secret of combination, it is gradually subverting the power of the politician and rendering him subservient to its purposes. More and more the legislatures and the executive powers of the Government are compelled to listen to the demands of organized business interests. That they are not entirely controlled by these interests is due to the fact that business organization has not reached full perfection. The recent consolidation of the iron and steel industries is an indication of the concentration of power that is possible. Every form of business is capable of similar consolidation, and if other industries imitate the example of that concerned with iron and steel, it is easy to see that eventually the government of a country where the productive forces are all mustered and drilled under the control of a few leaders, must become the mere tool of these forces.[14]

Another important development, which took place later (around 1920), was the coalescence of what the political scientist G. William Domhoff calls the "policy-planning network," a network of nonprofit organizations in which corporate leaders and members of the upper class shape policy debates in the United States. These interlocked foundations, think tanks, and policy-discussion groups were funded by the corporate community, whose members controlled their messages by serving on the boards of trustees. The bulk of the money came from just three members of the economic elite: the steel magnate Andrew Carnegie, the oil baron John D. Rockefeller, and a wealthy St. Louis merchant, Robert Brookings.[15]

During the fifty years after the end of the Civil War, the Northern business and political elites thus merged into a true national upper class. As the left-leaning historian Gabriel Kolko wrote in *The Triumph of Conservatism*, "The business and political elites knew each other, went to the same schools, belonged to the same clubs, married into the same families, shared the same values—in reality, formed that phenomenon which has lately been dubbed The Establishment."[16]

American Plutocracy Today

The idea that the United States is a plutocracy has been expressed by American presidents, social scientists, and public intellectuals.[17] And by me. But I use this term in its neutral meaning, simply as shorthand for a state dominated by economic elites. (The literal meaning of *plutocracy* is "the rule of wealth.") But what stands behind the label?

Simply put, at the top of the power pyramid in America is the corporate community: the owners and managers of large income-producing assets, such as corporations, banks, and law firms.[18] Several corporate sectors are so influential and cohesive in their influence on public policy that, over the years, they have acquired such names as the military-industrial complex, the FIRE (finance, insurance, and real estate) sector, the energy (oil and gas, electric utilities) sector, Silicon Valley, Big Food, Big Pharma, the medical-industrial complex, and the education-industrial complex. In 2021, twelve thousand lobbyists spent $3.7 billion influencing policy at the federal level, according to the nonpartisan OpenSecrets research group.[19] The top three industries, spending hundreds of millions of dollars on lobbying, are pharmaceuticals, electronics, and insurance.[20] Others are close behind.

According to this "class-domination" theory, the corporate community rules America indirectly.[21] Its "structural economic power" allows it to dominate the political class through lobbying, campaign finance, businesspeople running for political office, appointments of corporate leaders to key government positions, and the "revolving door"—the movement of individuals back and forth between government and industry positions. In fact, the two power networks, economic and administrative, are joined at the hip in a very thorough fashion, but the economic network is the dominant one.

The corporate community also controls the ideological basis of power through the ownership of mass media corporations and a policy-planning network made up of private foundations, think tanks, and policy-discussion groups. The remaining source of social power, the military, has been thoroughly subordinated by the political network throughout American history. Future officers are indoctrinated into a culture of obedience to their commanding political leaders, and at the highest levels, generals and admirals look forward to occupying well-compensated post-retirement positions on the boards of the companies that live off government contracts.

Conspiracy Versus Science

To say that America is a plutocracy is, to be clear, not a conspiracy theory. It's a scientific theory. What's the difference?

First, let's acknowledge that some conspiracies are real. History abounds with examples of groups of people who plotted in secret to advance their interests and goals at the expense of other groups or whole societies. Guy Fawkes and his conspirators indeed planned to blow up the House of Lords in 1605 because they wanted to replace James I with a Catholic monarch. The administration of Richard Nixon indeed committed a variety of illegal acts, such as bugging the offices of political opponents and harassing politicians and activists, then tried to cover it up. And sometimes people who try to expose real conspiracies are wrongly dismissed as conspiracy theorists, or even branded as mentally ill. This is what happened to Martha Mitchell, the "Cassandra of Watergate."[22] Thus, the discussion below concerns not conspiracies but conspiracy theories.

There are quite a number of conspiracy theories about shadowy, nefariously motivated groups that supposedly control the US government, or that want to create an oppressive global state. Such "shadow government" and "new world order" theories postulate that real political power is held by central banks, organized Jewry, Freemasons, Illuminati, Jesuits, the CIA, the United Nations, or the World Economic Forum. In the past, the favorite bogeyman was Soviet communists, but after the collapse of the Soviet Union, the focus of conspiratorial fantasizing shifted to Chinese communists (for the right) and Vladimir Putin's Russia (for the left). For example, Stewart Rhodes, the founder of the Oath Keepers, believes that the "Chicoms" have fully infiltrated the US government,[23] while Rachel Maddow's MSNBC show enjoyed huge ratings in 2017 by repeatedly claiming that the Russian government was pulling the strings of the Trump presidency.[24]

What are the features of conspiracy theories that distinguish them from scientific theories?[25] One, the conspiratorial theory is often vague about the motives of the behind-the-scenes leaders or assigns them implausible motivations. Two, it assumes that they are extremely clever and knowledgeable. Three, it places power in the hands of one strong leader or a tiny cabal. And, finally, it assumes that illegal plans can be kept secret for indefinitely long periods of time. A scientific theory, like the class-domination one, is very different. Let's go through these four points in the same order.

First, the motives of wealth holders are quite transparent. We don't need to be mind readers to understand that they want to augment their wealth rather than see it diminish. This is, of course, a great simplification. People are complex beings with multiple overlapping motivations. Different people are motivated by different mixes of materialistic and idealistic goals. But one motive that the wealth holders share as a class is, by and large, the wish to keep and increase their wealth. All theories (and models) oversimplify the messy reality, but this assumption is a good approximation.

Second, the class-domination theory also outlines empirically verifiable mechanisms by which the corporate class dominates the political class. It is done by setting up super PACs, funding lobbyists, making campaign contributions to candidates, and having members of the class run for office themselves. The officeholders are further influenced through the mainstream media, which are owned by the economic elites, generally speaking, and share a general understanding of what "news" is and isn't. The details of legislation are often written by think tanks and lobbyists, again controlled by the economic elites.

Third, there is no center. Economic elites are organized in a very different fashion than military elites, for example, with their elaborate command-and-control hierarchies and a commander in chief at the top. Instead, collective action is facilitated by the members of the power network being socialized at exclusive prep schools and colleges, country clubs and golf courses. They serve on corporate boards together and participate in various professional groups and gatherings, such as chambers of commerce, industry associations, and global convenings (e.g., Davos). Concrete policies are hammered out in the policy-planning network of interlocked think tanks, institutes, and charitable foundations. Again, there is no center—no supremo leader, no small inner cabal. Instead, power is distributed within a nonhierarchical network of thousands of individuals. And there are differences of opinion and even conflicts between different nodes of the network. The degree of unity and cohesion within the ruling class is a dynamic quantity; it changes with time. I will return to this point later.

Finally, there is secrecy versus transparency. Admittedly, members of the ruling class often attempt to keep their goings-on out of public view. They live in gated communities and socialize in exclusive clubs to which common people have no access. But the data, which sociologists use to study the inner workings of the ruling class, are a matter of public record. Organizations such as OpenSecrets have amassed a remarkable amount of data on the influence of money on US politics and policy.[26] Sociologists have painstakingly reconstructed the network of the American power elite—you can view it on whorulesamerica.net, Domhoff's web resource.[27]

The most important, indeed decisive, difference between conspiracy and scientific theories is that the latter make novel predictions that can be tested with data. The class-domination theory was first proposed by Domhoff fifty years ago, and there has been plenty of time since then for other social scientists to test its predictions.

Affluence and Influence

The theory of how the American state functions that is taught in school is neatly encapsulated by Abraham Lincoln's reference to government "of the people, by the people, for the people." Sociologists refer to this idea of governance as "majoritarian electoral democracy." This theory assumes that government policies are shaped by the collective will of common citizens, which is transmitted through the process of democratic elections. The theory predicts that policy changes, such as new legislation adopted by Congress, will primarily reflect the preferences of typical citizens, or "median voters." Class-domination theory, in contrast, predicts that policy changes will reflect only the preferences of the economic elites. So who's right?

The political scientist Martin Gilens, aided by a small army of research assistants, gathered a large data set—nearly two thousand policy issues between 1981 and 2002. Each case matched a proposed policy change to a national opinion survey asking a favor/oppose question about the initiative. The raw survey data provided information that enabled Gilens to separate the preferences of the poor (in the lowest decile of the income distribution) and the typical (the median of the distribution) from the affluent (the top 10 percent).[28]

Statistical analysis of this remarkable data set showed that the preferences of the poor had no effect on policy changes. This is not entirely unexpected. What is surprising is that there was no—zilch, nada—effect of the average voter. The main effect on the direction of change was due to the policy preferences of the affluent. There was also an additional effect of interest groups, the most influential ones being business-oriented lobbies. Once you include in the statistical model the preferences of the top 10 percent and the interest groups, the effect of the commoners is statistically indistinguishable from zero.

This doesn't mean that ordinary citizens always lose out. There are a number of policy issues on which they agree with the affluent, and these policy changes tend to be implemented. But, on the evidence, issues on which the common people and the economic elites disagree are always—*always*—resolved in favor of the elites. That is plutocracy.

So much for the majoritarian electoral democracy theory. Let me add that this analysis had several features that actually slanted the results against the class-domination theory. We would really want to distinguish the effects of preferences of the top 10 percent from those of the top 1 percent (and, even better, the top 0.01 percent). After all, the members of the power network, identified by Domhoff, constitute a tiny proportion of the population. But making such nuanced distinctions was not possible given the data that Gilens and his crew had access to. Another consideration is that this analysis addressed only what political scientists call the "first face of power": the ability of citizens to shape policy outcomes on contested issues. But the "second face of power," shaping the agenda of issues that policy makers consider, is a subtle but extremely powerful way for the elites to get their way. Finally, the "third face of power" is the ability of ideological elites to shape the preferences of the public.

The third face is the most subtle, perhaps even insidious, kind of power. My favorite example of its effectiveness is the "death tax" meme, invented by some brilliant, if evil, propagandist at one of the think tanks to kill the inheritance tax on top fortunes. Common people agitate against the government to "take your dirty paws off my money that

I am leaving to my children" without apparently realizing that the proposed tax would affect only the superrich.[29]

The brilliant research done by Gilens is a great example of how science works. Scientists take two or more rival theories (in this case, class domination and majoritarian electoral democracy), derive specific predictions from them, and then gather data to see which theory is correct. Majoritarian electoral democracy is a beautiful theory, but unfortunately, it is slain by the ugly facts.[30]

Immigration

Now that we have a better understanding of how power works in America, let's use it to reflect on one puzzle about American democracy: the contentious politics of immigration. According to multiple polls, Americans strongly oppose illegal immigration.[31] There is E-Verify, a Department of Homeland Security website that allows businesses to determine the work statuses of potential employees, but no federal mandate requires employers to use it. Many believe that such a mandate would be a much more effective and humane way to reduce illegal immigration than the current system. Obviously, there are many sides to this complex issue. Yet one has to wonder when a solution that involves spending billions of dollars on border security and detention of migrants is implemented—with imperfect results, to say the least—but a solution that involves cutting off the money that draws migrants to this country in the first place has never been adopted. Cui bono, as the Romans used to say.

"In the heightened emotions of America's public debate on migration, a simple moral and political dichotomy prevails," writes Angela Nagle in "The Left Case Against Open Borders."[32] "It is 'right-wing' to be 'against immigration' and 'left-wing' to be 'for immigration.' But the economics of migration tell a different story." Of course, economics is only one of the considerations that should inform public policy on immigration. It has become a hugely emotional issue. As Nagle adds:

> With obscene images of low-wage migrants being chased down as criminals by ICE, others drowning in the Mediterranean, and the worrying growth of anti-immigrant sentiment across the world, it is easy to see why the Left wants to defend illegal migrants against being targeted and victimized. And it should. But acting on the correct moral impulse to defend the human dignity of migrants, the Left has ended up pulling the front line too far back, effectively defending the exploitative system of migration itself.

Let's follow Nagle to look below the surface to structural issues— economics but, even more deeply, power.

The economic argument is very clear. Massive immigration increases the supply of labor, which in turn depresses its cost—in other words, worker wages. Clearly, such development benefits the consumers of labor (employers, or "capitalists") and disadvantages the workers.

Of course, as we saw in chapter 3, immigration is only one of the many forces affecting wages. My statistical analysis of long-term data trends indicates that immigration has been a significant contributor to the stagnation/decline of wages in the United States over the past several decades, particularly for workers without college educations, although far from the only one.[33] There is a reason why the greatest surge of immigration in American history in the late nineteenth century coincided with the first Gilded Age, the period of extreme income inequality and popular immiseration comparable only to our own. Any such external input into a social system, of course, has multiple effects. Immigrants to America during the Gilded Age enriched this country immeasurably, just as immigrants today do. But they also tilted the balance of power away from workers and toward owners, accelerating the wealth pump. Unless there are strong institutions protecting workers' wages, an oversupply of labor is going to depress wages—it is simply the law of supply and demand in action. In his 2016 book, *We Wanted Workers: Unraveling the Immigration Narrative*, the Harvard economist George Borjas (himself an immigrant) explains that the main effect of immigration is not on whether it benefits the economy or is a drag. (It has a slight positive effect.) Rather, it is that it creates winners and losers. A massive influx of unskilled immigrants depresses the wages of less educated native-born workers. Already disadvantaged communities, like noncollege-educated Black Americans, are particularly badly affected. But their lower wages translate into higher profits for those who employ immigrants—business owners and managers.[34]

As Nagle points out, this idea was clear to Karl Marx, who "argued that the importation of low-paid Irish immigrants to England forced them into hostile competition with English workers. He saw it as part of a system of exploitation, which divided the working class and which represented an extension of the colonial system." It was also clear to those who were negatively affected—the workers and their organizations:

> From the first law restricting immigration in 1882 to Cesar Chavez and the famously multiethnic United Farm Workers protesting against employers' use and encouragement of illegal migration in 1969, trade unions have often opposed mass migration. They saw the deliberate importation of illegal, low-wage workers as weakening labor's bargaining power and as a form of exploitation. There is no getting around the fact that the power

of unions relies by definition on their ability to restrict and with-
draw the supply of labor, which becomes impossible if an entire
workforce can be easily and cheaply replaced. Open borders and
mass immigration are a victory for the bosses.

Not surprisingly, the American economic elites were also well
aware that a continuing influx of immigrants allowed them to depress
worker wages and increase their returns on capital. In 1886, Andrew
Carnegie compared immigration to "a golden stream which flows into
the country each year."[35] During the nineteenth century, the corporate
community often used the American state to ensure that this "golden
stream" would continue flowing. Recollect that in 1864 (during the
Lincoln administration), Congress passed the Act to Encourage Immigration. One of its provisions was the establishment of the Federal Bureau of Immigration, whose explicit intent was "the development of a
surplus [my italics] labor force." Business leaders today are much more
circumspect.

To strip Nagle's main argument to its essence, globalization is
wielded by the governing elites to increase their power at the expense
of the non-elites. It's another wealth pump that takes from the workers
and gives to the "bosses." It is also a global wealth pump that transfers
wealth from the developing world to rich regions. Some of that extra
wealth is then converted into greater political power for big business.
Furthermore, antagonism between native-born and immigrant workers corrodes their ability to organize. As a result, Nagle argues:

Today's well-intentioned activists have become the useful idi-
ots of big business. With their adoption of "open borders"
advocacy—and a fierce moral absolutism that regards any limit
to migration as an unspeakable evil—any criticism of the ex-

ploitative system of mass migration is effectively dismissed as blasphemy.

"What Is" and "What Should Be"

Stepping away from the specific question of who rules America, in science—and in life—it's important to distinguish "what is" from "what should be," and not allow the second to cloud the first. Social scientists, such as Domhoff and Gilens, who have proven that our democracy is not quite as democratic as it is taught in civics classes, are not antidemocratic. Quite the opposite. They are motivated by a desire to make our society work better. And the only way we can improve things is by understanding how they really work, not by imposing some preconceived idea of how they should work. This is such an obvious thing to say. But it needs to be said, because scientists who made displeasing discoveries have been persecuted. Galileo had to recant, while Giordano Bruno was burned at the stake. Today, a scientist discovering some unpalatable truth may be branded as a purveyor of "hate facts." Closer to our topic, those who expose the workings of our ruling class run the danger of being accused as "class warriors."

CHAPTER 6

WHY IS AMERICA A PLUTOCRACY?

American Exceptionalism

The extent to which economic elites dominate government in the United States is very unusual compared to other Western democracies. Countries like Denmark and Austria have ruling classes that have been fairly responsive to the wishes of their population. During the postwar period, these countries were ruled by strong center-left parties, such as social democrats and socialists. Center-left parties rotated in power with center-right parties, but a strong consensus for the welfare state was shared broadly by the ruling elites in Western European democracies. Countries such as Denmark and Austria usually occupy the top positions when UN countries are ranked for their ability to deliver a high quality of life for their citizens. Until recently, they have largely resisted the worldwide trend of growing economic inequality. On many indicators of quality of life—life expectancy, equality, education—the US is an outlier in the Western world. Why?

The explanation lies in the effects of history and geography.[1] Two major factors are particularly important: geopolitical environment and race/ethnicity.

In order to understand the historical and geographical origins of the American plutocracy, let's start with a short excursus into the history of Western Europe during the last five centuries. Before 1500, Europe was occupied by more than five hundred states and statelets, some quite minuscule, such as free imperial cities and independent principalities. Apart from one theocracy (the Papal States), these polities were governed either by militocracies or plutocracies. Plutocracies were particularly common in the more urbanized swath that ran through the middle of Europe from Italy to the Rhine Valley and then along the Baltic littoral. Typical examples include the city republics in northern Italy and the members of the Hanseatic League that controlled Baltic trade.

During the next four centuries, this geopolitical landscape was utterly reshaped. First, the total number of states in Europe was drastically cut down, from more than five hundred to just about thirty. Second, most of the plutocracies went extinct and were swallowed up by militocracies. The reason? Three words: the Military Revolution.[2]

Gunpowder weapons underwent a rapid evolution during the fifteenth century and by 1500 had utterly changed the nature of warfare. Another important technological advance was the development of oceangoing ships that dramatically increased the geographic reach of the new powder empires.[3] Europe was the pioneer in these developments, which explains why Europe, together with its North American offshoot, had achieved global dominance by 1900. The conditions of intense warfare favor larger, more cohesive states. Small principalities and city-states could no longer hide behind their walls, which were easily breached by cannons. Intense military competition between European states weeded out those that couldn't raise large armies; produce muskets and artillery in quantity; and build expensive modern fortifications that could withstand cannon fire. The Military Revolution also triggered a revolution in governance and finance because successful states had to learn how to efficiently extract and use wealth from their populations. As the Romans liked to say two millennia ago, "Money is the sinews of war."[4] As a result, medieval militocracies gradually evolved into ruling classes that combined military and administrative functions.

Although most plutocracies rapidly went extinct, some lingered longer than others. The Republic of Venice, located on islands protected by its lagoon, lasted longer than the other Italian city-states. The Netherlands survived into the twenty-first century, in part thanks to its waterways and canals, which made offensive operations difficult.

Most interesting is the case of England. It emerged under Norman rule after 1066 as a typical medieval militocracy. But thanks to its protected position in the British Isles, once England conquered all of them, it could, and did, dispense with the standing army (at least within England itself). The squirearchy, which started as a military class, gradually lost its military character and became simply a class of landowners, from which members of the British Parliament were elected. A large merchant class evolved, thanks to the world empire forged by Britain. Unlike the other European great powers, which had to direct most of their resources into land armies or be conquered, the British Empire poured its resources into its navy. As a result, the United Kingdom came to be ruled by an elite that combined economic and administrative functions.

The antebellum ruling class in the US was a direct offshoot of the English squirearchy. Virginia, the Carolinas, and Georgia were settled by the Cavaliers, the faction of supporters of Charles I that lost the English Civil War. They brought with them their aristocratic ways and indentured servants. The latter were soon replaced by imported Africans, enslaved for life. After they won the Revolutionary War against the British Empire, the winners set about building their own state. Southern planters and Northern merchants largely copied the cultural forms of governance with which they were familiar. The early American Republic was an oligarchy modeled after the United Kingdom, although without a monarch (who, by that point, was on the way to becoming just a figurehead in the British Empire anyway). As a result, the United States inherited plutocracy as part of its "cultural genotype."

Of course, the US didn't become a huge territorial state in a fit of absentmindedness. From the establishment of the first European colonies in the seventeenth century to the end of the nineteenth century, territorial expansion came at the expense of the Native Americans in a conflict that reached genocidal intensity. America also fought against the British (in the Revolution and again in 1812). In the Mexican-American War (1846–1848), the US gobbled up half of Mexico.

But when the corporate plutocracy overthrew the antebellum ruling class in the Civil War, this process of continental expansion was nearly complete. (The frontier was pronounced a thing of the past, and Native Americans had all essentially been confined to reservations by 1890.) Neither Mexico nor Canada posed any danger to the US. North America is a giant island protected from any potential threats by two huge moats—the Atlantic and the Pacific Oceans. What militocracy the US had was destroyed in the Civil War, in which the overwhelming majority of American professional officers fought on the losing side. The bureaucratic apparatus, before 1914, was vanishingly small, with just 2 percent of the GDP captured by the federal government. In any case, the administrative apparatus, such as it was, was thoroughly dominated by the plutocracy. Thanks to the infamous "spoils system," between 1828 and 1900, most federal officials (down to local postmasters!) were replaced by the party winning the elections.

During its formative post–Civil War years, the plutocracy had no significant rivals, whether internal or external. Once it was entrenched, it became exceedingly difficult to displace without a social revolution. Thus, the rise of the American plutocracy can mostly be explained by its historical antecedents and geographical circumstances. But its continuing survival and efflorescence into the twenty-first century is largely due to a second cause—race and ethnicity.

And He Ate Jim Crow

To make this argument more concrete, let's compare America to Denmark. During the nineteenth century, industrialization in Denmark, as in other European countries, resulted in the creation of a working class concentrated in large factories, which made labor organization more efficient. The first social democratic party was founded in Copenhagen in 1871 by Louis Pio, Harald Brix, and Paul Geleff, who became known as the holy trinity of the Danish labor movement. They all came from non-elite backgrounds. Pio was a son of tenant farmers, while the other two were "petty bourgeoisie." But they acquired a good education, read lots of Marx, and worked as editors and publishers. The Social Democratic Party first entered the Danish Parliament in 1884. In 1924, it became the country's biggest party, with 37 percent of the vote. Its leader, Thorvald Stauning (from a working-class background), became prime minister. They governed only one term and were temporarily replaced by the liberals, but in 1929 they were back in power. Thus, it took sixty years for Danish social democrats to transition from counter-elites to established elites.

While Pio, Brix, and Geleff were radical hotheads, Stauning perfected the art of dialogue, melding radical and liberal ideas and achieving a compromise with the opposition. In 1933, Stauning negotiated the Kanslergade Agreement, which laid down the foundations of what became known as the Nordic model. The key feature of the Nordic model is tripartite cooperation between labor, business, and government, working together for the common good. Although each Nordic country followed its own unique path to social democracy, Denmark provided a blueprint and inspiration to others.[5] The Nordic model proved to be an enormously successful way of enabling societies to deliver a high quality of life to their members. Recently in the US, both center-right intellectuals (e.g., Francis Fukuyama) and progressive-left politicians (e.g., Bernie Sanders) have cited Denmark as the model for emulation.

For a while, the United States followed a similar trajectory. Although the Populist Party (People's Party) and the socialist parties that arose in America during the 1890s never gained power, their impact on mainstream American politics was undeniable. One of the mainstream parties, the Democratic Party, became a quasi-social-democratic party under the leadership of Franklin Roosevelt. As a result of reforms adopted during the Progressive Era and the New Deal, the United States in many respects became a "Nordic country." I'll discuss this trajectory in more detail later on in this chapter, but here let's talk about why the trajectories of Denmark and the United States diverged during the second half of the twentieth century.

A big part of the answer is race. Race has been one of the most important issues in American politics, all the way from its beginnings to this very day. Because of its importance, it has been hugely politicized and ideologized. Although, as I said a bit earlier, the Democratic Party of the FDR period can be thought of as a party of the working class, we must add an important qualification. It was a party of the white working class. In order to push his agenda through, FDR had to make a devil's bargain with the Southern elites, which essentially made the South immune from the tripartite bargain among workers, business, and government that the FDR administration forged. In particular, the segregationist regime in the South was left untouched. Black workers, especially in the South, were excluded from the social contract of the New Deal. As Heather Cox Richardson writes in *How the South Won the Civil War*:

> So the original American paradox of freedom based on inequality was reestablished. That restoration relegated people of color to inequality, but it also undercut the ability of oligarchs to destroy democracy. Black and brown people were subordinate, so wealthy men could not convincingly argue that they were commandeering government to redistribute wealth and destroy liberty. With that rhetoric defanged, white Americans used the government to curb wealth and power. From the presidency of Theodore Roosevelt in the early 1900s to that of Franklin Delano Roosevelt thirty years later, Progressives regulated the economy, protected social welfare, and promoted national infrastructure. That government activism, though, privileged white men over women and people of color. Even the New Deal programs of the Depression, designed to lift the poor out of desperation while reining in runaway capitalism, carefully maintained distinctions between women and men, black and brown and white.[6]

In the two decades after World War II, this situation began to change. Strong economic growth created enough prosperity to lift all boats; a sense of national unity argued against exclusion of people of color; and ideological rivalry between Cold War adversaries provided an additional push. (Constant reminders by Soviet propaganda of pervasive racism in the US were embarrassing.) Nurtured by these conditions, the civil rights movement became an irresistible force for social change.

The gradual expansion of the social contract to include Black workers, however, provided an opening for those plutocrats who were unhappy with America as a quasi-Nordic country in which their power was constrained by the other two interest groups: workers and the state. They used the Republican Party as a vehicle to push their own agenda, aiming to dismantle worker protections and reduce taxes on the wealthy. This agenda was translated into action by politicians such as Barry Goldwater and Richard Nixon, initially, and later by Ronald Reagan as the "Southern strategy," whose goal was to make the Republican Party the dominant party in the former Confederate states by appealing to Southern white voters using explicitly or implicitly racist issues.

Such a strategy couldn't succeed in Denmark, which has been a racially and culturally homogeneous country. But in the United States, the working class could be, and was, divided by race—white, Black, brown. As the old Romans said, divide et impera—divide and rule. In *The Sum of Us*, Heather McGhee writes:

> In the two-hundred-year history of American industrial work, there's been no greater tool against collective bargaining than employers' ability to divide workers by gender, race, or origin, stoking suspicion and competition across groups. It's simple: if your boss can hire someone else for cheaper, or threaten to, you have less leverage for bargaining. In the nineteenth century, employers' ability to pay Black workers a fraction of white wages made whites see free Black people as threats to their livelihood. In the early twentieth century, new immigrants were added to this competitive dynamic, and the result was a zero sum: the

boss made more profit; one group had new, worse work, and the other had none. In the war years, men would protest the employment of women. Competition across demographic groups was the defining characteristic of the American labor market, but the stratification only helped the employer.

This potential weak point for working-class solidarity was well understood by early labor organizers, such as the Knights of Labor, the first mass labor organization in the United States:

> When the Knights began organizing in the volatile years of Reconstruction, they recruited across color lines, believing that to exclude any racial or ethnic group would be playing into the employers' hands. "Why should working men keep anyone out of the organization who could be used by the employer as a tool in grinding down wages?" wrote the official Knights newspaper in 1880. With Black workers in the union, white workers gained by robbing the bosses of a population they might exploit to undercut wages or break strikes; at the same time, Black workers gained by working for and benefiting from whatever gains the union won. The Knights also included women in their ranks. A journalist in 1886 Charleston, South Carolina, reported on the Knights' success in organizing members in that city: "When everything else had failed, the bond of poverty united the white and colored mechanics and laborers."[7]

The Knights of Labor were part of the larger Populist movement that challenged the American plutocracy in the last decade of the nineteenth century. As Thomas Frank documents in his most recent book, *The People, No: A Brief History of Anti-Populism*, the Populists' ideal was

class-based political action across racial lines. But the Populist movement failed as a mass democratic movement. Why? One answer to this
question was offered by Martin Luther King Jr. In a speech at the conclusion of the 1965 march from Selma to Montgomery, Alabama, King
gave his fellow marchers a short lesson in history. He talked about how
the People's Party tried to unite the poor white masses and the former
Black slaves into a voting block that would threaten the ruling class's interests. But the plutocrats "took the world and gave the poor white man
Jim Crow":

> And when his wrinkled stomach cried out for the food that his
> empty pockets could not provide, (Yes, sir) he ate Jim Crow, a
> psychological bird that told him that no matter how bad off he
> was, at least he was a white man, better than the black man.
> (Right sir) And he ate Jim Crow. (Uh huh)[8]

The Progressive Era Trend Reversal

How does this all help us interpret the results of our investigation into
who rules America? First, let's avoid blaming the rich. The economic
elites are not evil—or, at least, the proportion of evil people among them
is not terribly different from that of the rest of the population. They are
motivated by self-interest, but Mother Teresas, if absent among the ruling class, are quite rare in the general population as well. Furthermore,
we know that many among the 1 percent are motivated by more than just
short-term self-interest. Nick Hanauer isn't alone; a group of wealthy
"Patriotic Millionaires" has been campaigning to raise taxes on the
very rich since 2010.[9] And nearly all billionaires donate to what they
consider worthy causes (although there may be some unintended con-

sequences of that, which we will discuss). Finally, while history is replete with examples of selfish elites running the countries they ruled into the ground, there are also examples of prosocial elites overcoming crises and rebuilding social cooperation. Here's one example.

Although the American political system has been dominated by corporate elites since the Civil War, in some historical periods the elites worked primarily for their own benefit, while in others they implemented policies that benefited society as a whole, even at the expense of their own short-term benefits. It is relatively easy to understand the periods in which the wealthy and powerful shaped the political agenda to suit their own interests, as happened in the Gilded Age, when economic inequality grew by leaps and bounds. But how can we account for the policies of the Great Compression era, roughly from the 1930s to the 1970s, during which inequality in income and wealth tended to decrease? What caused the reversal that ended the Gilded Age and ushered in the Great Compression?

Investigations of historical case studies suggest that the key role in such trend reversals is played by long periods of persistent political instability. Sometimes they ended in social revolutions, state collapses, or bloody civil wars. But in other cases, the elites eventually became alarmed by incessant violence and disorder. They realized that they needed to pull together, suppress their internal rivalries, and switch to a more cooperative way of governing.

Well, the two decades around 1920 were a very turbulent time in the United States.[10] Violent labor conflicts had become bloodier and more frequent since the Gilded Age and reached a peak during the "violent teens" and early 1920s. In 1919, nearly four million workers (21 percent of the workforce) participated in labor strikes and other disruptive actions aiming to force employers to recognize and bargain with unions. The worst incident in US labor history was the Battle of Blair

Mountain (1921). Although it started as a labor dispute, it eventually turned into the largest armed insurrection in US history, other than the Civil War. Between ten thousand and fifteen thousand miners armed with rifles fought thousands of strikebreakers and sheriff's deputies, called the Logan Defenders. The insurrection had to be ended by the United States Army.

Race issues were intertwined with labor issues, and in many episodes of political violence during this period, it is impossible to separate the two. In the East St. Louis Riot of 1917, at least 150 people were killed. Race-motivated riots also peaked around 1920. The two most serious outbreaks were the Red Summer of 1919 and the Tulsa Race Massacre in 1921. The Red Summer involved riots in more than twenty cities across the United States and resulted in something like one thousand fatalities. The Tulsa riot in 1921, which caused about three hundred deaths, in effect a mass lynching, took on an aspect of civil war. Thousands of Black and white Americans, armed with firearms, fought in the streets, and most of the Greenwood District, a prosperous Black neighborhood, was destroyed.

Finally, the 1910s saw the peak of terrorist activity by labor radicals and anarchists. A bombing campaign by Italian anarchists culminated in the 1920 explosion on Wall Street that caused thirty-eight fatalities. This was followed by an even worse incident, the 1927 Bath School disaster, in which forty-five people, including thirty-eight schoolchildren, were killed by a domestic terrorist.

Less violent, but ultimately more threatening, developments were internal electoral challenges to the ruling class from the surging socialist and Populist movements, as well as external threats resulting from the rise of communism and fascism in Europe. The economic elites perceived the gravest threat in the victory of the October Revolution in

Russia and the establishment of the USSR, a country with a militant universalizing ideology that directly challenged the foundations of the American political order. It did not help that many of the counter-elites in America—labor organizers, anarchists, socialists, and communists—were recent immigrants from Southern and Eastern Europe. The First Red Scare, which swept through the country from 1919 to 1921, was a reflection of elite fears that a Bolshevik revolution was imminent in America.

As we saw earlier, by 1920, America's economic and political elites had consolidated into a true upper class, which had acquired a number of institutions that promoted cohesive political action (elite boarding schools, Ivy League universities, exclusive country clubs, and, most notably, a policy-planning network). Gradually, a realization grew among many American leaders that in order to reduce instability, steps had to be taken to rebalance the political system, and better to do it by passing reforms from above than by revolution from below.

During the nineteenth century, American capitalists had shown no concern for the well-being of the working classes. Ideas of Social Darwinism and what we would now call market fundamentalism dominated the intellectual landscape. Things began to change after 1900, during the Progressive Era, and by the late 1910s, the idea that corporations needed to behave in socially responsible ways was starting to take hold. For example, this period saw the introduction of employee stock plans by several corporations.

A key development in shutting down the wealth pump was the passage of the immigration laws of 1921 and 1924. Although much of the proximate motivation behind these laws was to exclude "dangerous aliens," such as Italian anarchists and Eastern European socialists, their broader effect was a reduction in labor oversupply, something that business elites were well aware of. Shutting down immigration reduced the labor supply and provided a powerful boost to real wages for many decades to come.

Although these trends were initiated during the Progressive Era, they matured during the New Deal, helped along by the economic and social turbulence brought on by the Great Depression. In particular, new legislation legalized collective bargaining through unions, introduced a minimum wage, and established Social Security. American elites essentially entered into a "fragile, unwritten compact" with the working classes. This implicit contract included the promise that the fruits of economic growth would be distributed more equitably among both workers and owners. In return, the fundamentals of the political-economic system would not be challenged. Avoiding revolution was one of the most important reasons for this compact (although not the only one). When the United Auto Workers' president, Douglas Fraser, resigned from the Labor-Management Group in 1978, at the point when the compact was about to be abandoned, he wrote in his blistering resignation letter: "The acceptance of the labor movement, such as it has been, came because business feared the alternatives."[11]

In this account, it is important not to overemphasize the degree of unity among the American power elites. There was no hidden capitalist conspiracy, and there was no truly monolithic ruling class. In their analysis of the origin and implementation of New Deal reforms, Domhoff and Webber stress that there were at least six recognizable power networks that participated in shaping New Deal legislation.[12] It was a complex pattern of conflict and cooperation between these power actors that determined the success or failure of various reforms, and different legislation could be supported by different alliances.

The Progressive Era trend reversal introduced the Great Compression, a long period of economic inequality trending down. However, while such "quantitative" inequality declined, there was an underside to this arrangement. The social contract was between the white working class and the WASP elite. Black Americans, Jews, Catholics, and foreigners were excluded from the "cooperating circle" and heavily discriminated against. Nevertheless, while making such "categorical inequalities" worse, the compact made a dramatic reduction in overall economic inequality possible in the first place.

As we've seen, the exclusion of Black Americans from the contract was a result of tactical choices made by the FDR administration, which needed Southern votes to push its legislation against the resistance of conservative business elites (organizing around the National Association of Manufacturers), who were dead set against giving any ground to the working class. In retrospect, this decision to abandon Black workers also made it possible for the next generation of leaders, such as Jack and Robert Kennedy and Lyndon Johnson, to usher in a new civil rights era that eventually swept away the apartheid state the Southern elites had erected in the aftermath of the Civil War and the failure of Reconstruction.

The Great Compression

Cooperation is not costless. To produce public goods, cooperators have to sacrifice self-interest, to a greater or lesser degree. The prosocial policies during the Progressive and New Deal periods had to be paid for—and the costs were borne by the American ruling class. It is little appreciated just how much the economic elites had to give up to make it work. Between 1929 and the 1970s, top fortunes declined not only in relative terms (in comparison with median wealth) but also in absolute terms (when inflation is taken into account).

Kevin Phillips came up with a neat way to visualize how the fortunes of the rich changed during the course of the American Republic.[13] For different periods of American history, he found data on how much wealth the richest person had and divided it by a typical annual wage of an American worker. In 1790, the top wealth holder was Elias Derby with about a million dollars. The typical American worker earned forty dollars a year, which was a good wage. (Remember that at that time common Americans enjoyed standards of living high enough to make them the tallest people on earth.) The top wealth, then, was equivalent to the annual wages of twenty-five thousand workers. By 1912, when this indicator reached its first peak, the top fortune was $1 billion, and its lucky holder was John D. Rockefeller. It was equivalent to 2.6 million annual wages—two orders of magnitude (x100) greater! The great depressions of the nineteenth century, while imposing huge amounts of misery on the working classes, had no long-term effect on the triumphant march of the top fortunes.

But things changed during the Progressive and New Deal periods. The Great Depression, triggered by the New York Stock Exchange collapse of 1929, wiped out a third of the largest banks, which were members of the Federal Reserve System, and nearly half of all smaller banks. Membership in the National Association of Manufacturers collapsed from more than five thousand in the early 1920s to fifteen hundred in 1933. Overnight, thousands of business leaders plunged into the commoner class. (And some literally plunged to their deaths, jumping out of their offices on the top floors of office buildings.) In 1925, there were sixteen hundred millionaires, but by 1950, fewer than nine hundred remained. The size of the top fortune remained stuck at $1 billion for decades. In 1962, the richest man was J. Paul Getty, whose $1 billion was the same as Rockefeller's fifty years prior in nominal dollars, though the real worth of his billion was considerably smaller due to inflation. By 1982, when inflation had eroded the dollar even more, the richest American was Daniel Ludwig, whose $2 billion was equivalent to "only" ninety-three thousand annual wages.[14]

This reversal of elite overproduction was similar in magnitude to the one that occurred in the aftermath of the Civil War, but it was accomplished through entirely nonviolent means. No social revolution did this; the ruling class did it itself—or, at least, it allowed a prosocial faction within itself to persuade the rest of the elites of the need for reforms. To drive this home, let's follow the trajectory of the tax rate on top incomes. When the federal tax system was established in 1913, the tax rate on the top bracket was only 7 percent. During World War I, it jumped to 77 percent, but by 1929, it had declined to 24 percent. During the Great Depression, it went up to 63 percent, and toward the end of World War II, it soared to 94 percent. This was justified as a necessary sacrifice during a time of national emergency. But even after the war ended, the top rate stayed above 90 percent until 1964. Think about it—during the two peaceful decades after World War II, the very rich gave away to the government nine-tenths of their income!

In his most famous book, *Capital in the Twenty-First Century*, the French economist Thomas Piketty argues that, over the long term, the rate of return on capital is typically greater than the rate of economic growth, which results in growing economic inequality and concentration of wealth in the hands of the elite.[15] *The Great Leveler*, a book by my good colleague and friend Walter Scheidel, is about the opposite process that reduces inequality. Amassing an impressive number of historical examples, he argues that "death is the great leveler."[16] Typically, it takes a major perturbation to reduce wealth inequality, and this perturbation usually takes the form of a social revolution, a state collapse, a mass-mobilization war, or a major epidemic. As we shall see in chapter 9, where I review the results of the first one hundred cases in CrisisDB, Scheidel's pessimistic view is only 90 percent right.

The Great Compression in America is one of the exceptional, hopeful cases. There was no bloody revolution or state collapse, no catastrophic epidemic, and World War II was fought entirely overseas. The threats of internal revolution and external competition—against the Nazi regime during World War II and against the Soviet Union during the ensuing Cold War—were clearly instrumental in focusing the minds of the American ruling class on adopting the right mix of reforms, which shut down the wealth pump and reversed the inequality trend. But it would be unfair to think that fear was the only motive of American leaders from the Progressive Era through the New Deal to the Great Society. By the postwar period, most of the elites had internalized the values that promoted social cooperation—among the elites and between the elites and the common people.

As the historian Kim Phillips-Fein wrote in *Invisible Hands*, despite their initial resistance to the New Deal policies regulating labor-corporate relations, most corporate executives and stockholders had made peace with the new order by the 1950s. They bargained regularly with the labor unions at their companies. They advocated for the use of fiscal policy and government action to help the nation cope with economic downturns. They accepted the idea that the state might have some role to play in guiding economic life. The president of the US Chamber of Commerce told the Chamber in 1943, "Only the willfully blind can fail to see that the old-style capitalism of a primitive, free-shooting period is gone forever." To put this in perspective, today the Chamber of Commerce is one of the organizations of the economic elite that pushes for the most extreme forms of neoliberal market fundamentalism. In a letter to his brother, President Dwight Eisenhower wrote:

> Should any political party attempt to abolish social security, un-employment insurance, and eliminate labor laws and farm pro-grams, you would not hear of that party again in our political history. There is a tiny splinter group, of course, that believes you can do these things. Among them are H. L. Hunt . . . , a few other Texas oil millionaires, and an occasional politician or busi-ness man from other areas. Their number is negligible and they are stupid.

Need it be said that Eisenhower was a Republican?

Barry Goldwater ran against Lyndon Johnson in 1964 on the plat-form of low taxes and anti-union rhetoric. By today's standards, Gold-water was a mild conservative whose policies wouldn't be that different from those of, say, Bill Clinton. But he was regarded as a dangerous rad-ical, and business leaders abandoned his campaign in favor of Johnson. Goldwater was defeated by a landslide.[17]

The Fragility of Complex Societies

The American Republic has gone through two revolutionary situa-tions, as we've seen. The first one, which developed during the 1850s, was resolved by a social revolution, the American Civil War, which re-placed the antebellum ruling elites with the new corporate ruling class. The second one, which peaked during the 1920s, was resolved by the adoption of the reforms of the Progressive and New Deal periods.

Today, we are in a third revolutionary situation. How will it be resolved—by a civil war, by reforms, or by some combination of the two? This is the question to which I will return in chapter 8. But here let's talk about what lessons a "structural-dynamic" analysis (see chapter A3 for a detailed explanation of what that is) could yield for understanding our current age of discord.

The structural part of the analysis seems to be quite pessimistic—the wealth pump is so lucrative for the ruling elites, it appears that shutting it down would require a violent revolution. But when we shift to the dynamic part of the analysis, some hope emerges. It is possible for a ruling class itself—or, more accurately, for prosocial factions within it—to rebalance the system to stop the wealth pump and reverse elite overproduction in a relatively peaceful way. (Other such hopeful examples will be discussed in chapter 9.) But such an outcome requires prosocial forces to persuade economic elites to endure reforms that go against their self-interests in order to prevent an impending crisis. And we are not there—yet.

The fictional characters with which chapter 5 started, Andy and Clara, fine people as they are, work to undermine the pillars of the social order from which they benefit so much. They do so in two ways. Their support for politicians who advocate for lowering taxes starves the state of the revenue it needs to function. Their foundation supports well-meaning causes, working for social justice and equality. But our societies are complex systems in which different parts are interconnected in intricate ways. Well-meaning actions can have unintended consequences. By funding radical-left causes, the Clara and Andy Foundation may inadvertently increase the level of social discord and deepen societal polarization. This may lead to results opposite those intended.

Because the most recent period of social and political turbulence in the United States was the 1960s, which were very mild by historical standards, Americans today grossly underestimate the fragility of the complex society in which we live. But an important lesson from history is that people living in previous precrisis eras similarly didn't imagine that their societies could suddenly crumble around them.

Savva Morozov, one of the wealthiest industrialists in prerevolutionary Russia,[18] also couldn't envision such a disastrous outcome. He was a noted philanthropist and patron of the arts. At his opulent city residence (reputed to be the most expensive mansion in Moscow), he and his wife, Zinaida, entertained the cream of the Russian intelligentsia—famous writers, composers, and scientists. But Morozov also genuinely cared about the well-being of the workers employed by his textile manufactories. He instituted paid leave for pregnant women workers and stipends for students to study at technical colleges (including some abroad). He built a hospital and a theater for workers. More broadly, he advocated for constitutional reforms, including freedom of the press and of association, universal equality, and public control over the state budget. He was also in favor of the right of workers to join unions and to strike for better pay and working conditions.[19]

Morozov also supported radical parties, including the Bolsheviks. According to later reports, he gave hundreds of thousands of rubles (an enormous sum at the time) to the revolutionaries. He single-handedly financed the publication of *Iskra*, or *The Spark*, an underground newspaper published by the banned Social Democratic Party, which later evolved into the Russian Communist Party. Morozov's motivations in supporting the revolutionaries were, clearly, not to bring about a state collapse followed by years of bloody civil war and then the establishment of the Bolshevik dictatorship. Most likely, he wanted to use the radicals as a battering ram against the tsarist regime, forcing it to adopt genuine reforms that would transform Russia for the better.

When the first revolution broke out in January of 1905, the spiral of radical violence and state repression shocked Morozov. Unable to influence events, Morozov had a nervous breakdown and descended into depression. Following the advice of his doctors and family, he traveled with his wife to the French Riviera to undergo psychiatric treatment. But after checking into a hotel in Cannes, he apparently committed suicide by shooting himself with a handgun, although later there were persistent rumors that he was, in fact, murdered and his suicide staged. His wife, Zinaida, returned to Russia, where she continued to enjoy the huge fortune left to her by her husband. But her good life ended with the second revolution in 1917. The Bolsheviks confiscated all of her property, leaving her penniless. To keep penury at bay, she was forced to peddle the few pieces of jewelry that remained. In a final ironic twist, her opulent country estate, Gorki (The Hills), became the main residence of the leader of the proletarian revolution, Vladimir Lenin. It now houses a museum, Lenin's Gorki, displaying many possessions and other mementos of the first ruler of the USSR.

As we examine one case of state breakdown after another, we invariably see that, in each case, the overwhelming majority of precrisis elites—whether they belonged to the antebellum slavocracy, the nobility of the French ancien régime, or the Russian intelligentsia circa 1900—were clueless about the catastrophe that was about to engulf them. They shook the foundations of the state and then were surprised when the state crumbled. Let's talk now about state breakdown in deep history and in recent history.

Part III

CRISIS AND AFTERMATH

CHAPTER 7

STATE BREAKDOWN

Nero Wakes Up Alone

On a summer night in AD 68, Nero Claudius Caesar Augustus Germanicus, the ruler of the Roman Empire, woke up in his imperial palace in Rome and found that all his guardsmen had disappeared. Nero went looking for his supporters at the apartments they used in the palace, but they all were gone. When he returned to his bedroom, he discovered that the rest of his servants had also fled, "taking with them even the bed-clothing and the box of poison," as is related in Nero's biography by Suetonius. Nero realized that it was time to end his life, but fleeing servants had stolen the poison needed to do it painlessly, and he couldn't gather the courage to kill himself with a blade.

States die in a great variety of ways. Some go out in a bang of violence; others unravel quietly and die with a whimper. The Julio-Claudian dynasty, which ruled Rome from 27 BC to AD 68, ended with Nero muttering, "What an artist dies in me!"

Public intellectuals, politicians, and, well, people in general frequently and severely overestimate the power of rulers. This is reflected in commonly used language, such as "Saddam Hussein gassed his own people." Did Hussein fly the warplanes and drop chemical bombs on the Kurdish villages himself?[1] At best, this is lazy language, and at worst, it is bad sociology, which can lead to bad policy, as is inevitable when politicians obsess over the motivations of a single ruler rather than try to understand the power network within which that individual is embedded. As Nero's example shows, the emperor of a mighty empire becomes a nonentity as soon as he is abandoned by his network of power.

In the case of Nero, his power decayed in stages. First, there were rebellions in provinces far away, in Palestine, then closer to home, in Gaul and Spain. Legions in Germania attempted to proclaim their commander emperor, but he refused. When another pretender arose in Spain, the Praetorians, the personal guards of the emperor, switched their allegiance to him. Nero attempted to flee to the eastern provinces, but military officers refused to obey his orders. Suetonius reports that when Nero asked to use a military ship to make his escape, they replied: "Is it so dreadful a thing then to die?," more than hinting that it was time for Nero to bow out gracefully. Nero returned to his palace, only to wake up in the middle of the night to find out that he had been abandoned by everybody, including his servitors. Eventually, Nero accepted his fate, summoned the courage to drive a dagger into his throat, and bled to death.

State collapse, when the central authority suddenly and catastrophically disintegrates, is a frequent occurrence in history. A vivid, and more recent, example is the Cuban Revolution, which became an accomplished fact on January 1, 1959, when the dictator, Fulgencio Batista, simply ran away, taking a plane to the Dominican Republic. The revolutionary forces entered Havana and met with no opposition. The most recent example of the same kind of power implosion (at least as I write this book) is when the Islamic Republic of Afghanistan collapsed on August 15, 2021. Top officials, from the president down, ran away. The army partly melted away, partly defected to the Taliban. The police deserted their posts, and there was no one to stop looters in Kabul. Just as in the Cuban Revolution, the void at the center was immediately filled when Taliban troops entered Kabul unopposed.

An ironic twist to this story is that Ashraf Ghani, Afghanistan's president at the time, started as an academic who studied state collapse and nation-building. Together with Clare Lockhart, he even wrote a 2008 book on this subject, *Fixing Failed States*, which I happened to review at the time for the science journal *Nature*.[2] Unfortunately, this expertise didn't help him fix Afghanistan, although he became a very wealthy man in the process of trying. The problem with the state that Ghani ruled was that it was an extreme example of a kleptocracy, or a state ruled by thieves. In the case of Afghanistan, the state machinery, such as it was, was sustained only by the flow of international aid, most of which was diverted to the pockets of corrupt state officials and their cronies. Pure kleptocracies are rare because they are extremely fragile. The fragility of the Ghani regime was understood, with the CIA estimating that Kabul would fall within months after the withdrawal of American forces. But the speed with which this kleptocracy unraveled surprised American leaders; on the day after the state collapse, President Joe Biden commented that "this did unfold more quickly than we had anticipated."[3]

The "Nero moment," a sudden implosion of a state, as Batista and Ghani personally experienced, has been around ever since the first states evolved some five thousand years ago, and it is sure to happen again. It would be a mistake to assume that mature democracies in North America and Western Europe are entirely immune.

Stalin as Networker

Contrast Nero's fate with that of Joseph Stalin, perhaps the most successful dictator of the twentieth century. Stalin rose to power and then ruled by carefully placing people who were personally loyal to him in key positions. Then he appointed another layer of loyalists to watch the first group. Then he periodically repressed key subordinates and replaced them with ambitious underlings. When Stalin joined the Bolshevik Party, Russia was suffering from a huge problem of elite overproduction, which was a fundamental cause of the Russian revolutions of 1905 and 1917.[4] By 1941, when the Soviet Union entered World War II, Stalin had taken care of this problem by ruthlessly exterminating this elite "surplus." He essentially created a pipeline for ambitious aspirants to enter the elite, progress up the ranks, and then be executed or sent to labor camps.

This was a careful balancing act, which Stalin practiced to perfection. But fear and self-interest are not enough. Stalin also used Big Ideas to inspire his followers, such as his slogan of "building socialism in one country." What it really meant was the restoration of the Russian Empire as a great power under the guise of the Soviet Union. Stalin also proved his effectiveness as a manager by steering the successful industrialization of the 1930s. Without that industrial base, the Soviet Union would have lost World War II, just as it did World War I. Stalin was personally modest. Unlike other, unsuccessful dictators, he avoided ostentation in dress or female company. Unlike Mubarak (and innumerable other dictators), he didn't attempt to start a dynasty by passing the power to his son, Vasily. When his eldest son, Yakov, was captured by the Germans, he refused to exchange him. Yakov died in a German prison camp. Everything was subordinated to the needs of the state, including Stalin's personal interests.

Stalin ruled the Soviet Union for thirty years, leading it to victory in World War II and to superpower status. There was a genuine outpouring of popular grief when he died in 1953. Stalin achieved all of this because, unlike Nero, he was a master of building and maintaining a power network, with himself at its center. His huge power came from his influence over the elites and the common people. But even more importantly, the structural forces were on his side. New research by economists has shown that despite the brutality of Stalin's industrialization, the life of common people did get better during the 1930s, as hard as it may be to look past the millions of deaths from famine following mass agricultural collectivization.[5] After the devastating shock of World War II, life began improving again. When I grew up in the Soviet Union during the 1960s and '70s, life was visibly improving. My family moved from a one-room apartment (not one bedroom, one room!) to a two-room apartment, and then to a three-room apartment. We were certainly still poor compared to Americans, but the trend of well-being was up. Popular immiseration was decreasing, and elite overproduction had been taken care of earlier, in the crucible of the revolution and the purges that followed.[6]

The state that Stalin's Communist Party built proved to be quite durable, persisting through two generations of rulers (the Khrushchev and Brezhnev eras). When I left it in 1977, the Soviet Union looked to me like a monolithic juggernaut that would last for centuries to come. But I was wrong. It unraveled and collapsed in 1991. When I visited it in 1992, for the first time since I had left, I didn't recognize it—it looked like a failed state, and it was a failed state. During the 1990s, Russia continued on a disintegrative trajectory—in 1993, the adherents of the president fought the partisans of the parliament in the streets, and tanks shelled the parliament building. The next year, the First Chechen War started.

Social Breakdown: Sociological and Psychological Approaches

And this leads us to the central questions of this chapter: What explains social breakdown? Why do states collapse? How do civil wars start?

There are two opposite ways to approach these questions. The sociological approach is to ignore individuals and focus entirely on impersonal social forces that push societies into breakdown. But many people (who are not sociologists) find this approach unsatisfying. They want to know who was responsible. Whose fault was the French Revolution? Was it Louis XVI? Marie Antoinette? Robespierre?

An alternative to the sociological approach, then, is to analyze what leaders such as Louis XVI, Nero, and Gorbachev did wrong. This view is rooted in the great-man theory of history, which was particularly popular in the nineteenth century and is still the default mode for pundits, politicians, and the lay public.

An extreme version of this approach is the field of psychohistory,[7] which uses Freud's psychoanalysis to understand the emotional origins of the behavior of leaders. This "clio-Freudianism" is pseudoscience. Science advances theories and then gathers data to test them. Pseudoscience inverts this method. As the historian Hugh Trevor-Roper writes in his critique of Walter Langer's *The Mind of Adolf Hitler*, "[P]sychohistorians move in the opposite direction. They deduce their facts from their theories; and this means, in effect, that facts are at the mercy of theory, selected and valued according to their consistence with theory, even invented to support theory."[8]

The mind of another is an enigma—their motivations, intentions, and reasons for acting in a particular way are often inscrutable. We often don't understand our own motives; how could we possibly be sure of other people's? So it should come as no surprise to my readers that I find clio-Freudianism deeply flawed. As I've repeatedly argued in this book, we cannot understand societal trajectories without first dissecting how societal power structures work.

At the same time, I agree that leaders can matter. Although rulers are heavily constrained by the social structures within which they operate, they do have some leeway in nudging the trajectories of the states they lead, especially when supported by cohesive power networks working toward a common goal. We will talk more about the role of individuals later on, especially in the last chapter, where I review some of the "success stories"—societies that got into revolutionary situations but managed to exit them without major bloodshed. The positive role of prosocial leaders can be particularly visible when they succeed in steering the ship of state through rough waters.

But for now, let's continue with the sociological view, because it is more important to understand the social forces with which leaders have to contend than to understand their inner worlds. And without such understanding, whether it comes from cliodynamics or from the intuitive grasp of social dynamics by a gifted politician, we will not be able to navigate our own way out of a crisis.

In the past few decades, social scientists have devoted a lot of effort to studying the causes and preconditions of civil wars. They approach this area of study in an admirably scientific way—by collecting large data sets and running statistical analyses on them. Two important centers for this type of research are located in Nordic countries: the Peace Research Institute in Oslo, Norway, and the Department of Peace and Conflict Research at Uppsala University in Sweden. In the US, the most influential research project is the Political Instability Task Force (PITF). This project, funded by the Central Intelligence Agency, was initiated by Ted Robert Gurr at the University of Maryland, Jack Goldstone at George Mason, and about twenty other scholars. (Goldstone is one of the fathers of the structural-demographic theory that is a pillar of this book.) One PITF member, Barbara Walter, a political scientist based at the University of California in San Diego, published a book in 2022 called *How Civil Wars Start: And How to Stop Them*, in which she summarizes the insights from the PITF project and explains what they mean for the United States. Let's see what kinds of insights this research yields for our understanding of state collapse and civil war.

How Civil Wars Start

The best predictor of whether a country will be experiencing a violent internal conflict next year is whether it is already in conflict this year. This "prediction" simply follows from the observation that civil wars tend to drag on for many years, and it does not yield any understanding of why they start (and how they end). Thus, the interesting question, from the point of view of policy makers, is whether it is possible to predict the onset of a civil war, say, two years in advance. For a particular country that is currently at peace, what is the probability that it will still be peaceful two years from now, and what is the probability that it will slip into a civil war?

To answer this question, the PITF project collected data on onsets of political instability in all world countries from 1955 to 2003 and developed a statistical model that related country characteristics to the probability of a civil war starting there. The results of this study were published by Goldstone and his coauthors in 2010.[9] They discovered that their model was capable of predicting instability onsets with 80 percent accuracy. What came as a surprise was that, even though the researchers tested about thirty various indicators, the model needed to know only three or four country characteristics to achieve this level of accuracy.

The first, and most important, was the "regime type." Here the PITF researchers relied on the Polity IV project, which places countries on the autocracy–democracy spectrum, ranging from minus ten to ten, using such indicators as competitiveness of political participation and of executive recruitment, and constraints on the chief executive.[10] Each country-year (for example, Zimbabwe in 1980) is classified as a full democracy (score near ten), a full autocracy (score near minus ten), a partial autocracy (score between minus ten and zero), or a partial democracy (score between zero and ten).[11] The PITF project further divided partial democracies into those with and without factionalism. Factionalism is "sharply polarized and uncompromising competition between blocs pursuing parochial interests at the national level. This winner-take-all approach to politics is often accompanied by confrontational mass mobilization, as occurred in Venezuela in the early 2000s and Thailand prior to the 2006 military coup, and by the intimidation or manipulation of electoral competition."[12] Partial democracies with factionalism were exceptionally unstable political regimes; such countries were the most likely to descend into civil wars. Partial autocracies were intermediate in stability, and the remaining regime classes (partial democracies without factionalism, full democracies, and full autocracies) were relatively stable.

Other factors that increased the probability of civil war, as the PITF analysis showed, included high infant mortality, armed conflict in bordering states, and state-led repression against a minority group.

In *How Civil Wars Start*, Walter describes a similar set of causes resulting in the onset of political instability. As in the 2010 study, the first factor she brings up is the type of political regime: "It turns out that one of the best predictors of whether a country will experience a civil war is whether it is moving toward or away from democracy." She refers to such regimes, intermediate between full autocracies and full democracies, as "anocracies." The second factor is, again, factionalism, especially when it is based on ethnic or religious identity. Furthermore, danger of violence onset is especially high when one of the ethnic factions perceives itself as losing ground—economically, culturally, or in status. Government repression of a minority group further elevates the chances that the minority will resort to arms. The final factor in Walter's list of causes is the advent of the internet, the massive adoption of smartphones, and the rise of social media. In her view, the algorithms of social media serve as "accelerants" for violence by promoting a sense of perpetual crisis, a feeling of growing despair, and a perception that moderates have failed. "It's at this point that violence breaks out: when citizens become convinced that there is no hope of fixing their problems through conventional means."[13]

There is much of value in the approach advocated by the PITF group and in similar analyses using the violence data sets constructed by Nordic researchers. But there are also important limitations. It's granted that the short-term (two years ahead) predictors of instability are anocracy, factionalism, and state repression. But why does this kind of dysfunction develop? The most common cause of anocracy is either an autocracy trying to democratize itself under the pressure of intraelite conflict and popular mobilization, or a democracy backsliding into autocracy for similar reasons—the collapse of elite consensus and the rise of populism. But this means that the state in question is already in trouble. The two other precursors of civil war—factionalism and state repression—are similarly (and obviously) signs of structural instability. In other words, the PITF model relies on proximate indicators for predicting civil war, but it doesn't tell us why a particular country develops the divisive and dysfunctional politics that make it vulnerable to an outbreak of internal warfare.

Another problem is the shallow historical time depth of the data that the PITF group analyzed (going back only to 1955). The second half of the twentieth century, from which the bulk of PITF data comes, was in many ways an unusual time period. Most importantly, it fell in between major waves of political instability that tend to recur every two hundred years or so. As we saw in chapter 2, complex human societies typically go through an alternation of integrative and disintegrative phases. The High Middle Ages were followed by the Late Medieval Crisis, the Renaissance by the General Crisis of the seventeenth century, and the Enlightenment by the Age of Revolutions, which ended in the early twentieth century. Our own age of discord is only starting. The period covered by the PITF data was thus one of relative calm because it fell between the Age of Revolutions and our age of discord. There were plenty of civil wars, insurrections, and even a few genocides, but they tended to afflict the less developed parts of the world—regions where nation-building started relatively recently and where a sense of national unity was far from being formed. As an example, sub-Saharan Africa is today carved up into artificial states, which emerged after the tide of European colonization had receded. Most of these countries have haphazard collections of multiple ethnic groups. Worse, many ethnic groups are divided up among multiple states. Similar, though less extreme, conditions are found in the Middle East, where Kurdistan, for example, was divided among four different states. It is not surprising, therefore, that the most frequent civil wars in the past fifty to sixty years have been between different ethnic groups, and that ethnonationalism was the ideology that motivated the contending parties. Because of this bias in the PITF data, Walter greatly overestimates the importance of ethnic identity as the main driver of conflict.

When we expand the historical periods that our data cover (as we did with CrisisDB), we discover that the motivations of civil war combatants have varied much more in different historical eras and in different parts of the world. During the Late Medieval Crisis, most conflicts in Europe were dynastic—Lancasters versus Yorks, Orleanists versus Burgundians, and so on. (These civil wars were basically *Games of Thrones.*) In the General Crisis of the seventeenth century, by contrast, religion was the most salient ideology—Huguenots versus Catholics, Puritans versus Anglicans, and so on. The Age of Revolutions saw the rise of modern ideologies, such as liberalism and Marxism. At the same time, populism and class struggle are far from being purely modern inventions. Two millennia ago, the main contending parties of the late Roman Republic were the populares (the party of the people) and the optimates (the party of the ruling class). Ethnic conflicts, similarly, are not confined to the modern period—they were also present in the ancient world (for example, the Roman-Jewish Wars of the first and second centuries). The point is, specific ideologies and motivations of civil warriors are highly variable in time and space. They are also very fluid, liable to change during prolonged conflicts (as we discussed in chapter 4). Thus, basing a predictive model on only the last sixty years of history can be quite misleading. We now live at the beginning of the most recent wave of global instability, and the lessons of the postwar world may not be a good guide for what to expect in the near and medium future.

In fact, this is already turning out to be true—the PITF model has lost its ability to predict future conflict. As I've just related, the study that the project published in 2010 showed that the PITF model was able to predict the onset of civil war with 80 percent accuracy. How was this result obtained? The PITF group first built their statistical model using data from 1955 to 1994, then compared model predictions to what happened in the next decade (1995–2004). This is a sound scientific approach because it tells us how well the model can make "out-of-sample predictions." Essentially, the researchers put themselves back in 1994 and ensured that their model had no knowledge of the data to be predicted (the following decade).

So far, so good. However, ten years later another group of researchers replicated the PITF study by using their model to predict the decade of 2005–2014. Unfortunately, the PITF model did very poorly. In particular, it completely missed the uprisings of the Arab Spring, such as the 2011 Egyptian revolution (see chapter 5). Most importantly, Egypt and other Arab states, which were convulsed by severe outbreaks of political violence in 2011, were all autocracies (rather than anocracies, as the PITF model would predict). Additionally, ethnicity played no role in the Egyptian revolution, as all contending groups were Sunni Arabs. (Egypt also has an ethnic minority, the Christian Copts, but they played no role in the revolution except, episodically, as victims of Islamists.) What happened, in other words, was that the factors that worked well as advance indicators of instability before 2005 ceased to be good predictors afterward.

In a 2017 article on predicting violence—"Predicting armed conflict: Time to adjust our expectations?"—Lars-Erik Cederman and Nils B. Weidmann write:

> Ultimately, the hope that big data will somehow yield valid forecasts through theory-free "brute force" is misplaced in the area

of political violence. Automated data extraction algorithms, such as Web scraping and signal detection based on social media, may be able to pick up heightened political tension, but this does not mean that these algorithms are able to forecast low-probability conflict events with high temporal and spatial accuracy.[14]

And this leads me to the most important failing of an approach based on theory-free algorithms. As I have been arguing throughout this book, we cannot understand social breakdown without a deep analysis of power structures within societies. Who are the influential interest groups? What are their agendas? What are their sources of social power, and how much power do they wield to advance their agendas? How cohesive and well organized are they? These are the key questions to ask if we want to understand both social resilience and its opposite, social fragility. This is where the analysis by Barbara Walter in *How Civil Wars Start* often becomes woefully inadequate, and sometimes outright naive. Take her explanation of the 1917 Russian Revolution, which she contends "was driven by jarring political and economic inequalities as working-class Russians, serfs, and soldiers rose up against the monarchy to create the world's first socialist state." (For one thing, there were no serfs in Russia in 1917; see my discussion of the reform and revolutionary periods of Russia in chapter 9.) Or take her lengthier analysis of Ukraine's Euromaidan Revolution, which, according to her, was an uprising of "citizens—many of them young people from European-leaning western Ukraine" against Viktor Yanukovych, who sought to strengthen economic ties with Russia rather than the European Union.

What's wrong with such statements? "People" or "citizens" don't overthrow states or create new ones. Only "organized people" can achieve both positive and negative social change. Again, to understand

174

why a revolution was successful (or not), we need to understand what the contending interest groups were, how much power each wielded, how internally cohesive they were, and how they organized collective action. This is the essence of the structural-dynamic approach (which is explained in chapter A3).

To show that such a power analysis is necessary for understanding state breakdown (or lack of it), let's examine the divergent trajectories of three countries that were created in 1991 when the Soviet Union collapsed: Russia, Ukraine, and Belarus. In fact, the dissolution of the Soviet Union was a direct result of the agreement reached by three leaders of these (former) USSR republics: the Belovezh Accords. These three East Slavic countries share very similar cultures. Furthermore, in 1991, they were very similar according to the PITF criteria: each of them was an anocracy, moving from autocracy to democracy; they were all characterized by ethnic divisions; and they were all subject to the same "accelerants" of instability resulting from the rise of the internet and social media after 2000. Yet, despite these similarities, their trajectories diverged. Ukraine experienced not one but two successful revolutions after 2000. Russia and Belarus each experienced a massive wave of anti-government demonstrations (Russia following the 2011 parliamentary elections and Belarus following the 2020 presidential elections), but neither of them resulted in state collapse. What explains these divergent trajectories?

Post-Soviet Slavic States

The Soviet Union was really a giant corporation in which the state owned the wealth-producing assets (or the "means of production," to use Marxist terminology). When it collapsed in 1991, this huge capital was rapidly privatized by corporate managers—party bosses, factory directors, and their cronies (except in Belarus, as we will see below). Privatization was an incredibly corrupt and violent process, with the winners literally walking on the corpses of their less lucky competitors. In a darkly amusing anecdote, at a meeting between the two most powerful Russian oligarchs, Berezovsky and Gusinsky, one of them reportedly asked the other: "Why did you put a contract on me?" The response? "No, it was you who put a contract on me!" It turns out that each had hired assassins to eliminate the other.

As most of the wealth became concentrated in the hands of fewer than a dozen oligarchs, the well-being of the 99 percent collapsed. Russians were dying in droves from deaths of despair. By 1996, popular discontent became so intense that it was clear the incumbent president, Boris Yeltsin, had no chance of winning reelection—his approval ratings were in the single digits. The main challenger was the communist Gennady Zyuganov. The oligarchate became concerned that victory by the communists might create difficulties for their continued looting of the country. A group of the most powerful oligarchs, led by Berezovsky and Gusinsky, made a deal with Yeltsin: in return for his guaranteeing the privatization of state enterprises, they financed his campaign and threw their media resources behind him—by that point, they controlled all mass media. They also hired a team of American political campaign consultants (including the infamous Dick Morris) to manage Yeltsin's reelection. Even that was not enough, and in the end they had to resort to massive electoral fraud to reelect Yeltsin.

This is how Russia became an extreme plutocracy in 1996. Because the oligarchs had little regard for managing the state, the disintegrative processes gathered speed. The factory owners stopped paying their workers' salaries, and there was a wave of labor strikes during the autumn following the elections. A bloody war in Chechnya flared up again.

And in 1998, the country was hit by a severe financial crisis, which resulted in the devaluation of the ruble and a default on the state debt.

At this point, two main power networks formed in Russia. The ruling faction was the economic elites (the oligarchs), who thoroughly controlled the ideological elites by owning all major mass media. The second group included the administrative elites (the bureaucracy) and the military elites (the so-called siloviki, who included state security and military officers). In the ensuing power struggle, the alliance of administrative/military elites, led by Vladimir Putin, defeated the plutocrats. There was no sudden revolution; rather, the process was gradual, as one oligarch after another was exiled (Berezovsky and Gusinsky), imprisoned and then exiled (Khodorkovsky), or relegated to a subordinate position in the power hierarchy (Potanin). The oligarchs lost because they were not a cohesive ruling class, spending more energy on fighting each other rather than on advancing their collective interests. They also underestimated the importance of controlling the coercive apparatus. Finally, they lacked any legitimacy, and their kleptocratic ways were heartily disliked by the population.

The victory by the administrative/military elites represented a return to the historical pattern that has characterized power relations in Russia since at least the fifteenth century. As we have seen in other historical examples (e.g., Egypt and China), political culture tends to be resilient and usually reconstructs itself following even major perturbations.

The new (or restored) ruling class in Russia turned out to be quite corrupt and nepotistic. Its members enriched themselves enormously by stripping wealth-producing assets from the oligarchs and by diverting a large proportion of state expenditures into their own pockets. Somewhat surprisingly, despite the strong kleptocratic aspects of Russia's ruling class, its management of the state turned out to be somewhat less dysfunctional than that of the oligarchs who preceded it. The Putin regime enjoyed a number of successes, especially during the first ten years after it came to power. It ended the civil war in Chechnya, put the state finances on a sound basis, and even enabled (or, perhaps, did not interfere with) economic development. Economic growth was particularly rapid during the decade of 1998–2008 and resulted in a dramatic improvement of popular well-being. After 2008, economic growth slowed down and even experienced several reverses. But other indicators of quality of life, such as increasing life expectancy and declining homicide rates, continued to improve.

The mass protests, which started in 2011 and lasted into 2013, failed to shake the Putin regime. Most of the protesters were concentrated in the two largest cities, Moscow and St. Petersburg, while the rest of the country did not support the protests. Most importantly, the core of the ruling class (the siloviki) did not show any cracks in their support for Putin.

In Belarus, the oligarchs never gained power. During the first three years of the new republic, a young (in his thirties) former state farm manager and an anti-corruption crusader, Alexander Lukashenko, rapidly gained popularity, winning the 1994 presidential elections in a landslide (with 80 percent of the vote). Because the Lukashenko regime did not indulge in an orgy of privatization, the state retained ownership of major industrial corporations and prevented the rise of oligarchs. As a result, Belarus doesn't have even a single billionaire on the *Forbes* list. (There are a few Belarusians on the list, but they all made their fortunes in Russia.)

Following the presidential elections in August of 2020, mass protests against the Lukashenko regime flared up in Minsk and other large cities. For a while it looked (to outside observers) like the regime was failing. However, subsequent events proved them wrong. It became clear that Lukashenko had forged strong links with the military elites. (I use "military" in the general sense—not just the army but also the internal security apparatus.) There were no defections from Lukashenko's power network, and the regime survived. Several opposition leaders were imprisoned even before the elections, and others were driven into exile. The resolve of the regime not to bow to the demands, as well as mass arrests and detentions of demonstrators, gradually undermined their willingness to participate in the protests. Additionally, Lukashenko's support outside the capital remained strong. As a result, the protests gradually petered out, with the last one in March of 2021.

Ukraine: A Plutocracy

Let's now turn to Ukraine. During the 1990s, the political economy of Ukraine paralleled that of Russia. A group of oligarchs came to power by privatizing state-owned means of production. However, after 1999, the trajectories of the two countries diverged. In Ukraine, there was no overthrow of the oligarchate. Instead, the economic elites gained absolute power.

What has the oligarchic rule yielded for the well-being of common Ukrainians? Let's take a look at the Ukrainian GDP per capita on the eve of the 2014 revolution. According to the CIA's *World Factbook*, the Ukrainian GDP per capita (PPP) in 2013 was $7,400. That's far below Hungary's ($19,800), Poland's ($21,100), or Slovakia's ($24,700). It's also far below Russia's ($18,100), which is two and a half times larger than Ukraine's. This is a particularly striking observation given that before the collapse of the Soviet Union, Ukraine had a higher regional GDP per capita than Russia—or Belarus.

Perhaps Russia is not the best comparison, because it possesses vast mineral wealth in oil and gas. A better comparison is with Belarus, a country that lacks not only the mineral wealth of Russia but also the favorable climate and rich "black soils" of Ukraine. Nevertheless, Belarus's GDP per capita in 2013 was a respectable $16,100, more than twice that of Ukraine. Furthermore, because Belarus didn't even have any billionaires, the median Belarusian income was even higher compared to that of Ukraine (or Russia), as a more equitable division of wealth always elevates the median.

Although Ukrainian oligarchs ruled the country unrestrained by any other internal checks, they did not become a cohesive ruling class. Instead, they formed several factions that struggled against each other using as weapons electoral politics, semilegal seizure of property, and even imprisonment. When Yanukovych came to power in 2010, he jailed his rival, Yulia Tymoshenko, an oligarch popularly known as the gas princess. The internecine conflicts between the oligarchs made a mockery of Ukrainian democracy. No matter whom the Ukrainians elected, the officeholders did nothing for the common people, instead concentrating on transferring wealth and power from the losing oligarchs. The general dysfunction was further deepened by the country's electorate being split into two equally numerous groups with diametrically opposed ideas about where Ukraine needed to go. (This was also true, to a certain extent, of Belarus and Russia, each of which has large West-leaning minorities.) The western half of Ukraine wanted to join the European Union and NATO. The eastern half wished to keep and deepen cultural and economic links with Russia, and it was dead set against entering NATO. Different oligarchic factions appealed to one or the other of these electorates, but in reality they were all West-oriented, because they parked their wealth in Western banks, educated their children at Oxford or Stanford, purchased property in

London or on the Côte d'Azur, and rubbed elbows with the global elite at Davos.

In my rundown of the four structural drivers of instability (chapter 2), I pointed out that the last one, geopolitical pressures, can generally be neglected, for parsimony, in our cliodynamic models for historical megaempires and the most powerful contemporary states, such as the United States and China. But for a medium-size country like Ukraine, such factors can often be very important and need to be included in the analysis. There are two additional reasons why Ukraine is particularly vulnerable to external pressures.

First, it is located on a geopolitical fault line between the American sphere of interest (essentially, NATO) and the Russian sphere of interest (the "Near Abroad," as it is often referred to in Russia). In fact, the fault line runs right through the middle of Ukraine, with the western half leaning toward NATO and the eastern one toward Russia. One prominent American strategist, the late Zbigniew Brzezinski, considered independent Ukraine to be "a new and important space on the Eurasian chessboard, . . . a geopolitical pivot because its very existence as an independent country helps to transform Russia. Without Ukraine, Russia ceases to be a Eurasian empire."[15] An influential segment of the American foreign policy establishment considers the continued existence of weakened but still powerful Russia as the most important threat to American primacy (even greater than the rise of China).[16] Following Brzezinski, this segment has pushed for an extension of NATO to Russia, and by 2014, it was Ukraine's turn to be added to the alliance.

Second, the Ukrainian oligarchs were particularly vulnerable to falling under the control of Western interests. Because the plutocrats kept the bulk of their wealth in Western banks, it could be frozen, or even seized.[17] This is what Russian oligarchs discovered in 2022.[18] An even more direct threat is that of legal proceedings to extradite an oligarch to the United States for trial. Dmytro Firtash—a prominent member of the Donetsk clan of Ukrainian oligarchs and, before 2014, a powerful supporter of Yanukovych's Party of Regions—is currently (as of 2022) under house arrest in Vienna, fighting US extradition proceedings against him.

By 2014, American "proconsuls," such as veteran diplomat Victoria Nuland, had acquired a large degree of power over the Ukrainian plutocrats. This was not cheap—Nuland boasted that the Department of State had invested $5 billion in extending its influence over the Ukrainian ruling class.[19] In this, the American agents were aided by the deep animosities pitting the oligarchs against each other and dividing the oligarchate. Because the oligarchs were unable to agree among themselves, they required an external manager to set a common agenda. During the Revolution of Dignity in 2014, as we know from a transcript of the telephone conversation between them, Nuland and Geoffrey Pyatt, who was then the US ambassador to Ukraine, made decisions about who was to be appointed to various state positions (president, ministers, etc.).[20]

Over the thirty years since Ukraine's independence, its power structures have developed as a three-tiered configuration: people, oligarchs, American proconsuls. The masses of Ukrainian citizens voted in periodic elections, but whoever they elected pursued their private interests without any regard for the wishes of the electorate (except where the popular wishes coincided with the desires of the oligarchs). As a result, soon after being elected, each administration rapidly lost public support and became mired in scandal. With one early exception (Kuchma), no president managed to last more than one term. In the next round of elections, frustrated voters kicked out the previous crew and elected another one. There were two revolutions, one in 2004 and another in 2014. But the new politicians were also selected from among the oligarchs or people closely controlled by the oligarchs. The only thing that changed was that a different set of oligarchs fed at the trough.

The oligarchic factions vying for power are quite fluid, with individual oligarchs entering and switching alliances depending on the current situation. However, researchers have identified four main networks, or "clans," based on their geographic origins: Dnipro (formerly Dnipropetrovsk) and Donetsk in the southeast, Kyiv in the center, and Volhynia in the west. The election of Yanukovych as president in 2010, and the success of his Party of Regions in gaining the largest number of seats in the parliament, represented victory for the Donetsk clan.

Yanukovych started his political career as the governor of Donetsk province. The primary backer of Yanukovych and his Party of Regions was Rinat Akhmetov, the richest Ukrainian oligarch and the head of the Donetsk clan. He filled about sixty spots on the Party of Regions list with people personally loyal to him. The second supporter was Firtash, who chose thirty.[21] Once Yanukovych became president, he was expected to use his position to enrich his backers (not forgetting himself, of course). But instead of staying within the customary kleptocratic bounds, he embarked on a sweeping program of wealth redistribution in favor of his family. His son, in particular, was the recipient of massive wealth. It soon became clear to other oligarchs that Yanukovych aimed to build a new oligarchic clan, which was referred to as "the Family." If this was allowed to continue, Yanukovych would soon no longer need the support of Akhmetov and Firtash. The two came to the conclusion that they had to part ways with Yanukovych and started looking around for alternatives. As Christian Neef reported in February 2014, "Akhmetov, for example, had always gotten along well with Tymoshenko, in contrast with Firtash, and began supporting Arseniy Yatsenyuk, who took over the leadership of her Fatherland alliance when she was incarcerated. Firtash, for his part, backed Vitali Klitschko's party UDAR."[22] As a result, Yanukovych, who was already opposed by other oligarchs, lost the support of the Donetsk clan. Although he probably didn't realize this at the time, all that was needed to bring Yanukovych down was some kind of trigger.

In his summary of the events leading to the Euromaidan Revolution, the American journalist Aaron Maté writes:

> The spark for the Maidan protests was a decision by President Viktor Yanukovych to back out of a trade deal offered by the European Union. The conventional narrative is that Yanukovych was bullied by his chief patron in Moscow. In reality, Yanukovych was hoping to develop ties to Europe, and "cajoled and bullied anyone who pushed for Ukraine to have closer ties to Russia," Reuters reported at the time. But the Ukrainian president got cold feet once he read the EU deal's fine print. Ukraine would not only have to curb its deep cultural and economic ties to Russia, but accept harsh austerity measures such as "increasing the retirement age and freezing pensions and wages." Far from improving the lives of average Ukrainians, these demands only would have ensured deprivation and Yanukovych's political demise.[23]

The uprising began when tens of thousands of demonstrators gathered in Kyiv's Maidan Square to protest against government corruption and in favor of European integration. The oligarch Petro Poroshenko, a member of the Volhynia clan that was in opposition to Yanukovych,

later said in an interview: "From the beginning, I was one of the organizers of the Maidan. My television channel—Channel 5—played a
tremendously important role."[24]

At that point, Yanukovych still retained a large degree of popular
support, but his supporters were all in eastern Ukraine, whereas the
population of the capital was part of the western-leaning half of the
country, and most of this group had voted against Yanukovych in the previous election anyway. Even more importantly, tens of thousands of
western Ukrainians, among whom was a large contingent of far-right
extremists, traveled to Kyiv and turned a previously peaceful movement into a violent campaign of regime change.

As violence crested, both Akhmetov and Firtash realized that they
needed to abandon the sinking ship. Literally overnight, the two TV
channels they controlled, Ukraina and Inter, switched their support to
the opposition. In parliament, the members of the reigning Party of
Regions, who were appointed by Akhmetov and Firtash, broke party
ranks and joined the opposition. The security services, which had
battled far-right extremists, withdrew from Maidan Square, fearing
that they would be betrayed by Yanukovych. (Later events proved them
right.)

This was Yanukovych's Nero moment. Suddenly, his support melted
away, and he was left alone to face angry protesters. The billions that
he had looted from other oligarchs and from the Ukrainian people
could not protect him (and they were taken away from his family when
the new regime came to power). Yanukovych avoided Nero's end because he was able to run away to southern Russia, where he now lives
in exile.

The people had triumphed, and democracy was restored. At least,
this is how the Euromaidan Revolution was portrayed in the corporate

media. In reality, the 2014 Ukrainian revolution was no more a people's revolution than any other revolution in history. It was driven by the same forces that we have discussed in the pages of this book—popular immiseration and elite overproduction. The people didn't gain as a result of this revolution. Ukrainian politics continued to be as corrupt as before. The quality of life for the people did not appreciably increase. Petro Poroshenko was elected as president, but his administration rapidly lost public support. In the next elections (2019), less than 25 percent of the electorate gave him their vote.

The most catastrophic consequence of the 2014 revolution was a bitter civil war in the two Donbas regions of Donetsk and Luhansk, where the Donbas militia, aided by Russia, battled against the Ukrainian military and openly neo-Nazi volunteer brigades, such as the Azov Regiment.[25] By the time Russian troops invaded Ukraine on February 24, 2022, the war in Donbas had already claimed fourteen thousand lives.[26] It's too early to tell how this war will end. But the historical record suggests that this conflict will probably be the end of the Ukrainian plutocracy, one way or another. Most oligarchs have lost great chunks of their wealth, partly as a result of the economic collapse and partly as a result of the war's destruction.[27] Even more importantly, the oligarchs have been politically sidelined by war. The current Ukrainian president Volodymyr Zelensky's entry into politics was a result of rivalry between two oligarchs, Poroshenko (president of Ukraine between 2014 and 2019) and Ihor Kolomoisky (the head of the Dnipropetrovsk oligarchic clan), who needed a candidate to oppose Poroshenko.[28] But when the conflict escalated into a full-blown war on February 24, Zelensky reinvented himself as a wartime president and has vowed to fight until victory. Ukraine now faces a stark choice: either go down as a state or transform itself into a militocracy. Time will tell which of these futures becomes reality.

Take-Home Message

It is an ironic observation that of the three East Slavic republics formed by the collapse of the USSR, the most democratic one, Ukraine, has been the most impoverished and unstable, while the most autocratic one, Belarus, has enjoyed relative prosperity and stability. What are the implications of this observation? The obvious one is that autocracy works better than democracy. It is also wrong. There are plenty of dysfunctional autocracies with impoverished populations, and many of them collapsed in the past. And the best-governed countries with high levels of well-being for the vast majority of their populations, such as Denmark and Austria, tend to be democracies.

A better conclusion is that not all states with the trappings of democracy are run for the benefit of broad segments of the population. Some such pseudo-democracies are easy to detect, as when state officials decide which parties will participate in elections and who is going to win. But that was not the case in Ukraine—the politicians and the state officials were not the controllers; instead, they were closely controlled by the oligarchs and their private interests.

What is the take-home message from this analysis of past instances of state collapse? The political authority governing complex human societies is much more fragile than it may appear at a cursory glance. State collapse, a sudden disintegration of the power network that rules a society, is a frequent occurrence, both in history and in the contemporary world. Often a ruling class is deposed (and, at times, even exterminated) as a result of losing a war, or a battle, to an overwhelming force. This is the case in successful external invasions, as when Chinggis Khan's Mongols rode in, killed everybody, and piled their heads in a pyramid. Or it could be the attack of an organized group of revolutionaries or putschists. The Chilean president Salvador Allende died in a hail of bullets, assault rifle in hand, fighting to the death against the troops of General Pinochet that stormed the presidential palace. But the most frequent cause of state collapse (when it is not the result of an external invasion) is an implosion of the ruling network. The Nero moment with which this chapter started is perhaps the most vivid example. In the cases of the Cuban Revolution and the 2021 collapse of Afghanistan, there was pressure from a rival power network, but the ruling network disintegrated before the insurgents even entered the capital. Incidentally, the 1917 October Revolution in Russia unfolded according to the same scenario. Soviet propaganda glorified the Storming of the Winter Palace as the decisive break point, but the provisional government had already been abandoned by most of its troops, and its head, Alexander Kerensky, had already run away before the Bolshevik forces entered the palace. Finally, a political regime can collapse under the pressure of massive public protests, as was the case in Ukraine in 2014.

The contrast between the successful 2014 Ukrainian revolution and the unsuccessful 2021 uprising in Belarus is particularly instructive. The main factor explaining these divergent outcomes is the nature of the ruling group. In the Ukraine case, it was a collection of economic elites who hated each other, plotted against each other, and held a willingness to abandon the sinking ship at a moment's notice. In the case of Belarus, it was a cohesive administrative-military elite that weathered the public protests without showing any cracks. Ultimately, the difference between these two East Slavic countries stems from the different political-economic trajectories they went on two decades before the revolutionary situations of 2014 and 2021. Massive privatization of the state-owned corporations in Ukraine created a wealth pump that resulted in overproduction of oligarchs, inter-oligarch conflict, and repeated state collapses. In Belarus, there was no wealth pump, no oligarchs, no intraelite conflicts, and no state collapse.

All complex societies are vulnerable to the disintegrative force of elite overproduction, which is why they all experience periodic social breakdowns. But plutocracies, of which Ukraine is (was?) a rather extreme example, are particularly vulnerable. The main problem is that plutocrats, acting in their own selfish interests, tend to create institutional arrangements that favor the operation of wealth pumps. A wealth pump, on the one hand, increases popular immiseration and, on the other, elite overproduction (by creating more and wealthier plutocrats). In other words, a wealth pump is one of the most destabilizing social mechanisms known to humanity. Of course, America is no Ukraine. The American ruling class is unified and organized by a set of overlapping institutions, which we discussed in chapter 5. And this ruling class showed during the Progressive and New Deal periods that it is capable of acting against its narrow, selfish interests for the sake of common well-being. But how will it navigate the Turbulent Twenties? What are the possible trajectories that the United States might follow in the coming decades? That's the question to which I turn in the next chapter.

CHAPTER 8

HISTORIES OF THE NEAR FUTURE

Beyond the Cusp

Anyone watching the events of the past decade from afar—a space alien, say, or a future historian—will no doubt be impressed by how thoroughly the humans inhabiting the most powerful nation on earth have managed to screw up their society. Despite remarkable scientific progress, extraordinary technological change, and impressive economic growth, the well-being of most Americans has been declining. And even many of the winners are deeply anxious about being able to pass success on to their children.

As we have seen, human societies follow predictable trajectories into revolutionary situations. But how are these crises resolved? Now that America is in crisis, we want to know what could happen next. We understand that the future cannot be predicted with any great precision. For social systems in revolutionary situations, accurate forecasts are particularly difficult. We can use a physical analogy to explain this.

Think of the road to crisis as a valley with steep walls. A society, approaching crisis, is like a metal ball rolling down this valley. Its trajectory is constrained by the slopes and thus fairly predictable. But once the ball rolls out of the valley's mouth, it finds itself on a cusp (a revolutionary situation), with many potential routes leading away. Tiny pushes applied to the ball (actions by interest groups or even influential individuals) can nudge its further trajectory in either relatively benign directions or in a complete catastrophic one. This is why it is so difficult to predict what will happen after the cusp.

But there is a silver lining to this seemingly pessimistic conclusion. A relatively mild application of power may be all that's needed to direct the trajectory in a positive direction. The trick is to know where to push—after all, a seemingly obvious intervention may result in unexpected, and catastrophic, consequences. This is where verbal reasoning becomes completely inadequate. Ideally, we need a formal (mathematical) model that can tell us about what kinds of pushes result in what kinds of outcomes. Running the model forward to the end of the twenty-first century, we would be able to explore different scenarios resulting from the various possible choices available to interest groups within the state and, especially, the most powerful of them, the ruling elite. Following that, we would observe what collective choices were made and whether the model correctly predicted the long-term consequences of these choices.

Multipath Forecasting

As of yet, cliodynamics is nowhere near advanced enough to achieve such a feat of modeling. But over the past few years, my colleagues and I have been thinking along these lines. We call such an approach multipath forecasting, or MPF, for short.[1] A fully functional MPF engine will take as inputs various policies or reforms that are possible to adopt and forecast how the future trajectory will change as a result of such interventions. While such a device will take a lot of work and resources (money and people) to put together, I recently developed a "prototype" to show how it could work. The technically minded can see the details in the academic publication,[2] but in the next few pages I will describe it in words (no equations). My ulterior motive for delving into the inner workings of this prototype is to show how the general theory I explained in this book can work in a specific example. One thing all modelers know is that translating a verbal theory into a set of mathematical equations is a wonderful way to find all the hidden assumptions in it and bring them to light.

The heart of the MPF model, the engine that provides the impetus to all the moving parts within it, is the wealth pump. Here's how it works: First, the model keeps track of how many workers are looking for a job. The labor supply increases as a result of demographic growth (the balance of new workers entering the labor force and old ones retiring). Another important source of new workers is immigration. The model also needs to take into account the changing social attitudes surrounding work that have resulted in the massive entry of women into the workforce. (Between 1955 and 2000, the labor force participation of American women increased from 35 to 60 percent.) Second, the model tracks the supply of jobs, which is affected by factors such as globalization (resulting in jobs moving out of the country) and robotization/automation (shifting some jobs from people to machines but also creating other jobs in new economic sectors).

The overall labor trends during the past fifty to sixty years have resulted in an oversupply of workers, which tends to depress worker wages. At the same time, the institutional factors that could counteract this economic effect have become weaker. The proportion of workers belonging to labor unions has declined, as has the federally mandated real minimum wage. As a result, relative wages (wages in relation to GDP per capita) declined, especially for low-skilled workers but also for median ("typical") workers. In turn, declining relative wages drove the wealth pump, redistributing income from the working class to the economic elites, as we saw in chapter 3.

The beauty of this structural-dynamic approach (which is further explained in chapter A3) is that it allows us to understand how changes in one part of the social system affect the dynamics of other parts. The wealth pump has a major effect not only on the commoner compartment (causing immiseration) but also on the elite compartment. Elite numbers change as a result of demography (the difference between birth and death rates), but this is a relatively unimportant factor for us because demographic rates between the elites and the commoners are not that different in the United States. (It was a major factor for societies with polygamous elites.) The more important process is social mobility: the upward movement of commoners into the elite compartment and the downward movement of elites into the commoner compartment. And whether net mobility is upward depends on the wealth pump.

The mechanism here is simple. When corporate officers keep increases in worker wages slower than the growth of the company's revenues, they can use the surplus to give themselves higher salaries, more lucrative stock options, and so on. The CEO of such a company, upon retirement with a "golden parachute," becomes a new centimillionaire or even billionaire. For the same reason, the owners of capital get a higher return on it. The numbers of the superwealthy balloon.

This dynamic can also operate in reverse. When worker wages increase faster than GDP per capita (that is, when relative wages grow), the creation of new superrich is choked off. Some exceptional individuals continue to create new fortunes, but their numbers are few. The old wealth, meanwhile, is slowly dissipated as a result of bankruptcy, infla-tion, and division of property among multiple heirs. Under such condi-tions, the size of the superwealthy class gradually shrinks.

But such a gradual, gentle decline assumes that the social system maintains its stability. Analysis of historical cases in CrisisDB indi-cates that the much more frequent scenario of downward social mobil-ity, which eliminates elite overproduction, is associated with periods of high sociopolitical instability, the "ages of discord." In such cases, downward mobility is rapid and typically associated with violence. Po-litical instability and internal warfare prune elite numbers in a variety of ways. Some elite individuals are simply killed in civil wars or by way of assassination. Others may be dispossessed of their elite status when their faction loses in a civil war. Finally, general conditions of violence and lack of success discourage many "surplus" elite aspirants from con-tinuing their pursuit of elite status, which leads to acceptance of down-ward mobility. The MPF engine models such processes generically by assuming that high instability increases the rate at which elite individ-uals are converted into commoners.

Thus, the heart of the MPF model is the relative wage and the wealth pump that it powers. When the relative wage declines, it leads to both immiseration and elite overproduction. Both, as we now know, are the most important drivers of social and political instability. How-ever, outbreaks of instability—violent anti-government demonstrations and strikes, urban riots, terrorism, rural uprisings, and, if things really go to hell, state collapse and full-blown civil war—are the results of in-dividual people's actions. How does the model connect the structural drivers to people's motivations? It assumes that the key role in all such events is played by extremists, those who have been radicalized and primed for aggression. When such radicals are few in relation to the rest of the population, they offer no serious threat to the stability of the regime, because they are easily isolated and suppressed by the police. But if they are many, they start coalescing into extremist organizations, which can credibly challenge the ruling class. The number of radicals in proportion to the total population, therefore, is a key variable that the MPF model needs to track.

The process of radicalization works like a disease that, as it spreads, changes people's behaviors and makes them act in violent ways. The compartment of the MPF engine connecting structural drivers to unrest thus needs to model this dynamic of social contagion. It is quite similar to equations used by epidemiologists—for example, in forecasting the dynamics of COVID outbreaks.

The model keeps track of three kinds of individuals. The first is the "naive" type, corresponding to the susceptibles in the epidemiological framework. This is the class into which individuals are placed when they become adults. (The model tracks only individuals who are active adults; children and the retired elderly are not modeled, as they are assumed to have no effect on the dynamics.) Naive individuals can become "radicalized" by being exposed to individuals of the radical type (corresponding to infectious individuals in a disease model). The more radicals there are in the population, the higher the chance that a naive individual will catch the "virus of radicalism."[3]

When a high proportion of the population is radicalized, sociopolitical instability is also high. Riots are easily triggered and readily spread; terrorist and revolutionary groups thrive and receive support from massive numbers of sympathizers; and the society is highly vulnerable to an outbreak of civil war. However, the relationship between the degree of radicalization and the overall level of political violence (measured, for example, by the number of people killed) is nonlinear. As the proportion of radicals in the population grows, it becomes increasingly easy for them to link up and organize, potentially leading to an explosive growth of revolutionary parties. There is also a threshold effect. As long as the power of revolutionary groups is less than the power of the state's coercive apparatus, the overall level of violence can be suppressed to a low level. But should the balance shift in favor of radicals, the forces of the regime can suddenly implode, as we saw in numerous examples of state collapse in the previous chapter.

So far we've been speaking of "radicals" as though they are an interest group. But that's not the right way to think about it. In reality, radicals usually don't all belong to a single radical party. During periods of high political instability, there are many issues dividing the population and the elites. (We discussed this fragmentation of the ideological landscape in chapter 4.) Thus, there are many factions of radicals, each motivated by a different ideology and warring with other factions. Some become left-wing extremists, and others join right-wing organizations; still others become ethnic or religious extremists. And even within the right, as well as within the left, radical groups are splintered and may be more focused on internecine fighting than on fighting the opposite end of the ideological spectrum.

Generally speaking, an outbreak of political violence is dynamically similar to a wildfire or an earthquake. A single spark can start a prairie fire, as Mao famously said. But most sparks start little fires that go out before they manage to spread into conflagrations. Others grow to mid-size blazes. Only very few sparks start wildfires that sweep through all of the prairie. Complexity scientists have devoted a lot of attention to such processes in which the statistical distribution of the event size obeys a "power law." Whether we quantify these processes in square kilometers of prairie burned down or the strength of an earthquake on the Richter scale—or the severity of political violence events as measured in the number of people killed—they all have the same type of dynamics.[4] In a prairie fire, whether the initial fire caused by a spark spreads depends on how much combustible material is in reach, and whether fire can jump from one patch of dried grass to another. In a revolution, whether the initial revolt against the regime spreads depends on the number of radicals (analogous to combustible material) and how well they are connected, or how fast they can expand their networks of rebellion. As a result of such autocatalytic, self-driving dynamics, an initially small event can unexpectedly blow up into a rare, large-scale disaster—a "black swan" or a "dragon king."

Because the relationship between the radicalization quotient and the resulting scale of political violence is governed by a power law, normal statistics (e.g., the average level of violence) don't work very well, and the MPF model captures possible outcomes by assessing the probability of really severe events, such as the American Civil War or the Taiping Rebellion. Such extreme events may not be highly probable, but we need to worry about them, simply because they have the potential to cause unimaginable human misery. Is a 10 percent probability of a second American civil war high or low? Put it in personal terms: Would you take a bet that could cause your personal extinction with a probability of 10 percent? I would not, even if offered a huge reward. You need to be alive to enjoy the prize, no matter what size it is.

Let's get back to the MPF model. An additional element in the model is that a naive individual can become radicalized not only through contacts with other radicals but also through exposure to violence resulting from radical actions. For example, someone whose relative or friend was killed in a terrorist act perpetrated by right-wing extremists might join a left-wing revolutionary group. This second route to radicalization is also a kind of social contagion (but mediated by violence instead of radical ideology).

The third type of individual in the model, in addition to naïfs and radicals, is the "moderate" (corresponding to "recovered" in epidemiological models). This group comprises former radicals who have become disenchanted with radicalism and violence and have concluded that members of the society need to pull together and overcome their differences. The moderates differ from the naïfs in that they value peace and order above all, and they work actively to bring it about. In other words, naive individuals don't have an active political program, radicals work actively to increase instability, and moderates work actively to dampen things down.

In summary, new radicals are created when naïfs encounter the already radicalized ones or are exposed to violence. The more radicals there are (and therefore the higher the rate of violence), the more likely that a naive individual becomes radicalized. However, moderates also have a role: "infection" by radicalism declines as moderates increase in number and exert their moderating, instability-suppressing influence.

The numbers of radicals, however, don't grow without limit. As the level of violence increases, some radicals turn away from extremism and convert into moderates. The probability of a radical becoming disgusted with radicalism and turning into a moderate increases with the overall level of violence, but with a time delay, as high levels of political violence do not instantly translate into a social mood of revulsion against violence and a desire for internal peace. Violence acts in a cumulative fashion; several years of high instability, or even outright civil war, have to pass before the majority of the population begins to earnestly yearn for order.

The social contagion module of the MPF engine thus keeps track of the radicalization and moderation processes. Now it needs to connect to the dynamics of structural drivers of instability. This is done through the Political Stress Index (PSI), which combines the strength of immiseration and elite overproduction.[5] Popular immiseration is measured by inverse relative income (median family income divided by GDP per capita). Thus, when typical incomes fail to increase with economic growth, this factor causes the PSI to increase. Intraelite overproduction/competition is measured by the number of elites (including elite aspirants) in relation to the total population. The PSI "tunes" the probability that a naive individual becomes radicalized. When structural conditions result in high social pressures for instability, radical ideas fall on fertile soil and readily take root. Alternatively, if the PSI is low, an encounter between a naïf and a radical (or a naïf experiencing a political violence event) is unlikely to result in radicalization.

Now that we have the MPF engine, let's use it to investigate the possible trajectories that the American social system could take beyond the 2020s. Keep in mind that this is a model (even a prototype) and its predictions should be taken with some degree of skepticism. The goal is not to predict the future but to use the model to understand how possible actions may shape different futures. The MPF engine is a kind of "morality tale," like the story of a kind girl and an unkind girl, a narrative motif that is present in hundreds of traditional societies.

We start the engine in 1960 and first run it for the sixty years for which the history is fixed. From the MPF point of view, the most important trend during this time is the decline in the relative wage. The decline in the relative wage turns on the wealth pump, and elite numbers begin to increase in an accelerating manner. By 2020, both immiseration and elite overproduction, and thus the PSI, reach very high levels. The radicalization curve, tracking the number of radicals, which had been staying flat near zero, starts to grow after 2010 and literally explodes during the 2020s. So does political violence. At some point during the 2020s, the model predicts, instability becomes so high that it starts cutting down the elite numbers. Remember that MPF is a model, which means that it abstracts reality into mathematical equations. But in real life, instability causing declines in elite numbers is not abstract at all. Think about what happened in America as a result of the Civil War, when huge numbers of Southern elite men were killed on the battlefield and the rest were deprived of their elite status.

In the model, the cataclysm of the 2020s reduces elite numbers, which results in a decline in the PSI. Additionally, high levels of violence accelerate the transition of most radicals into moderates. The radicalization curve falls as precipitously as it rose and at some point after 2030 hits the minimum. Because radicals are the ones who drive violence, instability also declines. The social system regains its stability. But in this inertial scenario, the root cause of instability—the wealth pump—continues to operate. Gradually, elite numbers begin increasing. Meanwhile, the moderates who suppressed the 2020s peak of violence are slowly retiring and dying off. The uneasy peace holds for the next generation (twenty-five to thirty years), but then there is a repeat of the 2020s fifty years later.[6]

The inertial scenario thus predicts a rather grim future: an outbreak of serious violence during the 2020s and, if nothing is done to shut down the pump, a repeat every fifty to sixty years. What are the alternatives?

One assumption, which may strike readers as unrealistic, is the rather easy translation of high radical numbers into a full-blown civil war. After all, the coercive apparatus of the American state is very functional and shows no signs of crumbling. What happens if high levels of radicalization are not allowed to trigger a civil war? In some ways, that future is less dire, because civil war is avoided. But what happens instead does not look particularly bright either. The pump continues to operate, and the PSI is high due to high levels of both immiseration and elite overproduction. Most of the population is radicalized, and the radicalization curve does not go down, because conditions of civil war are what induce radicals to turn into moderates. The social system is indefinitely trapped in a state of high immiseration, elite conflict, and radicalization.

No, to bring the system to a positive equilibrium, the pump must be shut down. We can model this by driving the relative wage up to the point where upward and downward rates of mobility between commoners and elites are balanced (and then keeping it at this level by ensuring that worker wages increase together with overall economic growth). It turns out that this intervention will not eliminate or even have much of an effect on the 2020s peak—there is too much inertia in the social system. Furthermore, it will have an undesirable effect in exacerbating elite overproduction. Shutting down the pump reduces elite incomes, but it does not decrease their numbers. This is a recipe for converting a massive proportion of the elites into counter-elites, which will most likely make the internal war even bloodier and more intense. However, after a painful and violent decade, the system will rapidly achieve equilibrium. The PSI will reach its minimum, the proportion of the population that is radicalized will fall, and the surplus elites will be eliminated. The only memory of the Troubles of the Twenty-Twenties will be in the high proportion of moderates, who will gradually fade away toward 2070. The end result will be a "sharp short-term pain, long-term gain" outcome.

The MPF engine can be used to explore other scenarios. For example, if we very gradually increase the relative wage (over a period of twenty years, for example), then the Turbulent Twenties won't go away, but drastic impoverishment of elites can be avoided.

Perhaps the most important insight from the MPF model is that it is too late to avert our current crisis. But we can avoid the next period of social breakdown in the second half of the twenty-first century, if we act soon to bring the relative wage up to the equilibrium level (thus shutting down elite overproduction) and keep it there.

The Revolutionary Situation in America

The MPF model gives us a bird's-eye view of the range of possible trajectories that America can take during the 2020s and beyond. The model is quite abstract and follows such aggregated variables as immiseration, aspirant surplus, and radicalization. Let's now bring it down to earth and see what kinds of insights it can give us about the power dynamics of contending interest groups in the United States. For this we need to integrate the theoretical insights from the model with a much more concrete structural-dynamic analysis of contemporary American society.

As we discovered in chapter 5, the American ruling class is a coalition of the top wealth holders (the 1 percent) and the top degree holders (the 10 percent). Not all members of these groups are active participants in ruling the country. Many wealthy socialites (of the 1 percent) simply enjoy their wealth and status as members of the social upper class, a "leisure class." As for the degree holders, right-wing commentators love to fulminate against the evil influence of "liberal professors," but in reality, 99 percent of them have no power to speak of. A tenured professor at a good university is likely to enter the 10 percent by the time they retire. But most of them study things such as shark parasites and the systematics of bryophytes (congratulations if you know what a bryophyte is), obscure topics that have no relation to politics and power. Their students will forget most of their teachings a month after the final exam. And, of course, a large proportion of the credentialed are not even part of the 10 percent. Remember those law degree holders in the lower bulge of the bimodal distribution. The active part of the ruling coalition—CEOs and board directors of major corporations (like Andy), large investors, corporate lawyers (like Jane's father), top elected officials and bureaucrats, and the members of the policy-planning network—are the ones who rule.

We saw in chapter 5 how this ruling class acquired a network of interlocking institutions that enabled it to act as a (reasonably) coherent cooperative group. It overcame the divisions of the New Deal era and steered the country through World War II and the Cold War to superpower status. It also adopted a series of reforms that ensured a relatively fair division of gains from economic growth, which resulted in unprecedented—in the evolutionary history of our species—broadly based prosperity. During the 1960s, the ruling elites even made significant strides in overcoming the greatest source of inequity in American society, stemming from its history of slavery and racism. But after 1980, the social mood shifted away from broad-based cooperation and long-term goals toward short-term, narrowly selfish interests. The wealth pump was allowed to run at an increasingly frenetic pace.

The flood of wealth from the working classes to the economic elites ballooned their numbers and resulted in elite overproduction, bringing increasing intraelite competition and conflict, which started to undermine the unity and cohesion of the ruling coalition. In his 2013 book, *The Fracturing of the American Corporate Elite*, Mark Mizruchi observes that the corporate elite (top executives and directors of Fortune 500 companies), which was unified, moderate, and pragmatic in the postwar era, has become fragmented in recent decades. The economic leaders turned less moderate and less willing to contribute to the common good, which became a "significant source of the current crisis of American democracy and a major cause of the predicament in which the twenty-first-century United States finds itself."

One increasingly visible sign of polarization within the business community is the rise of charitable foundations pushing extreme ideological agendas. At one end of the spectrum are the ultraconservative foundations: Charles Koch, the Mercer Family, Sarah Scaife, and others. Domhoff calls them a "policy-obstruction network." Unlike mainstream think tanks, which develop policy proposals and help steer them through the legislative process, the goal of the policy-obstruction network is to "attack all government programs and impugn the motives of all government officials."[7] One example that Domhoff has developed at some length is the climate-denial organizations, such as the Heartland Institute, whose goal has been to sow doubt in the scientific foundations of climate change and undermine the emerging consensus on the role of fossil fuels in bringing about global warming and increasing incidences of extreme weather (such as Category 5 hurricanes). Another example is the creation and dissemination of the "death tax" meme (chapter 5). Ultimately, the policy-obstruction network contributes to the decline of trust in public institutions and of social cooperation in American society.

Appointments of Supreme Court justices and other federal judges have become another battleground among "radical billionaires." For decades, the ultraconservative foundations have contributed millions of dollars to the Federalist Society, which has "fundamentally reshaped the federal judiciary by training hundreds of the judges appointed to positions in the federal court system."[8] More recently, George Soros gave almost $20 million to fund dozens of progressive candidates in district attorney races throughout America.[9] Since 2017, Smart Justice California, funded by four wealthy Northern California donors, has channeled tens of millions of dollars toward criminal justice ballot measures and allied candidates, electing reformist district attorneys George Gascón (in Los Angeles) and Chesa Boudin (in San Francisco).[10] In the wake of the 2020 Black Lives Matter protests, reformist DAs have also been elected in several other large cities. But an unintended consequence has been increased conflict between progressive DAs and conservative police departments. Again, well-meaning initiatives by wealthy philanthropists have created more polarization, undermining social cooperation. (As always, this isn't a value judgment about the relative worth of one initiative or another; it is an analysis of their systemic impacts.)

Returning to Mizruchi, he concludes that the corporate elite, by "starving the treasury and accumulating vast resources for itself," is "leading us toward the fate of the earlier Roman, Dutch, and Habsburg Spanish empires. . . . It is long past time for its members to exercise some enlightened self-interest in the present."[11] So far, so good. But Mizruchi ends up overstating the degree to which today's corporate elite has become an "ineffectual group that is unwilling to tackle the big issues, despite unprecedented wealth and political clout." On the contrary, despite the ideological cracks that we discussed in the preceding paragraphs, the American ruling class continues to be very effective at advancing its narrow, short-term, parochial interests. With every piece of tax legislation, the tax code is becoming more regressive; today the effective taxes on corporations and billionaires are at the lowest levels since the 1920s. By successfully arguing that money is "free speech," corporations have largely dismantled constraints on using their wealth to shape American politics. The federal minimum wage continues to decline in real terms, despite inflation reaching levels not seen since the 1980s.[12]

The disagreements between the conservatives and the progressives within the ruling class focus almost entirely on cultural issues. The economic elites, who dominate the American polity, can tolerate a great diversity of views on such issues, as long as the consensus on promoting their collective economic interests (keeping their taxes and worker wages low) is strong.

The conclusion from this analysis, then, is that no existential challenges to the current ruling class are going to arise within it, at least not in the near future. Which interest group, then, is likely to be a credible threat to the current regime?

Social Action Needs Organization

Our structural-dynamic analysis has shown that there are two major groups whose well-being has been declining and, correspondingly, whose mass-mobilization potential is growing. The first one is the immiserated noncredentialed working class. The second one is the frustrated aspirants within the credentialed class. According to most pundits in the mainstream corporate media, the greatest threat to the status quo in today's America is noncollege-educated white Americans. Here's a typical call to arms from Stephen Marche, the author of the well-received 2022 book *The Next Civil War: Dispatches from the American Future*:

> An incipient illegitimacy crisis is under way, whoever is elected
> in 2022, or in 2024. According to a University of Virginia anal-
> ysis of census projections, by 2040, 30% of the population will
> control 68% of the Senate. Eight states will contain half the pop-
> ulation. The Senate malapportionment gives advantages over-
> whelmingly to white, non-college-educated voters. In the near
> future, a Democratic candidate could win the popular vote by
> many millions of votes and still lose. Do the math: the federal
> system no longer represents the will of the American people.
>
> The right is preparing for a breakdown of law and order, but
> they are also overtaking the forces of law and order. Hard right
> organizations have now infiltrated so many police forces—the

connections number in the hundreds—that they have become unreliable allies in the struggle against domestic terrorism. . . .

The white supremacists in the United States are not a marginal force; they are inside its institutions.[13]

However, a successful revolution requires a cohesive and organized revolutionary party with deep popular support. Think of Mao's Communist Party during the Chinese Civil War. There is no such organization in the United States, and one cannot be built while the federal police remain effective. The surveillance and coercive apparatus of the state is just too strong. The Bolshevik route to power—they sheltered their organization from the tsarist secret police in London and Zurich— is equally improbable. Where could a radical left party find refuge— China? Russia? It is hard to imagine any other country being willing to harbor a person designated as a terrorist by the United States. Moreover, the radical left is hopelessly disunited. A lack of unity and an absence of effective large-scale organizations has relegated the radical left to irrelevancy.

But the radical right is at least as disunited and impotent as the radical left. White supremacists, neo-Nazis, the Klan, the alt-right, the alt-lite, the alt-white, etc. are all tiny splinter groups that wink in and out of existence. According to the Anti-Defamation League (ADL) and the Southern Poverty Law Center (SPLC), two organizations that track far-right extremists, the KKK today consists of dozens of independent chapters that compete against each other. As popular immiseration has grown in the past decades, increasing numbers of noncredentialed males have become radicalized and joined far-right groups. The number of such groups has also grown, and with it, the incidence of terrorism.[14] But the far right is not just disunited; it also lacks any large-scale organizations to serve as vehicles for organizing revolutionary action. It poses no credible threat to the regime. Consider the plot to kidnap the governor of Michigan, Gretchen Whitmer.

The supposed plot leader, Adam Fox, worked as a contractor for Vac Shack, a job that barely kept his head above water. When his girlfriend kicked him out, he couldn't afford an apartment and moved to the basement of the Vac Shack shop. He wanted to start a revolution to overthrow the corrupt regime that was responsible for this immiseration. As *The New York Times* reported, he told an FBI informant, "I just wanna make the world glow, dude. We're gonna topple it all, dude."[15] But there was no revolutionary party for him to join. Instead, he and his buddies were infiltrated by the FBI. In the end, it was an FBI agent who proposed they kidnap the governor of Michigan. Nearly half of the paramilitary group that planned to kidnap, put on trial, and execute Whitmer were feds or informers. It is ironic that the organizational vacuum on the far right is so extreme that this far-right terrorist group had to be organized by the FBI.

Our fictional "deplorable," Steve, is far too intelligent to join any such plots. "Man," he told me, "as soon as there are three people in the plot, one of them is an FBI informant." Steve joined the Oath Keepers, but his main motivation was to protect his Second Amendment rights. He didn't go to Washington, DC, on January 6, 2021, because he felt that all such demonstrations were futile, given the power of the state. When he read in the news that Stewart Rhodes, the founder of the Oath Keepers, was arrested and charged with seditious conspiracy for his role in the January 6 attack on the Capitol,[16] Steve went to his car and scraped the Oath Keepers sticker off the bumper. Without effective organizations, the masses of immiserated working-class Americans are not a believable threat.

The Dissidents

If we arrange politically active Americans along a traditional left–right spectrum, the center is occupied by the ruling class and the politicians serving it faithfully. At the extremes are left and right radicals, who may dream of the overthrow of the reigning regime but lack the numbers and the organization to be a credible threat to it. Between the radicals and the center, however, are situated those who are critical of the regime but unwilling to use violent/illegal means to change it. Let's call them "the dissidents." Left-wing dissidents currently (as of the writing of this book) include Democratic politicians, such as Senator Bernie Sanders (Vermont) and Senator Elizabeth Warren (Massachusetts). Sanders had a real shot at being nominated as the Democratic candidate for president in 2016 and 2020, but he was passed over by the party in favor of candidates preferred by the ruling class. Sanders and other left-wing dissidents advocate for such populist policies as increasing the federal minimum wage and raising taxes on the rich. Rather uniquely among the established Democrats, Sanders has advocated against open borders. In a 2015 *Vox* interview with Ezra Klein, who asked if Sanders would approve of "sharply raising the level of immigration we permit, even up to a level of open borders," the senator responded with an emphatic no. "That's a Koch brothers proposal," he said. Sanders went on:

> What right-wing people in this country would love is an open-border policy. Bring in all kinds of people, work for $2 or $3 an hour, that would be great for them. I don't believe in that....[17]

In another interview that year, he continued on the theme.

When you have 36 percent of Hispanic kids in this country who can't find jobs, and you bring a lot of unskilled workers into this country, what do you think happens to that 36 percent of kids who are today unemployed? Fifty-one percent of African-American kids?[18]

Once the Democratic Party abandoned the working classes, which became a solid reality under Democratic President Bill Clinton (1993–2001), left-wing populists within the party ceased to have any influence on Democratic politics. In order not to lose elections, the reasoning goes, the party needs to move to the center. The "center," of course, is the policies favored by the ruling class.

On the ideological front, left-wing dissidents get very different treatment depending on the content of their critiques. Cultural left issues—race, ethnicity, LGBTQ+, intersectionality—occupy large swaths of the corporate media. Populist economic issues and, especially, critique of American militarism, much less so. A vivid example of this is how the ruling class deals with one of the longest-standing American dissidents, Noam Chomsky—he is simply ignored. There is no ban on his books or campus speaking engagements (as would happen were he a dissident in the Soviet Union), but he is never invited to appear on corporate media. As a result, such left-wing intellectuals remain marginal figures in the American ideological and political landscape.[19]

The situation is different with right-wing dissidents. Before 2016, the Republican Party was the stronghold of the ruling class, a vehicle for the 1 percent. But today, as I write this book, the Republicans are making a transition to becoming a true revolutionary party. (Whether this transition is successful or not, we will find out in the next few years.) The transition began with the unexpected victory of Donald Trump. Trump, of course, is not a revolutionary—he is a typical political entrepreneur who channeled popular discontent, especially of white Americans without college degrees, to propel himself to power. Once in power, however, he attempted to make good on his election promises (quite untypical for established politicians, which provides additional evidence that he is not one). Not all initiatives that he proposed went against the interests of the ruling class. Thus, his tax legislation succeeded, making the tax code even more regressive. He also appointed conservative justices to the Supreme Court, pleasing the conservative plutocrats, among other interests. But on other fronts, he went squarely against the priorities of the economic elites. His worst offense was his anti-immigration policy, as we've seen.

Other Trump initiatives included his rejection of the traditional Republican free market orthodoxy in favor of industrial policy, although he was not particularly successful at that. The left-leaning Economic Policy Institute observed that "Trump's erratic, ego-driven, and inconsistent trade policies have not achieved any measurable progress" in reshoring manufacturing jobs.[20] Finally, Trump's NATO skepticism and unwillingness to start new foreign (mis)adventures went against the consensus on "muscular" foreign policy goals broadly shared by the ruling elites. Trump was the only recent president who started no new wars.

While Trump doesn't see himself as a radical, one member of his team, the chief strategist Steve Bannon, is an avowed revolutionary (as we discussed in chapter 1). Bannon views himself as a "Leninist" who wants to "bring everything crashing down, and destroy all of today's establishment."[21] This view is not shared by his former boss. In *War for Eternity: Inside Bannon's Far-Right Circle of Global Power Brokers*, Benjamin Teitelbaum reports:

As he [Bannon] told me, "to Make America Great Again, you've got to . . . you've got to disrupt, before you rebuild." In Bannon's eyes, Donald Trump is "the Disrupter." I've heard him say "destroyer" as well. That's Steve's understanding, at least. Steve recalls having a quick conversation with Trump about it all in the White House in April 2017, following some media coverage of his reading of *The Fourth Turning*. The president wasn't amused. He saw his role as that of a builder rather than a destroyer, and was turned off by all the weird talk of doom and destruction and collapse. Steve didn't push it. It was just a quick exchange. And besides, there was no need to make Trump see the world the way he did.[22]

Trump may think of himself as a builder, but the subsequent course of his chaotic presidency (and even more so, its end) showed that Bannon's 2017 characterization of Trump as "the Disrupter" was just.

Trump and Bannon are both counter-elites, but Trump's evolution to becoming an anti-regime warrior followed the wealth route, while Bannon's followed the credential route. Bannon grew up in a working-class Virginia family and served in the US Navy. While serving in the navy, he earned a master's degree from Georgetown University and then an MBA from Harvard Business School. This led to an investment banker position at Goldman Sachs, then a launch of his own investment bank, and ventures into entertainment and media. Instead of assimilating into the ruling class, however, he became radicalized. (He describes himself during this phase of his life as an "outsider.") His loathing of the ruling elites and his desire to overthrow them seems rooted in his experiences living and working among them.[23] In his 2014 Vatican speech, he said:

I could see this when I worked at Goldman Sachs—there are people in New York that feel closer to people in London and in

Berlin than they do to people in Kansas and in Colorado, and they have more of this elite mentality that they're going to dictate to everybody how the world's going to be run. I will tell you that the working men and women of Europe and Asia and the United States and Latin America don't believe that. They believe they know what's best for how they will comport their lives.

In 2012, Bannon became the executive chairman of Breitbart News, a far-right online news site. "While at Breitbart, Bannon ran a popular talk radio call-in show and launched a flame-throwing assault on mainstream Republicans, embracing instead a fringe cast of ultra-conservative figures. Among them was Trump, a frequent guest of the show. They established a relationship that eventually led Bannon to mastermind Trump's populist romp to the White House."[24]

Getting to the Oval Office, however, turned out to be the peak of the pair's achievement.[25] Neither of them had the ability or discipline to "drain the swamp," as they had promised during the election campaign. Not only did Trump fail to implement a program of systematic reforms, but he also turned out to be very bad at simply governing the country, although, to be fair, everything that he tried to do against the interest of the ruling class was met with massive obstructionism by the same class. The story is well known and there is no need for the sordid details. Suffice it to say that Bannon and Trump had a falling out, at least partly as a result of Bannon's expressing unflattering opinions of Trump and his family.

Bannon was only one of many Trump associates who left his administration via scandal. In fact, it appears that the majority of the Trump team (such as it was) left it under a cloud. Many were indicted, and some even served time. Trump showed that he is much better at firing people than at building a cohesive and functional power network. Even his detractors, who accuse him of attempting to set himself up as a dictator, acknowledge that he proved to be remarkably inept at the business of despotism. In 2020, The Establishment ran a "counterinsurgency campaign," which succeeded at removing this irritant from the body politic. The storming of the Capitol on January 6, 2021, was the latest skirmish in that battle,[26] although by world-historical standards, this "insurrection" doesn't measure as much; it is certainly not close to a Bastille or a Winter Palace.

However, and this has implications for 2024, the Republican Party may be gradually evolving from the party of the 1 percent to a party of right-wing populism. Mainstream Republicans (read: loyal supporters of the ruling class) have been leaving the party in droves, some taking early retirement, others being challenged and defeated by "Trumpoid" candidates. It remains to be seen how successful this transformation is going to be. Will the Grand Old Party become a revolutionary organization aiming to overthrow the ruling elites, as Bannon wants? This is certainly a cause of great concern for the ruling class.

The radical right continues to be disunited and lacks a common ideology. Trump himself is hardly a unifying figure, and "Trumpism" is not a coherent ideology, but rather a wishful program to get one man back in power. Some politicians on the right are pure culture warriors, while others focus on populist issues. Currently, the most interesting phenomenon, which may or may not turn out to be the crystallization nucleus, is that of Tucker Carlson. Carlson is interesting because he is the most outspoken antiestablishment critic operating within the corporate media. Whereas media such as CNN, MSNBC, *The New York Times*, and *The Washington Post* are losing credibility among the general population (and especially among the noncredentialed Americans),

Carlson is growing ever more popular. He is currently the most listened-to political commentator in America. He is also interesting in that he has a clearly formulated and coherent ideology, which is conveniently laid out in his 2018 book, *Ship of Fools: How a Selfish Ruling Class Is Bringing America to the Brink of Revolution.*

At the beginning of the book, Carlson asks, "Why did America elect Donald Trump?" And he immediately answers:

> Trump's election wasn't about Trump. It was a throbbing middle finger in the face of America's ruling class. It was a gesture of contempt, a howl of rage, the end result of decades of selfish and unwise decisions made by selfish and unwise leaders. Happy countries don't elect Donald Trump president. Desperate ones do.

This answer, which is also a diagnosis, sets the tone for the rest of the book. America is in trouble; what are the root causes? His critique of the American ruling class in many places parallels our analysis of the social forces driving the United States to the edge. Although not necessarily using the same terms, his book is about the unraveling of social cooperation ("the glue strong enough to hold a country of 330 million people together"), popular immiseration ("the decline of the middle class"), and the selfish elites (well, "selfish elites"). He does, however, miss a key driver of instability—elite overproduction—and gets hung up on cultural issues. And it is one thing to intuitively understand the significance of various social forces I have discussed in this book, but it is quite another to grasp how these parts—the trunk, the tusks, and the columnar legs—are connected together to make a whole elephant.[27]

Because Carlson provides the closest thing to a common ideology for the "New Right," it's worthwhile to take a bird's-eye overview of *Ship of Fools.* Here are some of the main ideas of the book:

- The Democratic Party used to be the party of the working class. By 2000, however, it became the party of the rich. The two governing parties in the US have converged. "The marriage of market capitalism to progressive social values may be the most destructive combination in American economic history. . . . Bowing to the diversity agenda is a lot cheaper than raising wages."

- Mass immigration was always supported by the Chamber of Commerce (an organization promoting the interests of the employers). In contrast, no Democrat had doubted that a massive influx of "low-skilled" immigrant workers would reduce the wages of American workers, especially the less educated ones. By 2016, however, "there were virtually no immigration skeptics remaining on the left. . . . The change was purely a product of political calculation. Democrats understood that the overwhelming majority of immigrant voters would vote Democrat."

- The Republicans and Democrats are now "aligned on the wisdom of frequent military intervention abroad. . . . As a result, America has remained in a state of almost permanent war." Iraq, Afghanistan, Libya, Syria—each intervention was sold to the public as pursuing noble goals, such as replacing corrupt dictatorships with vibrant democracies. But the end result was a string of wrecked countries.

- "There was a time when the First Amendment qualified as secular scripture for educated Americans." Not anymore. Now both the left and right wings of the ruling class consider contrary opinions as a threat to their authority; "disagreement is the first step toward insurrection." Freedom of speech has been repudiated on campus, by Silicon Valley, and by the press. "Journalists had become handmaidens to power."

- "Why do we tax capital at half the rate of labor?" Why are working people dying younger? Asking questions like these is inconvenient to the ruling class. Instead of people blaming the governing elites, "[y]ou'd want people to blame one another. . . . The quickest way to control a population is to turn it against itself. . . . Identity politics is a handy way to do that."

Tucker Carlson is a very dangerous man. One clear sign that the established elites take him very seriously is a three-article series in *The New York Times* (*NYT*) in April of 2022.[28] *NYT* researchers did a truly mammoth amount of research for these articles, watching or reading transcripts of all 1,150 episodes of *Tucker Carlson Tonight* from November 2016 (when it first aired) to 2021. According to the *NYT* analysis, there are three main themes that Carlson talks about, again and again. Two of them are of direct relevance to the questions discussed in this book: "the ruling class" (which Carlson invoked in more than eight hundred episodes—that is, in 70 percent of shows) and "destruction of society" (six hundred episodes). The third one is "replacement" (mentioned in four hundred episodes, the idea that Democratic politicians want to force demographic change through immigration), which earned Carlson's program a designation by the *NYT* as "the most racist show in the history of cable news." The *NYT* series did not engage with the ideas Carlson laid out in *Ship of Fools* and instead focused entirely on his TV show.[29] Indeed, the contrast between the tone of the book and that of the show is so big that they could have come from two different people. The tone of the show has also evolved over time: appearances by guests who contradicted Carlson decreased, while monologues became longer and more frequent. The *NYT* suggests that this change in the show format was driven by the quest for greater TV ratings. Certainly, *Tucker Carlson Tonight* has become the most successful show in the history of cable news.

It should come as no surprise that Carlson is widely loathed by the rest of the corporate media, including commentators from his own Fox News. He has been called a right-wing provocateur, a "dishonest propagandist," a "dull racist," a "foreign asset," and even a traitor to his country.[30] Politicians and media personalities ("handmaidens to power") have called on Fox to fire him, so far without success.

Carlson is no lone voice in the wilderness. In addition to his trademark monologues, Carlson frequently has guests on his program, and their identities tell us much about the dissident insurgency criticizing the powers that be. In 2021–2022, Carlson's guests included Glenn Greenwald and Tulsi Gabbard on the left and Michael Flynn and J. D. Vance on the right.

The comedian and political commentator Jon Stewart once accused Rupert Murdoch, who owns Fox News and employs Carlson, of "trying to destroy the fabric of this country."[31] A more accurate charge would be that Carlson wants to overthrow the ruling elites. In many respects, he is a prototypical counter-elite figure. Should Murdoch take such appeals seriously, at least if he is interested in preserving the dominance of the economic elites (himself included, of course)? Apparently, however, Murdoch cares more about his personal bottom line than about defending his class.

The Next Battle

The ruling coalition prevailed in the first battle of the ongoing revolutionary war. The Democratic Party has controlled its populist wing and is now the party of the 10 percent and of the 1 percent. But the 1 percent is losing its traditional political vehicle, the Republican Party, which is being taken over by its populist wing. Tucker Carlson, rather than Donald Trump, may be a seed crystal around which a new radical party forms. Or another figure could suddenly arise—chaotic times favor the rise (and often rapid demise) of new leaders. Earlier I argued that a revolution cannot succeed without large-scale organization. The right-wing populists intend to use the GOP as an already existing organization to grasp power. An added advantage is that control of one of the main parties offers them a nonviolent, legal route to power.

This incipient right-wing populist faction goes by a variety of names, the most common currently being the New Right and the National Conservatives (NatCons). One of the rising NatCon stars is J. D. Vance, a newly elected Republican senator from Ohio. Vance's life trajectory has a lot in common with that of Bannon. Vance grew up in the Ohio Rust Belt, experiencing firsthand the devastating effects of deindustrialization on the working class, including such problems as domestic violence and drug abuse. His mother and father divorced, and he was raised by his grandparents. He enlisted in the US Marine Corps and served in Iraq. Then his life trajectory took a dramatic turn. After graduating from Ohio State, he received a juris doctorate from that forge of revolutionary cadres, Yale Law School.[32] When in law school, he was encouraged by a professor there, Amy Chua, to write a memoir, and the result was *Hillbilly Elegy: A Memoir of a Family and Culture in Crisis*, published in 2016. After graduation, he worked for a corporate law firm and then as a principal at Mithril Capital, one of Peter Thiel's venture capital firms. And now he has won a Senate seat running on a NatCon program. His candidacy was funded by Thiel, and he got sympathetic treatment on Tucker Carlson's program. Vance has also appeared several times on Steve Bannon's podcast, *War Room*. Another 2022 Senate candidate with a similar trajectory (although with a law degree from Stanford, not Yale) is Blake Masters. He was also funded by Thiel and endorsed by Carlson. These two are prototypical American counter-elite figures.

As of late 2022, we have no way of knowing whether Carlson, Vance, and, more generally, NatCons will succeed in taking over the Republican Party. But the NatCons are clearly reshaping the GOP, building on what has already been accomplished by Trump and Bannon. As Jason Zengerle wrote in *The New York Times*, "Depending on your point of view, NatCons are either attempting to add intellectual heft to Trumpism or trying to reverse-engineer an intellectual doctrine to match Trump's lizard-brain populism."[33] And even established Republican politicians are moving in the populist direction, having started to question their allegiance to big business. These politicians include Republican senators and 2016 GOP presidential candidates Ted Cruz and Marco Rubio. Cruz recently declared that he would not accept donations from corporate PACs. Rubio has not made a similar pledge, but he is voicing increasingly populist messages: "For the past several years, I have been making the case that far too many American companies were prioritizing short-term financial windfalls at the expense of America's families, communities and national security. More and more people are coming around to that viewpoint, both in the Republican Party and around the country."[34] Senator Josh Hawley (another graduate of Yale Law School) is pushing legislation that he says would "break up the big tech companies" and impose "tough new penalties" on companies that violate antitrust laws.[35]

The American ruling class today finds itself in the predicament that has recurred thousands of times throughout human history. Many common Americans have withdrawn their support from the governing elites. They've flipped up "a throbbing middle finger in the face of America's ruling class." Large swaths of degree holders, frustrated in their quest for elite positions, are breeding grounds for counter-elites, who dream of overthrowing the existing regime. Most wealth holders are unwilling to sacrifice any personal advantage for the sake of preserving the status quo. The technical term for it is "revolutionary situation." For the ruling class, there are two routes out of a revolutionary situation. One leads to their overthrow. The alternative is to adopt a series of reforms that will rebalance the social system, reversing the trends of popular immiseration and elite overproduction. The American ruling elites did it once, a century ago. Can they do it again? What does history suggest?

CHAPTER 9

THE WEALTH PUMP AND
THE FUTURE OF DEMOCRACY

Crisis Outcomes

Our analysis of the one hundred cases in CrisisDB on which we have gathered data so far shows that there is a fundamental difference in how societies enter and exit periods of crisis. If the entry is like a narrow valley, outcomes follow a fan of possible paths with widely different "severity." Our research team coded severity using a variety of indicators of negative consequences (twelve in total).[1] One set captures the demographic consequences: Did the overall population shrink as a result of turbulence following the crisis? Was there a major epidemic? We found that population declines are quite common—half of the exits from crisis resulted in a population loss. Thirty percent of exits were associated with a major epidemic.

Other indicators focus on what happened to the elites. In nearly two-thirds of the cases, the crisis resulted in massive downward mobility from the ranks of the elites to the ranks of the commoners. In one-sixth of the cases, elite groups were targeted for extermination. The probability of ruler assassination was 40 percent. Bad news for the elites. Even more bad news for everybody was that 75 percent of crises ended in revolutions or civil wars (or both), and in one-fifth of cases, recurrent civil wars dragged on for a century or longer. Sixty percent of exits led to the death of the state—it was conquered by another or simply disintegrated into fragments.

The overall conclusion is grim. There are very few cases in which societies managed to navigate their crises with no or few major consequences. In most cases, several disasters combined, and some societies experienced really severe outcomes. For example, Valois France experienced nine out of twelve severe consequences during the French Wars of Religion in the sixteenth century. Kings and dukes were assassinated; elites were exterminated on a number of occasions (such as the St. Bartholomew's Day Massacre); and it is estimated that three million people died from the violence, famine, or disease during this period of civil war. Other severe cases include the fall of the Tang and Song dynasties of China, the breakup of the Sassanid Empire, and the sixth-century crisis in the Eastern Roman Empire.

The historical record does, however, offer some examples of societies that managed to escape their crises relatively unscathed. Violence was minimal; sovereignty was maintained; there was little, if any, territorial loss; and most societal structures and institutions remained intact, excepting certain institutional or policy reforms. Somehow these societies managed to "flatten the curve" of spiraling unrest and sectarian violence that engulfed so many others. How, exactly, did these societies avoid more catastrophic outcomes?

Let's focus on the last complete wave of state breakdown, the Age of Revolutions, which was global in scope. In particular, the second half of the Age of Revolutions, between roughly 1830 and 1870, was an extremely turbulent period in world history. Nearly all major states experienced revolutions or civil wars (or both). They included the United States and China (as we saw in chapter 1). Europe was convulsed by a wave of revolutions in 1848. France managed to get three revolutions— in 1830, 1848, and 1871. In Japan, the Tokugawa regime fell in 1867. But there were two exceptions: the British and Russian Empires. Both experienced revolutionary situations but managed to deal with them by adopting the right set of reforms. Up until now, my book has been filled with "dismal science" about societies unraveling and states collapsing. It's time to look at the brighter side of things.

England: The Chartist Period (1819–1867)

After the end of England's seventeenth-century crisis (1642–1692, encompassing the English Civil War and the Glorious Revolution), the next century saw a dramatic expansion of its overseas empire, despite the loss of its American colonies. The population of the British Isles also grew as a result of high birth rates and gradually declining mortality. Much of that population growth ended up in industrial centers like London and Manchester, which became overcrowded hubs rife with disease and malnutrition. The cities' laborers worked long hours for low wages with few safety measures in place. Labor oversupply began depressing real wages after 1750. Popular immiseration led to a decline in average stature, a key indicator of general well-being. In 1819, a massive popular protest demanding full male suffrage and improvement of working conditions in Manchester was brutally suppressed by the authorities. Fifteen people died and hundreds were injured when the crowd of sixty thousand protesters was charged by the cavalry with sabers drawn. The Peterloo Massacre, as it became known, shocked the nation.

At the same time, industrialization, in which Britain was a pioneer, began gathering steam, generating an unprecedentedly long period of vigorous economic growth. The wealth pump began producing new economic elites. Another clear sign of elite overproduction was that university enrollments, which had been declining from their peak on the eve of the English Civil War, surged again after 1750. Fierce debates broke out within elite factions about how to address the unrest. In 1831, this conflict led to the British Parliament being dissolved, resulting in elections just one year after the previous elections and a victory for the reformers, although the issues remained contentious.

We can track the pressures for instability by the number of arrests and deaths at contentious public gatherings in Great Britain. There were only three such arrests in 1758, but they grew during the following decades, reaching a peak of eighteen hundred arrests in 1830. The number of deaths peaked in 1831, when fifty-two people were killed. The UK was clearly in a revolutionary situation. Turbulence lasted until 1867, when the franchise was extended to all male citizens. In between, several more riots and protests occurred, while a series of labor laws and other reforms aimed at improving the living conditions of the urban working poor were passed. The period is named after the 1838 People's Charter, a formal document of protestation calling for these reforms.

The mid-nineteenth century was undoubtedly a time of great stress and unrest in England. Scholars of the period generally agree "that these decades possessed a revolutionary potential and . . . that the country came as close as it had ever been to revolution since the seventeenth century."[2] Yet major civil war or outright rebellion did not materialize, and the scale of political violence was much lower than in other

European countries (or during England's previous age of discord, 1642–1692). What explains this happy outcome?

Part of the answer has to do with England benefiting from the resources afforded by its extensive empire. Millions of commoners emigrated from England during the Chartist period, primarily to possessions like Canada, Australia, and the (then already independent) United States of America. This was driven partly by the demographic and economic pressures facing a large segment of the population. The state also facilitated this outward movement by lifting emigration restrictions, starting in the 1820s, and subsidizing travel to areas seeking colonists, notably Australia and New Zealand. Not only commoners emigrated. Many elite aspirants frustrated with the saturation of prestigious and powerful positions at home went overseas—some to positions in the colonial administration, others as private citizens.

Arguably more significant in eventually ending the crisis were the institutional reforms of the period. In response to unrest, a sizable fraction of the English political elite became persuaded of the need for several critical reforms. In 1832, the franchise was extended to smaller landowners and some urban residents. The Reform Act of 1832 also shifted the balance of power away from the landed gentry (the squirearchy) in favor of the upwardly mobile commercial elites by removing "rotten boroughs" (with tiny populations controlled by wealthy patrons) and turning major commercial and industrial cities into separate boroughs. In 1834, the country's Poor Laws were amended in an attempt to increase state support for infirm and out-of-work laborers. When the new Poor Law failed to meet its stated aims, a fresh wave of riots and protests erupted, giving rise to the People's Charter. In response, a number of additional reforms were made during the next two decades. One of the most important measures that alleviated immiseration was the repeal of the Corn Laws that had imposed tariffs on the import of grains, benefiting large landowners but inflating the price of staple food products in domestic markets. Another important dynamic during this period was the struggle of workers to establish their right for trade unions. These different developments resulted in real wages regaining by 1850 the ground they had lost since 1750. After 1867, worker wages started growing at a historically unprecedented rate, doubling in the next fifty years.

The political process was messy. The concessions of English Parliamentarians came only after sustained public protest and (nearly) rebellion. It also took a long time—nearly fifty years—to put all reforms in place. Elites themselves were divided on how to deal with this unrest. Nevertheless, the ruling elites sought to meet, at least partly, the demands of the immiserated majority through institutional reforms. Their implementation also required large outlays of public spending to support the new welfare programs. As one historian put it, "From the 1820s onwards the British elite showed a remarkable ability to reform its institutions and move from a fiscal-military state to an administrative state capable of meeting the needs of an increasingly complex commercial and industrial society."[3]

Russia: Reform Period (1855–1881)

The historical trajectories of the early modern Russian and British Empires had much in common. Up until the seventeenth century, both were relatively insignificant, peripheral players in European power politics.[4] But during the eighteenth century, these states acquired large empires, land-based for Russia and sea-based for England. After they jointly defeated Napoleon's France, the British and Russian Empires became the "superpowers" of Europe and, indeed, the world (as the Qing Empire progressively crumbled from internal causes). In 1833, Russia was the mightiest European land power, with an army of 860,000. However, the industrial revolution that gathered steam in northwestern Europe after 1800 transformed the balance of forces within Europe. Because Russia lagged behind in modernizing its economy, it experienced a humiliating defeat to a military coalition, led by Britain, in the Crimean War (1853–1856). This defeat served as a trigger for the revolutionary situation in which the Russian Empire found itself during the late 1850s.

First, though, Russia was one of the last countries to abolish serfdom. How did this patently unfair social order develop? To understand why, we need to look back to the origins of the Russian Empire. Toward the end of the fifteenth century, the Muscovite state, the gentry, and the peasants forged a tripartite social contract, according to which the gentry would serve in the army, while the peasants would work to support these warriors and the state (which was minuscule, anyway, and staffed with gentry who were compensated in the form of land with peasants). Those gentry who couldn't, or wouldn't, serve had land (and peasants) taken away from them. This compact enabled Muscovy, which inhabited an extremely tough geopolitical neighborhood, surrounded by powerful enemies on all sides (except the north), to survive and expand into a powerful empire. The social contract was renewed under Peter the Great (ruled 1682–1725), who obligated all nobility to serve the state, either in the army or in the bureaucracy. But it was abandoned as a result of the "gentry revolution" of 1762, when Peter III abolished the service obligations of the noble landowners to the state. By 1860, the nobility had become a parasitic class, with only a minority of serf-owners serving in the army or in the bureaucracy. Thus, abolition of the serfdom restored a measure of social justice. But righting social wrongs doesn't happen on its own; it took a revolutionary situation to impel the rulers to force the needed reforms against noble resistance.

The root causes of this sociopolitical fragility were, as usual, popular immiseration and elite overproduction.[5] At the end of the seventeenth-century crisis in Russia, when the Romanov dynasty was established in 1613, the population of the country was less than five million. But by 1860, the Russian population in its fifty European provinces alone had grown to more than sixty million. Although Russia had at the same time expanded its territory, such massive population growth exceeded the stocks of arable land available to peasants, leading to reduced consumption of food per capita. A clear sign of popular immiseration was the decline in the average height of peasant recruits by four centimeters during the eighteenth century.

The elite numbers also increased in the run up to 1860, even faster than those of the peasants. As a result, the proportion of nobles within the general population grew during the eighteenth and the first half of the nineteenth centuries. At the same time, the elites increased their consumption levels. As the numbers and appetites of the elites expanded, they needed to extract more resources from the productive class. Because about half of the peasants in Russia were serfs (the rest being free "state peasants"), the nobles tightened the screws on serfs whom they owned. Most wealth pumps we've discussed so far were turned on by a shifting balance in economic power between workers and employers. In a serf-based economy, the elites had the option of using naked force to pump wealth from peasants.

Growing demands on the serfs during the first half of the nineteenth century were met with increasing peasant resistance. The great majority of rural riots were caused by new impositions on the peasants, such as increased quitrent or corvée, dispossession of land, and harsh punishments. The number of peasant protests increased from 10 to 20 per year in the early 1800s to 162 in 1848 (triggered by the news of European revolutions). The peak of peasant resistance was in 1858 (423 disturbances).

The increasing pressure from continued peasant rioting and agitation was an important factor in the decision of Alexander II (ruled 1855–1881) to free the serfs. The Third Department of His Majesty's Own Chancery (the political police) reported in 1857 that the peasantry was in an "agitated state" as a result of rumors of imminent emancipation and that massive unrest was likely. This is precisely what happened the next year.

The shock of the humiliating defeat in the Crimean War, which delegitimized the tsarist regime, coupled with fear that exploding peasant resistance might turn into a repeat of Pugachev's Rebellion[6] convinced the Russian ruling class that the serfs had to be emancipated. After reading de Tocqueville's book on the French Revolution, the emperor's brother, Grand Duke Konstantin, remarked, "If we do not carry out a peaceful and complete revolution with our own hands, it will inevitably happen without us and against us." In his address to the Moscow nobility, Alexander II himself expressed the same sentiment, stating, "We live in such an age that it will happen sooner or later. I think you are of the same mind as me: it would be better to begin to abolish the serfdom from above than to wait until it abolishes itself from below."[7]

The Great Reforms of the 1860s and 1870s not only freed the serfs but also transformed Russian society in a truly unprecedented way.[8] Not all interest groups in Russia welcomed them, however. The Emancipation Reform of 1861, in particular, pleased neither peasants nor noble serf-owners. Most freed serfs did not get enough land to feed their families, and they had to pay onerous redemption taxes to their former owners. The nobility were even bigger losers, as they lost their captive workforce. In the aftermath of emancipation, the majority of elites were forced to endure downward social mobility. This process created huge numbers of counter-elites, which fed the growth of radicals, such as anarchists and social revolutionaries. A wave of terrorist acts roiled Russia during the 1860s and '70s. Alexander II, who became known as Alexander the Liberator, paid the ultimate price for his liberalization policy—he was assassinated in 1881 by the Narodnaya Volya (People's Will) radicals, who hoped to trigger a popular revolution against the tsarist regime.

But although it took two decades for the reforms to work, they were eventually successful in reducing social tensions that brought about the mid-nineteenth-century crisis in the Russian Empire. The Russian ruling class successfully averted a revolution. In the post-reform period, the number of peasant disturbances declined, and while there were spikes of unrest toward the end of the century, these were usually associated with the ascent of a new emperor, which raised peasant hopes for land reform. (The problem of not enough land per peasant persisted.) Similarly, the wave of terror subsided by 1890. Because capital punishment in tsarist Russia was reserved for the most serious political crimes, such as terrorism, the number of executions per year provides a useful indication of revolutionary activity.[9] The temporal distribution of executions clearly delineates the post-reform peak of instability: zero in the 1850s, seventeen in the 1860s, twenty-two in the 1870s, thirty in the 1880s, and zero again in the 1890s.[10]

What can we learn from these two success stories? Despite obvious differences between Britain and Russia—one was a liberal empire, the other an autocratic one—they also shared certain similarities, which may help explain why they managed to navigate their mid-nineteenth-century crises without major revolutions, unlike the rest of the contemporary great (and not-so-great) powers. Possessing a growing empire was, undoubtedly, an important advantage, because each state could afford to export surplus population and elites to recently annexed territories. Additionally, building a large and durable empire is not simple. Success at this business suggests a certain competency of the ruling class and at least some degree of broadly based cooperation within society. This competency can be, and was, directed to the business of reforming the empire to face new challenges. At the same time, both empires were simply lucky in having leaders who were willing to sacrifice short-term selfish advantage for the sake of long-term collective good. Finally, both states faced stiff external competition, from each other and from other great powers. Nothing focuses the collective mind of a ruling class more than a twin existential threat—from within, the ruled population, and from without, geopolitical rivals.[11]

Success Stories in the Long Term

CrisisDB tells us that no past society has managed to go for long before running into a crisis. It is legitimate to ask, then, how long the stabilizing effect of the reforms implemented by Russia and Britain lasted.

In Russia, the calm lasted for only about a generation, from 1881 to 1905. The main problem was the one I mentioned earlier: freeing the serfs made the economic position of the nobility untenable. On the one hand, this was only just, but on the other hand, it had unintended consequences.

Most noble landowners, especially those who specialized in producing grain for the market with corvée labor,[12] were unable to adapt to the new conditions and failed. The estates belonging to ruined gentry were bought by wealthier peasants, merchants, and petty bourgeois. The main avenue through which impoverished nobles could compensate for lost land-based revenues was government service. Education provided credentials that gave an advantage in the competition for jobs, so the gentry youth entered colleges and universities en masse. Between 1860 and 1880, the number of university students more than tripled (from 4,100 to 14,100) and continued to increase for the next two decades.[13]

About half of the students were the children of nobles and government officials. Most of them were very poor. A combination of abject poverty and exposure to new social ideologies from Western Europe, such as Marxism, radicalized the students. This period saw the formation of a new social stratum, the intelligentsia, which grew in tandem with the expansion of education. Elite overproduction was the most important process underlying the formation of the intelligentsia, half of whom had their roots in the noble estates.

The state was unable to find employment for all gymnasium and university graduates because the size of the government bureaucracy increased by only 8 percent during this period (while the number of graduates quadrupled). Faced with poor employment prospects, many students found alternative pursuits, such as revolutionary activity, an attractive option. Sixty-one percent of the revolutionaries of the 1860s, the "nihilists," were students or recent graduates, and an even larger proportion (70 percent) were children of nobles or officials.[14]

The first wave of revolutionary ferment during the 1860s and '70s failed to overthrow the tsarist regime. Suppression of radical organizations during the reign of Alexander III, who succeeded to the throne after his father was assassinated, restored stability. But the process generating frustrated elite aspirants continued unabated, and during the reign of the next tsar, Nicholas II, tipped Russia into the revolution of 1905–1907. The trigger, as before, was the military defeats that Russia experienced, this time in the Russo-Japanese War (1904–1905). There was still a lot of resilience in the empire and, while bloody, the revolution was unsuccessful in overthrowing the Russian ruling class. It took the additional shock of World War I to bring on the 1917 Russian Revolution and the end of the Romanov dynasty.

Summing up, the Great Reforms of the 1860s and '70s were a genuine success story. They resolved the revolutionary situation that developed during the 1850s with relatively little bloodshed. For comparison, if during the reign of Alexander III (who was called the Peacemaker or, by the revolutionaries, the Strangler of Liberty) there were only thirty executions (and none during the 1890s), the suppression of the revolution of 1905–1907 required three thousand. The Romanov dynasty managed to "flatten the curve," giving Russia an additional half century to modernize. In the long term, however, the dynasty collapsed under the combined blows of elite overproduction and geopolitical pressure.

The British Empire fared better. The victory over Russia in the Crimean War removed the last threat to its position as an unrivaled world-hegemonic power. The Victorian era (1837–1901) was a period of cultural, technological, and scientific brilliance. But all such integrative eras end. Despite being a winner in World War I, in the postwar period, the British Empire began its slow decline (although this gradual disintegration avoided significant political instability and internal violence at the center). It lost the economic race to the United States and Germany. There was a successful revolution in Ireland, which created the Irish Free State in 1921. The process of imperial decay accelerated in the aftermath of World War II, with India, the "crown jewel of empire," becoming independent in 1947. Today it is not inconceivable that Scotland could become a separate state in the next decade or so. All empires eventually die, and the British Empire was no exception. But this observation in no way diminishes the achievement of the British elites during the Chartist period.

Why Democracies Are Vulnerable to Plutocratic Elites

Analysis of the success stories (Chartist Britain, Reform Russia, the Progressive Era in the United States, and other cases[15]) is a source of both optimism and pessimism. The optimistic take is that it is possible to shut down the wealth pump and rebalance social systems without resorting to a revolution or catastrophic war. Death may be the "great leveler," as Scheidel argues, but it is not the only one. Fear—or putting it a bit more charitably, intelligent foresight—can also work, and did work in the success stories.

However, more pessimistically, success stories are relatively rare in the historical record. But, more optimistically, we now have a much better understanding of the deep causes that drive social systems out of balance, and it is possible to forecast (if imperfectly) the likely outcomes of various interventions intended to bring them back into balance. On the pessimistic side, again, implementing the needed reforms is not easy, because the reformers always have to overcome the resistance of those interest groups that will be the losers.

Finally, there is no permanent solution. A balanced social system with the wealth pump shut down is an unstable equilibrium that takes constant effort to maintain—like riding a bicycle. This instability is due to one of the most fundamental principles in sociology, the "iron law of oligarchy,"[16] which states that when an interest group acquires a lot of power, it inevitably starts using this power in self-interested ways. We see this general principle operating in both premodern and contemporary societies. The early Russian Empire, for example, was a service state in which everybody served: the peasants, the nobility, and the ruler. (Peter I is a good example of a service tsar but not the only one.) However, the nobility had more power than the other players, and they eventually subverted the tripartite compact by freeing themselves from service. Then they turned on the wealth pump—because they could— oppressing the peasants and becoming a parasitic class. We see the same process, again and again, in all historical states, which is why instability waves always recur.

Unfortunately, modern democracies are not immune from the iron law of oligarchy. The United States successfully shut down the wealth pump during the Progressive Era/New Deal but then allowed self-interested elites to turn it back on in the 1970s. The United Kingdom followed a trajectory that was similar, even if a few years behind. In that country, the downward slope of the relative wage began after 1975.[17] There are now numerous signs that several other Western democracies are stepping on the same slippery slope.

One clear and obvious sign is that after a long period of income and wealth compression during most of the twentieth century, economic inequality has begun growing again within Western democracies (as well as in much of the rest of the world).[18] Western Europe also suffers from an increasingly acute problem of overproduction of youth with advanced degrees.[19] Another worrying sign has been the spread of neo-classical market fundamentalism, promoted by influential international publications, such as *The Economist*, and by international organizations dominated by the US, such as the International Monetary Fund.[20]

An even more worrying development is the transition in Western democracies from "class-based party systems" to "multi-elite party systems." Earlier in the book (chapter 8), we discussed this transition in the United States, where the Democratic Party, a party of the working class during the New Deal, became by 2000 the party of the credentialed

10 percent. The rival party, the Republican Party, primarily served the wealthy 1 percent, leaving the 90 percent out in the cold. Amory Gethin, Clara Martínez-Toledano, and Thomas Piketty studied hundreds of elections and found that political parties in other Western democracies also increasingly cater to only the well educated and the rich.[21] When political parties abandon the working classes, this amounts to a major shift in how social power is distributed within society. Ultimately, it is this balance of power that determines whether the selfish elites are allowed to turn on the wealth pump.

What is little appreciated is that although democratic institutions are the best (or least bad) way of governing societies, democracies are particularly vulnerable to being subverted by plutocrats. Ideology may be the softest, gentlest form of power, but it is the key one in democratic societies. The plutocrats can use their wealth to buy mass media, to fund think tanks, and to handsomely reward those social influencers who promote their messages. In other words, they wield enormous power to sway the electorate toward the opinions that promote their interests. Cruder forms of power, such as swaying elections and lobbying politicians, are also quite effective in promoting the political agendas of the rich. Finally, just as in war, money is the most important fuel powering organizations. Naked enthusiasm is not enough for a sustained, long-term effort, although money plus enthusiasm is better than just money. The plutocrats can afford (literally) to plan, and implement their plans, for the long term.

All of this sounds quite pessimistic. And the United States provides Europeans with a cautionary tale, as all of these processes driving the transition from democracy to plutocracy have been running here at full throttle for decades. But some grounds for optimism remain. Despite having strong cultural similarities and despite belonging to the same supranational organization, EU countries exhibit a remarkable degree of variation in country-specific trajectories. Let's do a quick survey to illustrate this point, focusing on one particular statistic in the World Inequality Database: the share of income going to the top 1 percent.[22]

Germany, as the largest economy in the EU, is the logical starting point. For many decades since 1945, the share of income going to the top percent has fluctuated around 10 percent. It was 9.5 percent as late as 2003, but then it rapidly increased to above 13 percent and stayed there. This shift occurred later, and was not as extreme, as in the United States. In America, the share of the top percent was close to 10 percent during the 1970s (as in Germany), but after 1980 it grew rapidly and has been above 19 percent for a decade now. But keep in mind that America is an outlier among Western democracies—not only in its degree of economic inequality but also in its dismal well-being statistics (although the two are clearly related). Germany has a lot of distance to travel to match America, but it's on the slippery slope.

France provides us with an interesting counterpoint to Germany. The share of income going to the top percent in France reached an absolute minimum during the 1980s (around 8 percent), then increased to above 11 percent during the early 2000s. But then it remarkably declined and is currently just below 10 percent.[23] Germany and France are the two most important and influential players in the EU, yet their inequality trajectories are quite different. Clearly, their elites are pursuing different courses.

What about Denmark and Austria, the two countries that I've used as examples of well-governed states? Austria appears to be doing well and managed to keep its inequality on a remarkably even keel. The share of the top percent was around 11 percent in the 1980s; it increased slightly to around 12 percent during the early 2000s, but then it declined and is now at 10 percent, just as in France. In Denmark, the trajectory has been quite different. As we saw in chapter 6, Denmark was the first of the Nordic countries to implement a tripartite agreement. This compact achieved a remarkable degree of income compression, so around 1980 the share of the top percent dipped below 7 percent. But the 1980s saw a trend reversal, and the top percent's fortunes started improving. Today its share is just under 13 percent, in the same ballpark as that of Germany.

The most important conclusion from this survey is not in the specifics of trajectories followed by different countries but in the fact of variation itself. Why is it important? From the scientist's point of view, having enough variation is key for developing a better understanding of the causes driving the dynamics. Nearly every country in the World Inequality Database has followed its own unique trajectory. There are many theories that economists and other social scientists have proposed to explain why inequality sometimes increases and sometimes decreases. The more variation there is, the more informative the data are for testing these theories against each other. Furthermore, we have clearly entered a particularly turbulent period of world history. In the coming years, the resilience of countries will be severely tested by climate change, pandemics, economic depressions, interstate conflicts, and massive immigration flows. Will those countries that did not permit their inequality levels to increase be more resilient to such shocks? We need to know.

The final thought with which I want to end this book is that humanity has come a long way since our species appeared some two hundred thousand years ago. The last ten thousand years have seen a particularly rapid evolution. Despotic elites who oppressed common people repeatedly arose and were repeatedly overthrown. We are now again in the disintegrative phase of this cycle, but while we live through our own age of discord, it's worth remembering that humanity has learned from previous such debacles. Cumulative cultural evolution equipped us with remarkable technologies, including social technologies—institutions—that enable our societies to deliver an unprecedentedly high—and broadly based—quality of life. Yes, this capacity is often not fully realized—there is great variation between different states in providing well-being for their citizens. But in the longer term, such variation is necessary for continuing cultural evolution. If societies don't experiment in trying for better social arrangements, evolution will stop. Even more importantly, when selfish ruling classes run their societies into the ground, it is good to have alternatives—success stories. And it falls to us, "the 99 percent," to demand that our rulers act in ways that advance our common interests. Complex human societies need elites—rulers, administrators, thought leaders—to function well. We don't want to get rid of them; the trick is to constrain them to act for the benefit of all.

ACKNOWLEDGMENTS

This book is a result of a long journey. Over the past two decades I have enjoyed and was enlightened by conversations with many colleagues and friends: Jim Bennett, Chris Chase-Dunn, Georgi Derluguian, Kevin Chekov Feeney, Sergey Gavrilets, Jack Goldstone, Dan Hoyer, Vladimir Ivanov, Ludmila Korepin, Andrey Korotayev, Gavin Mendel-Gleason, Angela Nagle, Georg Orlandi, and Nina Witoszek.

I especially would like to thank Dan Hoyer, Jim Bennett, and Kevin Chekov Feeney, who read and commented on a complete draft of the manuscript. Andy Poehlman and Kate Kohn provided invaluable help with chasing down the sources and checking the factual basis of the claims I made in the book.

This book couldn't be written without CrisisDB, the large database on past societies sliding into crises and emerging from them. Many thanks to my colleagues who helped build it: Dan Hoyer, Jill Levine, Samantha Holder, Jenny Reddish, Robert Miller, and Majid Benam.

I want to express gratitude to my agent, Andrew Wylie, and the rest of the Wylie Agency team. Scott Moyers not only steered the publication process at Penguin Random House but also was a major influence in shaping the book manuscript. Following his feedback on the initial text version, I extensively restructured and streamlined the story line. He also made many excellent suggestions throughout the manuscript that greatly improved it. Thanks are also due to the production team at Penguin Random House for their superb professional handling of the book manuscript.

As always, my greatest debt of gratitude is to my wife, Olga, for her support, encouragement, and (constructive) critique.

APPENDIX

A NEW SCIENCE OF HISTORY

A Meeting of the Babbage Society[1]

The chalk in Phineas' hand scrawled a mathematical curve across the slate. "Those are the figures for the last few decades. I've run them through the engines and fit them to an equation. Here is the projection. . . . Slavery is dying. The next fifty years will see the end of the whole sorry business. Am I not right, Brother Eli?"

Eli shifted and shrugged. "Do we know even that much? How confident are we in our very data? Our equations may be grotesquely wrong."

Jedediah Crawford's cane thumped the floor like a judge's gavel. "We know enough that to do nothing would be cowardice of the worst sort. Every year that slavery persists is another year closer to disaster. . . ."

Jedediah pushed himself to his feet and hobbled to the slate board, where he slashed an S-shaped growth curve atop the slavery decay curve. "We cannot wait for slavery to expire. . . ."

"If the South secedes," Eli told Isaac quietly, "the North will fight. . . . Not for abolition, but to preserve the Union. No good can come from that."

"Fight?" Meechum laughed. "If the South leaves the Federal Union, the North will dare nothing. Southron gentlemen are trained to combat from birth. How can a nation of shopkeepers and mechanics stand up to them?"

"How?" asked Isaac, amusement in his voice. He rose and walked to the chalkboard. Taking the chalk, he wrote a set of equations on the board and stepped back.

Davis studied the equations and felt his heart grow cold.[2]

Cliology, Psychohistory, Cliodynamics

Charles Babbage was an English mathematician and engineer who invented the Analytical Engine, a machine capable of general-purpose computation. The first description of the Analytical Engine was published in 1837. Over the next decades, until his death in 1871, Babbage attempted to build a working version several times, but each time he failed due to lack of funds and personnel conflicts. Today it is generally agreed that Babbage's design was sound and could be built with the manufacturing technology available in his time.

The premise of Michael Flynn's science-fiction novel *In the Country of the Blind* is that an Analytical Engine was, in fact, built by a group of antebellum American scientists and engineers, led by Jedediah Crawford, one of the characters in the vignette with which this chapter begins. For reasons that are not entirely clear in the novel, these researchers decide to keep their work secret. (Well, if they didn't, that would destroy all the suspense elements of the plot, and there would be no novel to write.)

Two years before Babbage described his Analytical Engine, the

Belgian mathematician and statistician Adolphe Quetelet published a book, *A Treatise on Man and the Development of His Faculties,* or *Essays on Social Physics*, in which he describes an approach to understanding human societies using statistical laws. Inspired by the ideas of Quetelet and the French philosopher Auguste Comte (the father of modern sociology), Crawford and his colleagues form the Babbage Society, whose goal is to develop a science of human history, which they call cliology (from *Clio*, the name of the Greek mythological muse of history). They write mathematical models for social processes using differential equations. Some of the simpler models can be solved with pencil and paper, but more complex systems of equations have to be run on the Analytical Engine. The cliologists also invest a lot of effort into collecting data that are then fed into their mechanical computers. These data allow them to anchor their mathematical equations in reality.

As their work progresses, the Babbage Society gains the ability to predict the future trajectory of American society, even if imperfectly, as we saw in the vignette. They can predict some things, like the eventual victory of the North, should a civil war happen, with a great degree of certainty. But the breakout of the Civil War itself was to them a horrible surprise. As one of the characters says later in the novel, "The Civil War . . . We still don't know why that happened. Something was overlooked in the equations." Still, some ability to predict is better than none. As the proverb goes, in the country of the blind, the one-eyed man is king.

I learned about Michael Flynn's book when I was already quite advanced in my own quest for an analytical, predictive history. A reader of my book *Historical Dynamics: Why States Rise and Fall*, published in 2003, in which I proposed this new science, alerted me to cliology. Flynn's novel has a much more famous predecessor—Isaac Asimov's

Foundation, which I read many years ago, when I was twenty. I found it fascinating, but it didn't inspire me to become a psychohistorian (psychohistory being what Asimov called his version of the science of history). At that time, I was on track to become a mathematical biologist. I love the outdoors and animals, so I combined my passions for nature and for "practical mathematics" (that is, using math not for the sake of math but as a tool kit for understanding the world) to become a population ecologist.[3] It was only twenty years later, at the age of forty, that I decided to switch from ecology to cliodynamics, and although Asimov's *Foundation* continued to be an inspiration, it didn't play a role in my decision to switch.

There are many differences between Asimov's imaginary science of history and the reality of cliodynamics, as we now practice it. Asimov wrote *Foundation* in the 1940s—way before the discovery of what we now call mathematical chaos. In Asimov's book, Hari Seldon and psychohistorians develop mathematical methods to make very precise predictions decades or even centuries in advance. Due to discoveries made in the 1970s and '80s, we know that this is impossible.

In Asimov's vision, psychohistory, quite appropriately, deals not with individuals but with huge conglomerates of them. It basically adopts a "thermodynamic" approach in which no attempt is made to follow the erratic trajectories of individual molecules (human beings); instead the goal is to model averages of billions of molecules. This is in many ways similar to the ideas of Leo Tolstoy (as we will see later in this chapter), and indeed to cliodynamics, which also deals with large collectives of individuals.[4]

What Asimov did not know is that even if you can ignore such things as individual free will, you still run against very strict limits to predictability. When components of a complex system interact nonlinearly, the resulting dynamics become effectively unpredictable, even if they are entirely deterministic. This is, by the way, why weather cannot be predicted more than a few days in advance. For complex systems like human societies, this possibility becomes a virtual certainty: they are complex and nonlinear enough and, therefore, must behave chaotically and unpredictably.

The hallmark of mathematical chaos is "sensitive dependence on initial conditions."[5] In a climate scenario, this means that a butterfly deciding to flutter its wings (or not) can ultimately cause a hurricane to veer from its predicted path, with a major effect on local weather.

But this limitation on predictability is, paradoxically, a source of optimism. It means that human individuals are not as powerless as Asimov imagined them. Exercising one's free will can have major consequences at the macro level, just like a butterfly fluttering its wings can affect the course of a hurricane. However, such optimism should be tempered by a large helping of realism. Although each of us affects the course of human history, most of us have a very slight effect, and any large effects are probably a result of a completely unforeseen concatenation of events. To make a big effect, an individual has to be at the right place at the right time, and it is very difficult, perhaps impossible, to predict such "cusp points." A more realistic way to achieve positive results is to cooperate with other people.

In short, making precise predictions about events in human societies decades or centuries in the future is pure science fiction. It seems that Asimov himself became uneasy with the mechanistic unfolding of future history according to the Seldon Plan, which his first book portrayed. He solved the problem in the second book in the series, *Foundation and Empire*, by throwing in the Mule—a mutant with frightening mental powers who derails the train of actual history from the course predicted by Seldon.

In actuality, we are all "Mules." By exercising a multitude of choices throughout our lives, we constantly send the train of future history in unpredictable directions.

The impossibility of precise long-term prediction doesn't mean that the dynamics of our societies are simply "one damn thing after another."[6] Both systemic forces and the myriad actions of individuals are combined to produce the actual outcome. You can see it vividly if you run a model that is in a chaotic regime on a PC. For example, I once played with one of the first chaotic models, proposed by Edward Lorenz. But in addition to solving the equations numerically, I periodically added some stochastic perturbations. The trajectory, thus, was constantly buffeted by these random forces, but when I plotted it in the phase space, it still traced out the famous shape of the Lorenz attractor that looks like a butterfly. To put it in simple terms, if you have a peak coming, then individual actions can delay it, or advance it, or make the peak a little higher or a little lower, but there will be a peak in one form or another.

Another interesting issue is Asimov's insistence that any knowledge of psychohistorian predictions must be kept hidden from the people—otherwise, when people learn what's in store, that will affect their actions and cause the prediction to fail. There are several things wrong with this notion. For one, most people couldn't care less about what some eggheaded scientist predicts. As an example, here's what I wrote in my blog on September 3, 2012, referring to the forecast I made in 2010:

> I feel quite safe making the prediction that there will be a peak of political violence in 2020 (plus/minus a few years). If this prediction fails, it will be a result of the theory going wrong, or some massive unforeseen event affecting the social system, or something completely unforeseen (the "unknown unknowns," in the

brilliant characterization of Donald Rumsfeld). But I am fairly certain it will not be because the American policy makers suddenly take a note of what an obscure professor wrote and take action to avoid this undesirable outcome.

And if they do, I will be quite happy. Prediction is overrated. What we really should be striving for, with our social science, is ability to bring about desirable outcomes and to avoid unwanted outcomes. What's the point of predicting [the] future, if it's very bleak and we are not able to change it? We would be like the person condemned to hang before sunrise—perfect knowledge of the future, zero ability to do anything about it.[7]

Of course, this prediction about prediction, or "metaprediction," also turned out to be true. Nobody paid any attention to my 2010 forecast until it actually happened in 2020. But let's return to *In the Country of the Blind*.

Because Flynn wrote his book much later than Asimov, Flynn's discussion of the possibility of analytic, predictive history benefited from the new understanding of dynamical systems resulting from the "chaos revolution" of the 1970s.[8] His ideas were also informed by the personal computer revolution, which placed huge amounts of computing power in the hands of individual researchers. (Not surprisingly, these two revolutions are closely connected, as it was the advances in computers that drove the progress in understanding nonlinear dynamical systems.) As a result, the discussions of cliology by the characters in his book read much less quaintly than the explanation of psychohistory given by Hari Seldon. You may not want to read the book itself—it was the first book Flynn wrote, and has many flaws typical of a first opus, but I recommend Michael Flynn's essay "An Introduction to Cliology," which was originally published in *Analog* magazine and is included as a postscript in the book's second edition. In it, Flynn discusses the many precursors of cliology (and cliodynamics). He actually did some original empirical research on recurrent patterns in history. Because he is not a research scientist, his results wouldn't be publishable in an academic journal and, as a result, did not lead anywhere. But his arguments countering critics of the idea of history as science are well worth reading.

In the final analysis, the proof is in the pudding. As we saw at the beginning of this chapter, Isaac, the cliologist from the Northern states, writes a set of equations on the blackboard that convinces Davis, the Southerner, that there is no chance of the South winning the Civil War, should it happen. War is the most demanding of human undertakings and perhaps the most unpredictable process in human history. How plausible is being able to predict its outcome?

Mathematics of War

Flynn doesn't tell us what equations Isaac writes on the blackboard, but I have a pretty good idea of how I would go about building a model of the American Civil War—I would use the Osipov-Lanchester equations as the starting point. This mathematical model was independently discovered by the Russian military officer Mikhail Osipov in 1915 and the English engineer Frederick Lanchester in 1916. The model is quite simple, especially from our point of view a century later, but it yields at least one unexpected insight. (This is what mathematical models are good for.)

The main variables, which the model keeps track of, would be the sizes of the two armies fighting each other. Once a battle is joined, the number of soldiers in each army starts going down because fighting inflicts casualties. The rate at which casualties are inflicted on the enemy is proportional to the number of soldiers. To see this, imagine a simple scenario in which each soldier shoots his rifle at the enemy. Not every bullet finds a mark, but the more bullets you pour into the opposing force, the more casualties you inflict. The quality of the weapons is a big factor, of course, because soldiers armed with automatic rifles can pour many more bullets into the enemy than soldiers armed with muzzle-loaders. In the Civil War, however, military technology was about the same on each side, so I'd keep the model simple and ignore this potential complication. ("The model should be as simple as possible.") At the same time, soldier skill matters, because better-trained soldiers hit targets more often. This is where the South had an advantage.

Though the Osipov-Lanchester equations are a good starting point, I would need to add a few other factors to the model, because we need to understand not just a single battle but the whole war with many battles. Between battles, each army strives to replace casualties; thus, its current size reflects a balance between forces subtracting and adding soldiers. Accordingly, I would add a recruitment rate to the model. At the beginning of the Civil War, the Confederate Army was nonexistent, while the Union Army was nearly so (consisting, mainly, of US Cavalry chasing Native Americans in the West). Thus, the recruitment rate would be of paramount importance in determining which army can make up the losses due to soldiers being killed, wounded, captured in battle, dying of disease, or defecting. I don't want to forget the last two factors, which are often more important than the casualties inflicted by the enemy. Here's where the North had an advantage, as its population on the eve of the Civil War was around twenty-two million, while the population of the South was only nine million (of which three and a half million were slaves).

Soldiers need rifles and cannons, and these engines of death need ammunition. The North, with its well-developed industries, had a huge advantage in producing and replacing arms and munitions—for every rifle constructed in the South, Northern factories churned out thirty-two.[9] Soldiers also need to be fed, clothed, and moved to the battlefield. I would add a detailed logistics component to my model. The South also got most of its arms from the outside, mainly via Britain. But these arms had to be run through a blockade imposed by the North. This factor is so important that I would probably build a dynamical "submodel," also based on the Osipov-Lanchester equations, that pits Southern blockade-runners against the Northern navy.

Finally, there is the issue of morale. As we just saw, much of what happened in history can be readily expressed in numbers—how many soldiers make up each army, the rate of recruitment, the rate of weapon production, and so on. But there are also "soft," even "squishy," variables that are hard to give numerical values. Hard doesn't mean impossible, however, and I will return to this point later in the chapter. But for now, it is enough to acknowledge that this is where the South held a large advantage over the North. Whereas the Southerners were defending their land, their homes, and their way of life, the Northern recruits were fighting to preserve the Union, a more abstract ideal. Furthermore, the United States was a deeply racist country, and the plight of slaves was not a main motivator for most Northerners, apart from a tiny minority of abolitionists.

And these are the major outlines of the model that I would build. Depending on your background, you might think that the model is hopelessly complicated (most physicists would say so) or hopelessly oversimplified (most historians would be in this camp). Both extreme views are mistaken. There is no single rule that determines how complex (or how simple) a model should be. Model complexity depends on how complex the modeled dynamics are, how much and what kind of data we have, and how precisely we want to know (or can know—remember the discussion on the limits of predictability) the answer. Over my research career, I have built many models of this kind. I always start with the simplest possible design and then add "stuff" to it. It's like cooking a soup. You first get the water boiling and then add meat, vegetables, spices, etc. You keep cooking until the soup tastes great, and then you are done. You need just the right amount and variety of ingredients and seasonings for the best soup, and no more than that. The same goes for the best model. What often happens is that once you get the model to the right level of complexity, adding more stuff to it does not help; in fact, it makes the model worse. And the models that are as simple as possible, but no simpler than that, can be remarkably good. As an example, some years ago, together with my colleagues, I built a model of state formation in the Old World during the ancient and medieval periods (the three millennia between 1500 BC and 1500 AD). Despite its relative simplicity, the model did a remarkable job of predicting where and when "macrostates" (large states and empires) formed and how they spread. (Look at the maps in the article.)[10]

For the model of the American Civil War, I can take a shortcut by avoiding most of the intervening steps and cutting straight to the answer. In this I am aided by the remarkable insight arising from the Osipov-Lanchester model. Remember that the North has a large advantage over the South in terms of manpower. To be precise, it is fourfold (twenty-two million Northerners to five and a half million white Southerners). One might think that giving a twofold advantage to the Southerners because of their skill, and another similar advantage due to their higher morale and motivation, would be just enough to match the numerical preponderance of the North. Getting arms is a problem for the South, but they could (and did) rely on overseas imports. Thus, the South has an even chance of winning the war, right?

Wrong. Although the numerical advantage of the North is four, it actually translates into a warfare advantage of four squared, which is sixteen. This mathematical result is known as Lanchester's square law. It sounds counterintuitive, but once the mathematical result is derived from the Osipov-Lanchester equations, it is easy enough to explain in words. (I do this in chapter 8 of my 2016 book *Ultrasociety*.[11])

Actually, giving a fourfold advantage to the Southerners, due to better skill and morale, is probably overly generous. But overcoming the sixteenfold advantage held by the North due to the square law is essentially hopeless.

Once Davis saw the equations—if, indeed, Isaac wrote the Osipov-Lanchester model on the blackboard, as I surmised—no wonder he despaired.

In real life, the course of the American Civil War went much as the Osipov-Lanchester model would have predicted. The Confederate Army won most of the battles, thanks to better Southern marksmanship and horsemanship, as well as better-trained officers and generals. But the North mobilized 2.1 million soldiers against 880,000 Southerners. The Union Army still had to endure heavy casualties; it lost 360,000 soldiers against 260,000 Confederates. But after four years of bloody, bitter struggle, the North ground up the South and won the war.[12]

Factoring in Morale

I promised to return to the question of how we can factor morale into our equations. Let's talk about this difficult, but by no means impossible, task.

One of the earliest attempts to express morale in numbers was made by, of all people, the great Russian novelist Leo Tolstoy. Few people realize that Tolstoy's magisterial opus, *War and Peace*, which he started writing in 1863, just at the peak of the American Civil War, has a second appendix in which he discusses a science of history. I discuss Tolstoy's ideas in greater detail in chapter 10 of my book *War and Peace and War*—you can guess what inspired this title—so here let's only touch on his thoughts about expressing morale in mathematical terms. In a passage dealing with the guerrilla war in Russia against Napoleon's troops, he wrote:

> In military affairs the strength of an army is the product of its mass and some unknown x....
>
> That unknown quantity is the spirit of the army, that is to say, the greater or lesser readiness to fight and face danger felt by all the men composing an army, quite independently of whether they are, or are not, fighting under the command of a genius, in two- or three-line formation, with cudgels or with rifles that repeat thirty times a minute. Men who want to fight will always put themselves in the most advantageous conditions for fighting.
>
> The spirit of an army is the factor which multiplied by the mass gives the resulting force. To define and express the significance of this unknown factor—the spirit of an army—is a problem for science.
>
> This problem is only solvable if we cease arbitrarily to substitute for the unknown x itself the conditions under which that force becomes apparent—such as the commands of the general, the equipment employed, and so on—mistaking these for the real significance of the factor, and if we recognize this unknown quantity in its entirety as being the greater or lesser desire to

fight and to face danger. Only then, expressing known historic facts by equations and comparing the relative significance of this factor, can we hope to define the unknown.

Ten men, battalions, or divisions, fighting fifteen men, battalions, or divisions, conquer—that is, kill or take captive—all the others, while themselves losing four, so that on the one side four and on the other fifteen were lost. Consequently the four were equal to the fifteen, and therefore $4x = 15y$. Consequently $x/y = 15/4$. This equation does not give us the value of the unknown factor but gives us a ratio between two unknowns. And by bringing variously selected historic units (battles, campaigns, periods of war) into such equations, a series of numbers could be obtained in which certain laws should exist and might be discovered.

Actually, Tolstoy did not get the calculation quite right. (He was a genius at writing great books, not at doing math.) But the core idea of estimating factor x by analyzing many, many battles is spot on. Much later, this approach was used by the American military historian Trevor N. Dupuy. In his 1987 book, *Understanding War: History and Theory of Combat*, Dupuy equated the combat power of an army to the product of three quantities: force strength (the number of troops modified by the quality and quantity of their equipment), operational and environmental modifiers (terrain, weather, posture—defensive versus offensive), and combat effectiveness. The last one is Tolstoy's factor x.

Dupuy then analyzed several wars for which he could obtain data on multiple battles. As an example, his analysis of the eighty-one engagements between the German and British or American forces in 1943 and 1944 showed that the combat efficiency of the Germans was 1.45 times greater than that of the British. This means that if the British wanted to get an even chance at winning a battle against the Germans, they had to bring 45 percent more troops (or arm them more heavily in the same proportion). Americans did better than the Brits, but not by much. They still had to amass a third as many troops as the Germans in order to have a fifty-fifty chance of victory.[13]

Turns out we can make a lot of progress in quantifying the fighting spirit. More recently, my colleagues within the field of cultural evolution have been probing the psychology of readiness for extreme sacrifice, using such concepts as "devoted actors," "sacred values," and "identity fusion."[14]

History as Science

Osipov disappeared after the October Revolution. Perhaps he himself became a casualty of the Russian Civil War. So it fell to Lanchester to become the father of the new discipline: operations research. While the philosophers and the lay public continued to believe that history couldn't become a science, military officers and researchers were quietly mathematizing and analyzing that part of history that is one of the most difficult ones to model and predict—warfare. The stakes are too high—millions of deaths and national survival—to leave it to amateurs. Operations research has developed as a vibrant research field with its own academic journals, research grants handed out by defense departments, and teaching positions at military colleges and general universities. In 2011, I got an introduction to this research community when I was invited to give a keynote address on cliodynamics at an annual conference organized by the historical research unit of the UK's Defense Science and Technology Lab near Portsmouth. The focus of the meeting was on how history can be used to inform defense. As an example, the next speaker after me, Brigadier Andrew Sharpe, talked about nature, character, and rhymes in history. Defense establishments in many countries take the possibility of history as science very seriously.

Stepping back from military history, let's look at how the idea of a general science of history has very deep historical roots. Aristotle wrote treatises on both natural and social sciences. Ibn Khaldun, the great medieval Arab historian, developed a remarkable theory explaining the rise and fall of states. I have already mentioned Quetelet and Tolstoy. Nicolas Rashevsky's book *Looking at History Through Mathematics* came out in 1968. But neither Quetelet's ideas on social physics nor Rashevsky's mathematical history started a new scientific discipline. Science is a collective endeavor. It needs more than a single brilliant individual. For a scientific discipline to take off, there needs to be a community of scholars feeding ideas off each other and, importantly, criticizing each other's concepts and results. As the ancients said, truth is born in argument, and you cannot have a good argument with yourself, or even with a small, secret cabal that too easily develops into an "echo chamber." This is one of the reasons why Michael Flynn's cliology is pure fiction. In our universe, cliodynamics could only start gaining traction around the year 2000. The question of why is interesting not only for the future historians of cliodynamics but also because it has a bearing on one of the major objections to the possibility of history as science.

The great-man theory is the most "anti-cliodynamic" theory of history I can think of. In the words of the Scottish philosopher Thomas Carlyle, who is widely credited with advancing it:

> Universal History, the history of what man has accomplished in this world, is at bottom the History of the Great Men who have worked here. They were the leaders of men, these great ones; the

modellers, patterns, and in a wide sense creators, of whatsoever the general mass of men contrived to do or to attain; all things that we see standing accomplished in the world are properly the outer material result, the practical realization and embodiment, of Thoughts that dwelt in the Great Men sent into the world: the soul of the whole world's history, it may justly be considered, were the history of these.[15]

Whereas both fictional psychohistory and cliology, as well as real cliodynamics, are primarily concerned with large human collectives and impersonal social forces, the great-man theory rejects this focus as misguided. It is not societies that make Great Men, it is Great Men who remake societies, as the psychologist William James later argued.[16] Although this nineteenth-century theory is currently mainly discredited, its traces linger in the popular understanding of how science is moved ahead by the Great Minds. A corollary of this idea underlies one of the objections that the famous philosopher of science Karl Popper made to a science of history: it is logically impossible to know the future course of history when that course depends in part on the future growth of scientific knowledge (which is unknowable in advance).[17]

But is the future growth of scientific knowledge really unknowable— or merely unknown, given our current lack of understanding of how knowledge cumulates? To me the second alternative sounds more plausible, and here's why I think so. It's truly remarkable how many scientific discoveries were made simultaneously by more than one scientist. This is not a pattern that we would expect if science were moved by rare towering geniuses. (Why would such geniuses make the same discovery within a year of each other?)

We have already talked about Osipov and Lanchester, who discovered their eponymous equations within a year of each other. Other examples abound: the independent invention of calculus by Newton and Leibniz; the independent formulation by Darwin and Wallace of the theory of evolution by natural selection; the discovery of the model of dynamic cycles by Alfred Lotka and Vito Volterra; and many more. Probably the most revealing example concerns the discovery of genetics. As we all know, genes were discovered by the Bohemian monk Gregor Mendel. But his discovery came too early—the scientific world was not ready for it, and his article on the genetics of garden peas, published in 1866, was completely forgotten. Here was a towering genius who failed to remake science. But when the time was right, in 1900, the principles of heredity were independently discovered by Hugo de Vries, Carl Correns, and Erich von Tschermak. The only reason we call genetics "Mendelian" and not "de Vriesian" is because Correns, when he realized that his rival might be credited for this discovery, made sure to point out that Mendel had beaten them all to it.[18]

Mendel's experience, albeit with a much happier end, was repeated by one of the key members of the cliodynamic community, my good colleague Jack Goldstone, with whom I have coauthored a number of papers. Goldstone started his scientific career hoping to become a physicist. As an undergraduate at Caltech, he received a solid foundation in mathematics, but then he became interested in understanding social systems—their history and dynamics. It was as a graduate student in the sociology department at Harvard that he conceived the "demographic-structural theory" of revolutions (which provides the foundations of the cliodynamic approach to understanding why societies experience recurrent crises).

Early on in graduate school, Goldstone became interested in explaining revolutions. At that time, the prevailing view was that revolutions were just random conjunctures of intraelite conflicts, popular uprisings, and state failure brought on by foolish rulers, or particularly costly wars, or the rise of unusually potent heterodoxies or radical ideologies. Because of his background in natural sciences, Goldstone found such special-case pleading unsatisfactory. By a stroke of luck, he was introduced to the field of demography (because he was engaged as a teaching assistant in a course on this subject, which is how graduate students put bread on their tables). He started looking into what was known about population dynamics during the early modern era. In a recent reminiscence, "Demographic Structural Theory: 25 Years On," published in the journal *Cliodynamics*, he relates what happened next:

> As I gathered up the data, a clear pattern emerged. Before every major revolution or rebellion between 1500 and 1900, I found that indeed, population had grown substantially in the prior half century. This was true for the European countries involved in the "General Crisis of the 17th Century" (Portugal, Spain, England, Italy, France), the Ottoman Empire during the Celali Rebellions, and China prior to the collapse of the Ming Dynasty. It was also true for the Atlantic Revolutions of the late 18th century (America, France, the Netherlands), the European revolutions of the 19th century (in 1830 and 1848), the Ottoman Empire in the 1830s and 1840s, and prior to the Taiping Rebellion in China. Even more important, during the periods in which revolutions and major rebellions were absent in Europe, the Ottoman Empire and China, roughly from 1450 to 1550 and from 1660 to 1760, population growth was almost nil. In the earlier interval this was due to the slow recovery from the Black Death, and in the second was due to a global reversal and stagnation of population growth stemming from severe weather and a second wave of major diseases, including plague, typhoid, and respiratory illnesses.[19]

Although today, forty years later, we know much more about the demographic and structural causes of revolutions, rebellions, and civil wars, this initial insight remains valid. What followed, however, was not a tale of scientific triumph (not for a long time, at least) but an epic of adversity and perseverance.

Jack's first detailed dissertation proposal to research the relationship between population growth and revolutions was flatly rejected by his graduate committee. Goldstone then reconstituted his dissertation committee and scaled back his proposal to focus on just the English Civil War of the seventeenth century. Two years later, he successfully defended his thesis, but when he submitted it to a journal, it was summarily rejected. It took two years of further review and argument to finally publish it as the article. Publishing additional articles was a constant uphill battle. A decade later, Goldstone wrote a book that finally communicated his vision, conceived in graduate school. In the book he showed that the demographic-structural theory accurately identifies the timing of the English Revolution, the French Revolution, the English Reform Movement during the Chartist period, the Revolutions of 1830 and 1848, the Ming–Qing transition, the Taiping Rebellion, and the crisis of the Ottoman Empire. This book was quickly rejected by Cambridge University Press. Goldstone persevered, and eventually it was accepted for publication by the University of California Press. After additional mishaps and reverses, *Revolution and Rebellion in the Early Modern World* was finally published in 1991, and it is now a cliodynamic classic. Yet for a decade following its publication, it was almost completely ignored, and the UC Press didn't even bother to bring it out in paperback.[20]

Like Goldstone, I also started my scientific career as a natural scientist. But my switch to social science came much later, in 1997, when I was already in a tenured position at the University of Connecticut. Initially I expected that my foray into history would be ignored or, at best, subjected to withering criticism. And there was some of that, to be sure. But overall, and to my surprise, the new science of cliodynamics, which I launched in 2003, started getting immediate traction. Something happened around 2000 that made cliodynamics not only possible but also necessary. What was it? In a word: data. And that's what we will talk about next.

CHAPTER A2

A HISTORICAL MACROSCOPE

Centaurian Xenosociologists

A thousand Terran years ago, the physicists on the fourth planet circling Alpha Centauri invented a wonderful instrument—the macroscope. Using this device, they were able to peer through the light-years separating their planet from the nearest inhabited planet in their galactic neighborhood—Earth—and observe the rise and fall of empires built by the Terrans. The invention of the macroscope sparked a new scientific field in Alpha Centauri: xenosociology.

One hundred and seventy years ago, Woql-X!jt-URS3DF, at the time a graduate student in Centaurian University's department of xenosociology, published a dissertation that examined the social and political trends within a recently formed state, which the Terrans called the United States of America. Using the data that Woql gathered with the macroscope, Woql built a mathematical model of antebellum society (although the term *antebellum* was not yet used by historians, as the American Civil War was still ten years in the future).

One foundational equation in the model tracked the growth and movements of the American population. In the eighteenth century,

Americans had much larger families than Europeans because each farmer had plentiful land to support many children. Americans ate well and grew tall, becoming the tallest people on earth at that time. But large families translated into rapid population growth. By 1850, when Woql submitted its[1] dissertation to its graduate committee, the Eastern Seaboard states had become crammed with people. Forests had been cut down and replaced with fields, even on relatively poor soils that yielded sparse harvests. A substantial chunk of young adults found that they could not make a living off the land anymore, so they moved away.

Some went west, where there was land for the taking. Others went to the cities. At that time, America had begun industrializing, and there were new jobs created all the time. Woql's model suggested that the twin forces of industrialization and colonization of the West could absorb the burgeoning supply of workers and thus keep American society in a rough equilibrium. However, there was an additional factor that needed to be added to the equation. By the mid-nineteenth century, overpopulation in Europe had become much worse than in America, and many "surplus" Europeans chose to migrate across the Atlantic, ending up in the same cities that were absorbing the American rural population surplus. Immigration to America, which was a mere trickle before 1830, became a mighty current during the 1840s, driven by such disasters as the Irish Potato Famine and the wave of revolutions in 1848 and 1849. The immigrants competed with citizens for a finite pool of jobs. As a result, the supply of labor overwhelmed the demand, even though demand was growing due to industrialization. As it happens in economics, when the supply of a good exceeds the demand for it, the price tends to go down. In this case, the "good" was labor. As the cost of labor went down, worker wages stagnated and declined. The decrease in general well-being was reflected in declining life expectancies and decreasing statures of even native-born Americans. The growing immiseration, in turn, translated into increasing social instability and conflict. Watching from Alpha Centauri, Woql saw an explosion of urban riots as well as rural insurrections in America.

The second fundamental equation in Woql's model focused on the elite dynamics, while taking input from the demographic part. Industrialization increased the productivity of workers and resulted in sustained growth of GDP per capita. But the conditions of labor oversupply pressed down on worker wages. As worker wages stagnated, or even declined, the fruits of economic growth had to go somewhere else. They were not reaped by the state, which was very rudimentary in the nineteenth century, taking just 2 percent of the overall GDP. Instead, economic gains went to the elites—to the economic segment of them, specifically. Big fortunes were made and lost, but overall, the trend was rapid growth of top fortunes. But not only the rich grew richer—the numbers of the wealthy rapidly expanded. Many a skilled worker could start their own shop and enter the moneymaking game. Most failed, but some of these budding entrepreneurs, profiting from low wages, bootstrapped themselves into the big leagues and joined the ranks of the millionaires. Woql's equations indicated that this trend of increasing numbers and wealth among the elites would continue showing runaway growth as long as the wealth pump, resulting from the oversupply of labor (and lack of any institutions protecting workers), continued to operate.

By the time Woql started gathering data and building a model for antebellum America, other xenosociologists, using the macroscope, had amassed data on about one hundred earthly societies going into crises and then emerging from them. Previous research had identified several general principles that explained why these periodic social breakdowns occurred: popular immiseration, elite overproduction, state weakness, and geopolitical environment. The last two processes Woql decided not to include in its model. The United States was the most powerful polity in North America. Canada, Mexico, and various Native American tribes were no match. In fact, the US was expanding at the expense of Mexico and the Native Americans. The state was so rudimentary that it also was not a player. That left the first two factors: immiseration and elite overproduction. Both were trending in alarming directions. When Woql submitted its thesis, it included a prediction. According to Woql's model, the worsening immiseration and elite overproduction trends would degrade the social resilience of antebellum America to such a low point that a major breakdown was almost certain to occur by 1870 or thereabouts. Woql also pointed out that this forecast had a large degree of uncertainty. Thus, the likely breakdown could happen a decade before or after 1870. Also, based on the statistics from the one hundred cases thoroughly studied by other xenosociologists, there was a 10–15 percent chance that a major outbreak of violence, such as a revolution or civil war, could be avoided, provided that the governing elites could pull together and adopt a set of policy measures that would reverse the forces pushing antebellum America to the brink. Most importantly, they would have to stop the wealth pump. But Woql did not see any signs in 1850 that the ruling elites were even aware of the problem, or would be willing to address it should they become aware of it. (After all, keeping wages down was highly lucrative for them.) Finally, Woql's model could not make any predictions about the identities of individuals responsible for the likely rupture, as it tracked social forces, not individual people.

As we see, unlike the fictional cliologists, our (equally fictional) Centaurian xenosociologists did predict the American Civil War. As it happened, the Civil War broke out even earlier than Woql's model anticipated. Soon after Woql defended its thesis, things unraveled in America at an accelerating pace. Outbreaks of collective violence spiked during the second half of the following decade. Looking at just major outbreaks (those that resulted in ten or more fatalities), Woql saw that between 1855 and 1859, there were three Know-Nothing riots (hitting Baltimore, Washington, DC, and New Orleans); a citywide gang war in New York (also known as the Dead Rabbits riot); election riots (Bloody Monday in Louisville, Kentucky); and the culmination of the Mormon War (the Mountain Meadows Massacre). Direct preludes to the Civil War included a murderous struggle between proslavery and antislavery forces in Kansas (Bleeding Kansas) and John Brown's raid on the federal armory at Harpers Ferry, Virginia. This was immediately followed by the disputed election of 1860; the bombardment of Fort Sumter in Charleston, South Carolina; and the ensuing years-long bloodbath of the Civil War.

Today Woql is a distinguished senior scholar who holds the chair of the department of xenosociology at Centaurian University.[2] It does not do research itself, but it supervises graduate students who do. One of these is Ziql-M&rw-ALF6GR, who has been studying the contemporary US. Following in the footsteps of its teacher, Ziql used the macroscope to gather a ton of data on the dynamics of population well-being and elite overproduction between 1970 and 2010. The model Ziql built in 2010 was similar in spirit to Woql's antebellum model, but it took into account the dramatic changes that American society experienced between 1850 and 2010. In particular, Ziql added another model equation to account for the much more important role that the American state began playing after World War II. But the prediction from Ziql's 2010 model was eerily similar to Woql's 1850 one: the United States was on track for a serious outbreak of political violence that would peak in the early 2020s. There was nothing that Ziql wanted to do more than alert the earthlings to their impending doom. But the macroscope is a one-way instrument, so Ziql could only helplessly observe as the trajectory that its model predicted was realized.

How to Build Our Own Macroscope

Unfortunately, the macroscope I describe in this vignette is pure science fiction. In real life, our physicists cannot build an instrument that allows us to peer back through the mists of time.

So what can we do? I cannot overstress how much we need data. Yes, mathematical models are an essential part of cliodynamics. And, of course, sometimes even a purely abstract model can yield an unexpected and powerful insight—as we saw with Lanchester's square law (chapter A1). But models work best when they are fed data.

To get the data, we need not physicists but historians. Unfortunately, many historians take a dim view of cliodynamics, fearing that its goal is to replace them. These fears are fed by many a journalist who puts pen to paper on the subject of cliodynamics without understanding what it is about. Nothing could be further from the truth. Cliodynamics needs history and cannot exist without historians doing what they know best—broadening and deepening the store of our knowledge about past societies.

Historians, archaeologists, and other scholars of the past have collectively built a huge store of knowledge. This information needs to be translated into a form amenable to analysis with the tools of cliodynamics. It's not an easy thing to do. There are many gaps—a lot of historical territory is mostly or even completely dark to us. Quantitative estimates are hard to get, and where we have them, they come with much uncertainty. Historians themselves often disagree, sometimes over quite fundamental issues. But we can overcome these difficulties.

I can say this with confidence because a successful "historical macroscope" has, in fact, been built. It is called Seshat: Global History Databank.[3] It's imperfect, and a lot more work is needed to improve it further, but the Seshat project has already proven that getting historical data is possible. Furthermore, Seshat is not the only project that has been converting the knowledge of historians into data.

I'll use Seshat to illustrate how we can go about gathering historical data, because it is the most sophisticated project (in my humble opinion) and because it is the one I know from the inside out. But later in the chapter, I will talk about other similar projects. Running a little ahead of the story, I can say that the sudden blossoming of data-based approaches to history explains why cliodynamics became not only possible but also required after 2000.

Proxies

How do we create historical databases? Paraphrasing Thomas Edison, we need both inspiration and (a lot of) perspiration.[4] Let's talk about inspiration first.

For past societies, unlike for modern ones, we don't have an abundance of data yearly churned out by government agencies and private pollsters. The further we go back in time, the less there are systematic data directly measuring quantities that we need to feed into our models. Where we possess such sources, such as the Domesday Book[5] or Chinese local gazetteers,[6] we eagerly squeeze them for any information they can yield. But where such troves are not available (which is the usual case), we have to rely on indirect indicators, or "proxies."

The use of proxies is most familiar in such historical sciences as paleoclimatology. Paleoclimatologists use a variety of proxies to reconstruct climate dynamics on Earth reaching thousands and millions of years back: ice cores, sediment cores, tree rings, and pollen counts. Because these are all indirect indicators of climatic conditions prevailing during various historical periods and geologic eras, much care needs to be taken to identify and remove various biases affecting the measurements. For this reason, a multi-proxy approach is best, as it allows us to see how well different proxies agree (or disagree) with each other and to make an informed judgment about how to combine them in the best way.

In the study of human history, the use of proxies is even more widespread because there are many more things we want to know about earlier societies than simply what the temperature or precipitation was at some point in the past. For example, one of the most fundamental things we need to know about any particular society is its size, which is also a key variable in the cliodynamic models of social resilience or breakdown. How many lived in the Roman Empire? And how did this population change from one generation to the next? Each person leaves traces that persist after they die. People eat—and defecate. They typically live in houses or in other kinds of dwellings. They wear clothes and shoes, and they work tilling land or making pots and jewelry. Each different activity leaves traces that could provide a potential proxy for measuring population change.

Thus, a growing population in a particular region requires more food, which necessitates clearing more land for agriculture. As forests are cut down, the composition of pollen blown by wind to lakes, where pollen grains settle to the bottom, changes from that dominated by tree species to that of crops, weeds, and grasses. By examining cores taken from lake bottoms, palynologists (pollen specialists) can reconstruct the environmental history of the region and infer periods when the regional population burgeoned and, alternatively, when it dwindled.

Another way to measure population rises and declines is to look at new house construction, whether resulting in village growth or the founding of new villages. By coring the large beams that have been preserved (even after the original structures collapse), dendrochronologists (tree-ring specialists) can determine the precise year when the trees from which the beams came were cut down. By collecting hundreds or even thousands of such dates, we can determine when there were spurts of building activity, indicative of a growing population that needed additional housing.

People generate a lot of waste. This is true today, and it was true in the past, even though the nature of trash has changed. The rate at which garbage—well, perhaps I should use the more scientifically correct *anthropogenic rubbish!*—accumulates is indicative of how many people there are. Potsherds are one of the most useful indicators of this. Potsherds are essentially eternal—it would require a geological submergence to get rid of them. They can be dated. Potsherds are generated because pots are constantly used in cooking and food storage, and sooner or later, pots inevitably break.

I could keep going on, but the point is clear. Not all proxies for population are available in any particular region or historical era, but we can often develop several of them. Each proxy may suffer from a systematic problem (bias), but it is possible to reconstruct population dynamics by comparing and contrasting multiple such indicators with different biases. As a result, there are currently decent reconstructions of both regional and global population dynamics.[7] They are far from perfect, but they already provide us with a lot of insight into how populations changed in the past. Even more importantly, this is a very intense area of current research, and thus these estimates are constantly being refined and getting better.

The Bones of History

One particularly rich source of proxies, even if a rather macabre one, is human remains. Human skeletons have a remarkable staying power. Those of you who watched the popular television series *The Sopranos* may recollect the scene in which two Soprano gangsters are sent by their boss to dispose of the remains of several victims, previously buried on a farm in upstate New York.[8] They dig up the skeletons, break the bones with hammers, and then throw the pieces into the lake. As many murderers know, disposing of dead bodies is hard work.

Skeletons easily persist over hundreds and even thousands of years (provided they are not deposited in acidic soil). Each skeleton is a trove of information. My readers surely know that we can now reliably extract and sequence ancient DNA, a technology that has literally revolutionized the study of our past.[9] Old theories have been overthrown and new ones advanced, thanks to the steady flow of ancient DNA (aDNA) data, and we've just started. But the old bones yield many other clues about the past.

One of the easiest measurements that we can take is the overall height of the person whose bones we are lucky to have. If the skeleton is incomplete, no worries. By measuring the length of one of the major bones (e.g., a femur) and using a table of correspondences, we can estimate the overall height quite accurately. Human height is a great indicator of biological well-being. People living under environmental stresses, such as malnutrition, high disease or parasite burdens, or poor living conditions (lack of fresh air and sunlight), grow up stunted. Of course, height is affected by many other factors—in particular, how tall your parents are. But when we average the heights of each generation that lived in a particular region, we buff out individual variations and obtain a remarkably accurate proxy for general population well-being. Population crowding and pressure on resources, for example, reliably reduce the average height. In chapter 1, I mentioned that one of the reasons we know why American workers faired poorly in the nineteenth century is because the average height of native-born Americans declined by a whopping five centimeters. These height data were obtained by measuring living people, but nothing prevents us from getting the same data from the dead. There are millions of skeletons in just European museums alone, covering thousands of years of European history. These skeletons yielded remarkable insights into the population history of Europe.[10]

But we are not done yet. Using methods of modern forensic science, archaeologists have been studying not only how people lived in the past but also how they died. Violent death often leaves telltale marks on skeletons. A stone or metal arrowhead stuck in a vertebra is, of course, a dead giveaway (pun intended). Lethal sword and axe cuts are also easy to detect. The effects of being pummeled with a club are a bit harder to identify with confidence, because bones can be broken as a result of falls and other accidents. But an unusually high frequency of breaks on the left ulna (forearm) are good indicators of violence committed with blunt objects. Just imagine your reaction if someone were about to hit you with a baseball bat. Your arms would likely go up in an attempt to protect your head, and if your attacker was right-handed, you would be hit on the left forearm.

Of course, not all cases of violent death leave detectable marks on the bones. An arrow piercing the stomach is a sure and painful way to die. If the arrow is removed, no traces remain once the soft tissues decay. But again, our interest is not in what happened to a particular person. Each death is a tragedy, of course, but a thousand deaths give us data.[11] If in one generation the proportion of skeletons with clear evidence of violent death is 3 percent, and in the next 30 percent, clearly the level of violence has exploded.

Skeletons can also tell us about where people were born and whether they moved; what kind of diet they ate; and something about the diseases from which they suffered. And this is just one, if unusually rich, source of proxies.

What Parish Registers Can Tell Us About the English Revolution

Inspiration, then, is needed to come up with clever proxies that allow us to detect how different variables we are interested in change over time. But the rest—99 percent of it—is perspiration. We don't have smart robots capable of reading and understanding a tax return written in crabbed handwriting on molding vellum using medieval Latin, at least not yet. So the job has to be done by professional historians. Most nonhistorians don't understand the significance and huge value of this work. And the amount of training needed to perform it well. Can you read what's written on a Babylonian clay tablet? Very few people can.

But what is the value of unearthing facts about some long-dead people? What does it have to do with us? For example, who cares that Susannah, daughter of William Dunkhorn and Martha, his wife (late Allen spinster), was born on November 21, 1796, and baptized privately on November 27, 1796?[12] Or that Mr. George Knaggs, gent of Pollington, aged seventy-four, was buried on December 25, 1723? The death of Mr. Knaggs might or might not have been a tragedy (after all, he passed away at the ripe old age of seventy-four), but a thousand such burial records is surely a statistic. And this statistic, when combined with other data and placed within the framework of cliodynamic equations, can tell us a lot about what's happening to the society we want to understand, including whether it is approaching a crisis.

Parish records are the raw data for a demographic technique of family reconstruction that was developed by the French demographers Louis Henry and Michel Fleury in the 1950s. Before computers became ubiquitous, researchers had to do everything by hand. First, they traveled to parish churches and transcribed on cards the events recorded in the parish records (baptisms, marriages, and burials). Next, back at their universities, they sorted the cards in different ways several times, following a specific protocol. This procedure enabled them to link events belonging to the same family and then summarize them on the family card. For example, one card tells us that Martha was born in 1796. Another one tells us that she was married in 1828. The burial register says that she died in 1860. She had four children, whose life trajectories we trace in the same way. As we add more and more individuals to our database, we get an increasingly better idea of how the overall population grew (or declined).

There are many practical difficulties in implementing this approach. Parish books got damaged (eaten by mice) or lost (when churches burned down, for example). Names were misspelled by clerks recording the events. Family records are often incomplete because people moved in and out of the parishes. One way of dealing with this is by doing more work. The more parishes you add to the database, the fewer gaps there will be in the data. Of course, if a family moved to a different country, you would still lose sight of them. In any case, no data set, especially a large one, is perfect. There are always data gaps and errors, but they don't negate the value of the data; we just need to take care of such problems during the analysis stage.

This is how parish records allow demographers to study the population history of a country before official censuses. For example, in Great

Britain the first census was run at a very early date compared to other nations—1801. Thus, we have detailed understanding of the population history of the UK for the last two centuries. But parish registers were introduced in England in 1538. The Cambridge Group for the History of Population & Social Structure started working on them in the 1960s. In 1981, two members of the group, E. A. Wrigley and R. S. Schofield, published *The Population History of England, 1541–1871: A Reconstruction*, thus extending our knowledge of the demographic dynamics in England (and Wales) back in time for nearly three centuries before the first modern census.

At the same time that the Cambridge demographers were completing their analysis of the population trends in early modern England, Jack Goldstone, as we learned in the previous chapter, had hit the first roadblock in his quest to develop the demographic-structural theory of revolutions and rebellions. Following the disastrous meeting of his PhD committee, in which his professors summarily rejected his initial, ambitious proposal, Goldstone retreated to his apartment to lick his wounds and decide what to do next.

Thanks to the work of the Cambridge Group, Goldstone felt that he was on solid ground with data on population dynamics—the key driver in the theory he proposed—for at least one of his cases, the English Revolution of 1640. In particular, the high-quality demographic data from the Cambridge Group confirmed that the population of England grew rapidly before 1640 and declined thereafter. There was also solid data on wages, elite mobility, and royal finances. The trends in these data were all perfectly in line with Goldstone's theory. Goldstone scaled down his PhD proposal to focus on early modern England, and this less ambitious proposal was accepted by his committee. It was the availability of large quantities of quality data on early modern England that made the difference.

The Personal Computer Revolution

Another and seemingly unrelated event that happened in 1981 was the introduction of the IBM PC, which became the first truly mass-market computer. Remember that the data Goldstone used in his PhD thesis was a result of incredibly labor-consuming research. Gradually, the plentiful computer power and storage revolutionized data sciences, introducing the era of Big Data. Historians were latecomers to this feast, but they gradually became enthusiastic participants. Digital history is now an established discipline with academic journals and its own department at a number of universities.

Seshat

Unlike Goldstone, I decided to become a cliodynamicist after I had already had a successful career as a theoretical biologist. I was in a tenured position at a good university and could thus afford a risky change of field. In my previous field, population dynamics, I had already encountered resistance to mathematical models from the empirical biologists, with their emphasis on studying organisms in the field. But my other mathematical ecology colleagues and I learned how to persuade empiricists of the value of models. We could point to the success of such population-ecology models as the Lotka-Volterra equations for predator-prey cycles. Before the independent discovery of this model by Alfred Lotka in 1925 and Vito Volterra in 1926 (one of these cases of simultaneous scientific breakthrough), ecologists were puzzled by why the populations of many animals—for example, Norwegian lemmings—go through repeated boom-and-bust cycles. They hypothesized that it could be due to climate fluctuations, but weather records did not support this idea. The discovery that the population interaction between predators and prey could generate cycles "endogenously," without being driven by external, or exogenous, factors was a huge surprise. As I already mentioned in relation to Lanchester's square law, one of the values of mathematics is that it can give us purely logical insights into a problem or puzzle we are trying to solve. Mathematical equations, and more recently computer models, are a wonderful crutch for the mind.

When I started studying the dynamical processes in human history, I fully expected that an "alien" invasion onto the historians' turf would generate enormous resistance. Rather than conducting a frontal attack, to borrow a military metaphor, I instead resolved to make a flanking maneuver. While the great majority of historians have been resolutely opposed to mathematical approaches to history, experts in a variety of related disciplines that could broadly be called historical social sciences were much more receptive to such ideas. By 2000, many social scientists interested in understanding history were chafing under the constraints imposed on their research by the "cultural turn" that denied the value of, or even the need for, quantitative approaches. These swings in collective mood are quite typical in the social sciences. The cultural turn was a reaction by young generations of scholars against the quantitative approaches fashionable during the 1970s, such as cliometrics (quantitative economic history) and processual archaeology (whose adherents advocated a rigorous application of the scientific method). The critics prevailed then and established a new orthodoxy, but now it was their turn to be criticized by the next generations. The seed of cliodynamics thus fell on prepared soil.

It didn't take much time to find allies in historical sociology (including Jack Goldstone), in environmental and economic history, and in evolutionary anthropology. We did not necessarily agree on what were the main drivers explaining various empirical patterns we saw, but we agreed that theories need to be buttressed by models, and that theoretical predictions need to be tested with data.

By that point, roughly 2010, there was a sea of information to swim in, thanks to computers becoming widely used by historians and archaeologists, as was signaled by the rise of the digital humanities. In fact, we were embarrassed by the riches rather than crushed by poverty. Building grand theories was much easier in the days of Karl Marx, when so little data on historical societies were available (and a Eurocentric focus ensured that data came from similar societies). But building better theories was made possible by the new abundance of data.

But how to get at all that knowledge? Some of this knowledge was already converted into data—numbers arranged in rows and columns within spreadsheets, which could be downloaded and fed into analysis. But even such digitized information was not problem-free, because it often lacked what data scientists call metadata, or data about data, that explained what the numbers meant. For example, columns in the spreadsheet could have uninformative headings like "Var23," "Var24," etc., referring to the variables number twenty-three, twenty-four, and so on. But what did "Var23" stand for?

And only a small proportion of knowledge was digitized. Most of it was spread across books and articles in academic journals, or in the hard to get "gray literature," such as archaeological site reports. Some of it simply resided in the heads of individual scholars. It would have been great to have had a spiderbot that crawled through experts' brains and harvested from them the information we needed. But that's science fiction, again. So we had to do it the hard way.

The real-life historical macroscope is called Seshat: Global History

Databank. The Seshat project was launched in 2011, when I met social anthropologist Harvey Whitehouse at a meeting. When I ran the idea of a historical database by Harvey, he immediately saw its great potential, and we agreed to add it as a component to a large grant proposal he was putting together at the time. Fortunately for us, the proposal was funded, and we started recruiting research assistants, experts, and a postdoc. The project expanded by adding anthropologists, historians, archaeologists, and data scientists to help us with the technical aspects of database building.

Initially, our idea was that all data in Seshat would be collected by experts—academic historians, archaeologists, and other scholars of the past. However, we quickly discovered that this approach had serious drawbacks, even with historians who were very enthusiastic about the Seshat project. For example, asking experts to fill in hundreds of boxes is a horrible misuse of their expertise. For many variables, once you have established an effective coding scheme, 80–90 percent of data can be accurately entered by well-trained research assistants working with standard texts. Consequently, we realized that the time and effort of experts is a highly valuable resource, and it should be deployed strategically, where it is truly needed—resolving difficult coding issues and locating elusive information. Furthermore, only an expert can make the judgment that the field doesn't know about a particular variable— that it is a true knowledge gap.

Most of the data entry into Seshat is thus done by research assistants (RAs). At the beginning of the project, we experimented with different types of assistants. We discovered that using temporary undergraduate student labor was not a viable approach. It simply didn't make sense to invest several months into training RAs, determining their accuracy and efficiency, only to then lose them for good. As a result, we shifted resources to hiring long-term RAs who work on the project for at least a year, and usually for many years. All of our RAs have at least bachelor's degrees or the equivalent; many have master's degrees, and some even have PhDs.

The third crucial element in our data-gathering process is the close supervision of RAs by PhD-level social scientists, who include Seshat postdocs, regional editors (each with expertise in a certain part of the world), variables coordinators (who each focus on a particular set of Seshat variables), and Seshat directors (currently consisting of three historians, an anthropologist, an archaeologist, and a complexity scientist). Their role is to train the RAs, check their coding decisions, and ensure consistent application of the coding schemes. It would not be possible to have generated so much high-quality historical data, as we have done, without the incredible hard work of our RAs and the extreme generosity of our expert collaborators, who donate their time and knowledge to help our project.

We discovered that our best data are collected when all three groups (RAs, expert scholars, and social scientists) work together. When we begin coding a particular Seshat "polity" (a politically independent society bracketed by a start date and an end date), we get expert help in suggesting a set of standard texts and answers to general questions. For example, what dates should we use as the start and end dates for this polity? RAs are then instructed to get as much data coded from standard sources as they can, using a "low-hanging fruit" approach. In other words, if they do not quickly discover an answer, they stop researching the question and add it to a list of issues to resolve later with expert help. Once this phase is over, we go back to the experts with a list of questions addressing data gaps and difficult coding decisions. We also often run specialized workshops that bring together members of the Seshat project with experts who focus on either world regions (e.g., Egypt, South-east Asia) or specific variables (e.g., ritual and religion, agricultural productivity).

In summary, expanding the Seshat Databank, and especially finding data for difficult-to-code variables, is a result of collaboration among experts and the Seshat staff. This process combines experts' special-ized knowledge of particular historical societies with our experience in translating historical knowledge into data.

As mentioned above, establishing an effective coding scheme is a key feature of making the Seshat project work. If variable definitions are too vague, or too abstract, or require too much interpretation, then they become difficult to code, and the chances that there will be dis-agreements between coders increase. For example, when gathering data into Seshat, we avoid forcing information about a past society into an arbitrary scale (e.g., "rate the social complexity of this society on a scale from 0 to 10"). Prior to collecting the data, we run a workshop, usually involving experts, that develops an understanding of how to code a particular aspect that we aim to capture in Seshat. Generally speaking, we aim to use a quantitative variable (e.g., an estimate of the population of the coded polity) or break up complex variables into mul-tiple simple variables that can be coded in a binary fashion (e.g., absent/present). The initial coding scheme is then tested by Seshat RAs, who apply it to several test cases, working in consultation with the experts. The coding scheme is then refined, based on suggestions from both ex-perts and RAs, and applied to the whole sample. Sometimes we dis-cover that we must adjust the coding scheme after a substantial number of polities have already been coded using the old one. Switching to a better definition results in a certain amount of inefficiency, as RAs have to go back to already coded polities and recode them using the new scheme. This process takes time, and such old codes sometimes linger in the databank until eventually encountered and corrected.

Before using Seshat data in statistical analyses, we run a systematic data quality check. Every data point is checked by an RA other than the one who entered it.

Seshat is a massive, complex, "living" entity that constantly evolves. In a project as large and multifaceted as Seshat, and with an underlying database as vast as this one is, there will inevitably be some practical constraints on obtaining accurate or representative values or codes for specific variables because, for example, a particular bit of information has been published in an obscure source, or there is new information of which we are not yet aware that changes the coded value. We don't wait until this "cleaning" process is over—because it is never over. Our approach is thus to address such remaining problems as we discover them, gradually making the databank better, while understanding that there will always be some errors in the data. The suggestions and critiques of other scholars are very useful in this regard. We all benefit by bringing these issues out into the open—the systematic nature of Seshat helps concentrate these discussions and identify where there are disagreements, uncertainties, and gaps in knowledge. Further, as new historical and archaeological knowledge becomes available, we aim to include it in Seshat.

CrisisDB

Until 2020, the main thrust of our data collection and statistical analysis of the collected data was to answer one particular Big Question. At the beginning of the Holocene, roughly ten thousand years ago, all humans lived in relatively egalitarian small-scale societies of hundreds or several thousand people. Today nearly all people (with the exception of a few indigenous groups in Amazonia and other faraway places) live in large-scale societies, with two, China and India, having populations exceeding one billion people. A new form of political organization, the state, arose in the mid-Holocene and has by now taken over the world. Technology has become very sophisticated and economies highly productive, increasing the quality of life for many people. On the darker side, increased well-being has not been evenly shared, and complex societies, both in the past and today, are highly unequal. The Big Question we wanted to answer was: How and why did this "great Holocene transformation" happen? Although I can't claim that we answered this question to the satisfaction of everybody, we certainly made a lot of progress. Many theories proposed by modern social scientists, as well as by great philosophers from the past, have been rejected by the data we collected in Seshat. As the field of supported theories narrows, we gain an increasingly better understanding of the driving forces that transformed our societies into what they are today.[13]

As data collection needed to answer this particular Big Question wound down, we gradually switched to a new Big Question: Why do complex societies periodically get into trouble? What are the factors explaining recurrent waves of high internal instability, state breakdown, and outright civil war? This question is usually formulated as: Why do complex societies collapse? In the last decade, a whole new scientific discipline, appropriately called collapsology,[14] has arisen to answer this question. To tell the truth, I am not much enamored of this new direction. What's "collapse," anyway? As I discuss in chapter 2, which relays what our macroscope sees in the past, outright collapse is only one possible outcome when societies get into trouble. Sometimes civil wars, massacres, and breakdowns of productive infrastructure, accompanied by epidemics, do indeed destroy the fabric of societies, resulting in huge population declines, simplification of governing institutions, and partial loss of knowledge. But some past societies emerged from their crises in a relatively bloodless way by implementing the right set of institutions that addressed the deep structural forces driving them to the edge. And most exits from crisis fall in between these two extremes. Why focus only on collapse? Aren't we interested in knowing how societies managed to avoid it so that we can draw lessons of possible relevance to us today?

This is why we decided to name the Seshat offshoot CrisisDB ("DB" stands for "database"). We have identified about three hundred cases of crisis, spanning from the Neolithic period to the present and located in all major continents of the world. Our goal is to test theories about why societies go into crisis. But equally important, we aim to understand why some exits from crisis were truly horrible, while others were relatively benign. What did the leaders and people do wrong in the first set of cases? And what did they do right in the second set?

Data collection for CrisisDB follows the approach that we have already refined for "classic" Seshat. This is a long, arduous process, and we are not done with it yet. Currently, we have good data on about one hundred of the crisis cases, or a third of what the database will eventually contain. This is enough for us to discern the main patterns. These "lessons from history" are the subject of chapter 2.

THE STRUCTURAL DYNAMIC APPROACH

Cherry-Picking and the Bed of Procrustes

The main purpose of historical examples, which I have used profusely in this book, is to illustrate how different parts of the cliodynamic theory of social breakdown and renewal work. The approach here is very different from that of books written by specialist historians and books written by what I'll call amateur armchair theorists.

Narratives, written by historians who have delved deeply into a period and region that they know best, are always illuminating. But no single scholar, no matter how brilliant she is, can master more than a limited number of historical case studies. As a result, we can gain from a historian's narrative a deep understanding of how a particular society slid into a crisis and then emerged from it, but we cannot separate the special circumstances, pertaining to here and now, from general principles applicable to there and then. And we need to understand general principles if we want to apply the lessons of history to help our own society weather the crisis in an optimal way. After all, each society is unique, and mechanically transferring what we learned by studying the Late Medieval Crisis in France, or the Taiping Rebellion in China, or even the American Civil War to the current crisis in the USA, or the predicaments of France and Germany, is not going to work. To learn from history, we need to separate the specifics and peculiarities from general principles. Also, we need to gain a general understanding of how certain special features of a society interact with general mechanisms of crisis and renewal. As an example of such an interplay between the general and the specific, we learned in chapter 2 that the degree of polygamy among the elites has a strong effect on the rate at which elite overproduction develops. Our general theory, therefore, needs to be able to identify other special characteristics of societies that shape the breakdown/renewal cycles.

While historian narratives can be deeply informative (even if they cannot help us with the problem of separating the general from the specific), the work of amateur armchair theorists is generally useless. These authors are typically not historians, and they often know very little history. Ignorance is liberating, but not enough. Amateur theorists use two "techniques" to build their grand narratives. The first one is cherry-picking, selecting only historical examples that fit their pet theories. The second one is the Bed of Procrustes, which enables them—stretching a little here, cutting off a bit there—to force various historical examples to conform to fixed cycles postulated by their theories. Ninety-nine percent of "cyclic history" suffers from one or both of these problems. It's so bad that I tend to avoid the word *cycle* in my professional articles because it comes with so much negative baggage. (Instead I talk about "oscillations," "boom-bust dynamics," etc.)

Cliodynamics is different. It assembles the huge body of knowledge collected by professional historians and then uses it in an objective scientific way. We want to know both what the general patterns are and how much variation around them is exhibited by different societies and different historical eras. Theoretical ideas must be translated into explicit dynamical models so that we can be sure about what assumptions lead to what predictions. And these predictions are tested against the data. This is a lot of work, and no single individual is capable of doing everything. It requires a whole scientific field, division of labor, constant trial and error, and constructive disagreement and debate. We are at the beginnings of this new science of history, and much more work is needed. But the insights that have already come from cliodynamics, despite the youth of the discipline, show that the endeavor is not hopeless. We need to continue working because the stakes are so high. Social breakdown and internal warfare kill people, wreck economies, and roll back human achievement. We must develop a clear-eyed understanding of why it happens so that we can avoid the endless cycle of recurrent waves of instability and violence.

Social Dynamics as an Aggregate

When cliodynamicists want to understand why, and how, our societies end up in crisis, and how we can get out of crisis with the least amount of bloodshed, they build mathematical models. These models track the internal workings of social systems by aggregating the myriads of individuals, each unique and having free will. Many traditional historians and laypeople find this approach wrongheaded or even distasteful because it appears to somehow dehumanize real people. Nevertheless, if we want to understand social dynamics and predict the effect of possible solutions, we have to do it. Why? Because it works.

Demographers working for such agencies as the Social Security Administration (SSA) must make projections about how much money the SSA will need next year, in five years, and further in the future. They use models that aggregate people by their ages and by how much

Social Security taxes they have already paid. Each individual is unique, but demographic models are remarkably accurate at forecasting what will happen to the aggregate population of retirees in the future. When you buy a car, your insurance premium will be calculated based on your generic characteristics. If you are a twenty-year-old male, prepare to be charged a higher insurance rate. This may be unfair, because you may happen to be a particularly careful driver, but if you want to drive, you will have to pay. If you get a speeding ticket, your premium will be increased. Each traffic accident is unique, but actuaries are exceedingly good at figuring out how to balance the risks so that the insurance companies, for which they work, don't go bankrupt.

Cliodynamicists use a similar approach. We know that people in a particular group (e.g., men without college degrees with earnings in the fifth decile of wage distribution) are not the same. But a model making this assumption works, just as demographic and actuarial models work.

At the same time, I don't want to limit the ideas and insights I discuss in this book to only tracking impersonal social forces. All social action is a result of summing together the acts of individual people. And impersonal forces shape the lives and attitudes of individuals. We want to understand both societies and people. So what to do?

The approach I chose for this book was to shift the focus of the narrative between the individual point of view and what happens at the aggregate, societal level. This is why chapters 3, 4, and 5 start with vignettes tracing a particular member of a social stratum, or class, that the chapter is about. Each individual is entirely fictional but based on my more than four decades of studying American society from the inside (my apologies to my non-American readers, but I must write about what I know best). At the same time, I did not grow up in this country, having immigrated to America when I was twenty. But, I would argue, this is actually an advantage—just as a xenosociologist observing Earth from Alpha Centauri has an analytic advantage over the humans who live through an age of discord and whose reason is often clouded by partisan passions. You, the reader, will be the final judge of whether I succeeded in this.

Structure and Dynamics

From the point of view of complexity science, human societies are complex dynamical systems. Scientists studying such systems have developed a set of theoretical tools that allow them to understand how these societies function and evolve. This understanding provides a basis for making forecasts about possible future trajectories and, more importantly, predicting possible systemic responses to various interventions.

Complexity science works. We know this from its successes in understanding biological systems (such as ecosystems) and physical systems (for example, global climate). The study of social systems is not quite as advanced as that of natural systems, but we are making great strides here too. In this book I use the theoretical tools developed by complexity scientists. How does this work in practice?

The first question we need to ask about a system is: What is its structure—its internal composition? Societies are not like containers with ideal gas beloved by statistical physicists. Unlike molecules, each human being is unique. Furthermore, all people belong to various kinds of groups, and those can belong to other, larger-scale groups. A society can be thought of as a group of groups of groups. People belonging to the same group may share collective interests, which makes this collection of individuals an interest group. One particular interest group on which this book focuses is ruling elites, or the "ruling class." These are the people who concentrate most of the social power within a state in their hands. They are the ones who make decisions at the level of the whole society on matters such as war and peace, social and economic policy, taxation and redistribution of resources, and legislation and law enforcement.

Interest groups vary in their ability to advance their collective interests. Partly this is due to how much power is wielded separately by each individual belonging to the group. For example, for economic elites, we want to know an individual's wealth (wealth being a kind of power). For military elites, such as medieval nobility, we want to know how well these warriors are armed, armored, and trained, and how large their military retinues are. But individual power is just the beginning. The power of an interest group critically depends on its social cohesion and political organization. If members of the group work at cross-purposes, or even actively struggle against each other, no matter how powerful individuals are, the collective power will be zero. Similarly, all effective collective action requires good organization. A disciplined, well-structured army will always defeat an unorganized mob of individually powerful warriors. Similarly, by virtue of being already organized into a corporate hierarchy, the bosses have a structural advantage over the workers, unless the workers organize in a labor union. Organization, if not everything, is one of the most important things you want to know to gauge an interest group's power.

Understanding how a society is structured—what the various interest groups are and how much relative power they have—is the first step in this kind of analysis. The second question concerns dynamics. How does an interplay of contending or cooperating interest groups affect the change at the system level over time? How do interests and relative capacities of groups evolve? This is where history matters. In order to answer such questions as "Is this society on the brink of collapse?" we need to understand how it got to the current stage of fragility (or, vice versa, resilient stability). What are the trends affecting the interests and power levels of various groups, and are they likely to undergo a trend reversal or continue developing in the same direction?

This structural-dynamic approach is quite standard in complexity and systems science. It's an important part of the tool kit of cliodynamics because it is explicitly historical—this is where the dynamics part comes in. It also allows us to better understand how individual actions percolate up to the societal level, because individual action is mediated by the interest groups to which the individual belongs.

Let's now talk about what I mean by "interest." The approach I follow is quite materialistic. It assumes that humans want to increase their well-being. Put simply (nearly) everybody prefers to have more money. Thus, workers favor higher wages, while employers prefer to pay lower wages. This is a good start, but we humans are complicated creatures, and there is a lot of heterogeneity among us in our values and preferences. Some people place a higher value on leisure and others on money. Some are motivated by purely material concerns, while others give more weight to intangibles like fairness and cooperation. People can also act against their material interests because they misunderstand them, or are misled by manipulative others. Asking people about their interests by, for example, sociological polls does not always work, because responders often lie about their motivations (sometimes even to themselves). The mind of another is an enigma wrapped in darkness (at least until we learn how to read minds).

Fortunately, many of these problems go away when all we need to know is group interests. Large enough groups are likely to have a mixture of different types, with altruistic and antisocial elements mostly canceling each other out. Groups, especially organized ones, may also use internal communication channels to agree on common goals. As a result, groups often converge on a common denominator of the shared material interests.

Material interests, however, are not limited to just economic well-being. Antebellum Northern businessmen, for example, saw their wealth increase, but they lacked power to influence national policy in the directions they favored (for example, on the tariffs and internal improvements). Group interests thus may include economic and political dimensions, as well as military (concern for security or domination) and ideological (maintaining legitimacy and status) ones. Furthermore, a group may be focused on its narrow, parochial interest, or it may adopt a more prosocial stance, taking the long view. For example, employer organizations may fight against unions' demands for higher wages to the death or agree to compromise, understanding that paying higher wages increases the purchasing power of workers, which is an important driver of economic growth, ultimately benefiting the whole society. This dilemma between short-term selfish advantage and long-term broad interest is particularly acute for ruling classes, whose selfishness may be punished when their polities go down.

Motivation by prosocial concerns is one possible reason why a group doesn't push its narrow interests. Another reason why groups may not act in their interests is because they are swayed by effective propaganda. A much-discussed, if somewhat controversial, example of this can be found in *What's the Matter with Kansas?: How Conservatives Won the Heart of America*, in which Thomas Frank explains why working Americans have started to vote against their economic interests.

This brings me to the last issue we need to resolve—lying. My general stance here is that, as long as a technology for reading minds is absent, the "real" motivations of people are unknowable. Again, the mind of another is an enigma wrapped in darkness. Fortunately, the "group mind," a process of collective decision-making, is knowable. And that's what we really care about. Group minds are a result of collective discussion and working out of a consensus, which can be listened to (unlike an unreadable mind). Arriving at a common program of action often leaves physical traces, such as meeting minutes and programmatic documents. Of course, some groups are quite secretive about their inner decision-making processes. Here's where whistleblowers like Julian Assange and Edward Snowden become essential for a sociologist of power.

Where we lack such inside information, we are thrown back to deducing a group's agenda by the consequences of its actions. Pragmatically, though, it is always a good idea to start by assuming that a group will pursue the material interests of its members. Those who claim otherwise—that the group is behaving prosocially, in the interest of a larger society or the whole of humanity—need to go an extra mile to show that they are not feeding us a load of bullshit. Equally, when a group goes against its interests because its members are misled by propaganda—again, we need evidence supporting this claim. This stance may strike my readers as cynical, but I think it works as a research agenda. I don't claim that people always act in their self-interests. (I wrote a whole book about it, *Ultrasociety*.) But when investigating interest groups (rather than individuals), and especially elite ones, it's the approach I take in this book.

NOTES

PREFACE

1. For the origins of this quote, please see https://quoteinvestigator.com/2015/09/16/history/.

CHAPTER 1: ELITES, ELITE OVERPRODUCTION, AND THE ROAD TO CRISIS

1. Calculated from 2019 US Federal Reserve Board data, a net worth of $1,219,126 is the threshold for entry into the top 10 percent in the US. See "Average, Median, Top 1%, and all United States Net Worth Percentiles" DQYDJ, accessed August 10, 2022, https://dqydj.com/average-median-top-net-worth-percentiles/.
2. Calculated using *24/7 Wall St.*'s 2020 peak wealth estimates and a ~$10 million net worth threshold. See Michael Sauter, Grant Suneson, and Samuel Stebbins, "The Net Worth of the American Presidents: Washington to Trump," *24/7 Wall St.*, March 2, 2020, https://247wallst.com/special-report/2020/03/02/the-net-worth-of-the-american-presidents-washington-to-trump-3/.
3. Jennifer Taylor, "Here's How Much Every Living US President Is Worth: Where Does Biden Rank?" GOBankingRates, May 30, 2022, https://www.gobankingrates.com/net-worth/politicians/heres-how-much-every-living-us-president-is-worth/.
4. This is a compression of the actual quote. See Andrew Robinson, "Did

Einstein really say that?" *Nature* 557 (2018): 30, https://doi.org/10.1038/d41586-018-05004-4.

5. Note that I use the term *class* not in a Marxist sense (where it is defined by the role of individuals in the production process) but in the sense of a group of individuals who have the same socioeconomic status—most importantly, similar levels of wealth and educational attainment.

6. Edward N. Wolff, "Household Wealth Trends in the United States, 1962 to 2019: Median Wealth Rebounds . . . but Not Enough." NBER Working Paper No. 28383, National Bureau of Economic Research, Cambridge, MA, January 2021, https://www.nber.org/system/files/working_papers/w28383/w28383.pdf.

7. But not by all. See Kevin Phillips, *Wealth and Democracy: A Political History of the American Rich* (New York: Broadway Books, 2002); Paul Krugman, *The Conscience of a Liberal* (New York: W. W. Norton, 2007); and Joseph E. Stiglitz, *The Price of Inequality: How Today's Divided Society Endangers Our Future* (New York: W. W. Norton, 2012).

8. "Election Trends," OpenSecrets, accessed August 10, 2022, https://www.opensecrets.org/elections-overview/election-trends.

9. From the 1970s to the 2010s, US government spending, as a percentage of the GDP, fluctuated between 19 and 21 percent. See "Federal Net Outlays as Percent of Gross Domestic Product," Economic Research, Federal Reserve Bank of St. Louis, last modified April 1, 2022. https://fred.stlouisfed.org/series/FYONGDA188S.

10. See figure 3.4 in *Ages of Discord*. Peter Turchin, *Ages of Discord: A Structural-Demographic Analysis of American History* (Chaplin, CT: Beresta Books, 2016).

11. Anne Case and Angus Deaton, *Deaths of Despair and the Future of Capitalism* (Princeton: Princeton University Press, 2020). More on this in chapter 3.

12. Zachary Crockett, "Donald Trump is the only US president ever with no political or military experience," *Vox,* January 23, 2017, https://www.vox.com/policy-and-politics/2016/11/11/13587532/donald-trump-no-experience.

13. The technical term is *hyperactive agency detection*, or *hypersensitive agency detection*; see Karen M. Douglas et al., "Someone Is Pulling the Strings: Hypersensitive Agency Detection and Belief in Conspiracy Theories," *Thinking & Reasoning* 22, no. 1 (2016): 57–77, https://doi.org/10.1080/13546783.2015.1051586.

14. David Barstow, Susanne Craig, and Russ Buettner, "Trump Engaged in Suspect Tax Schemes as He Reaped Riches from His Father," *New York Times*, October 2, 2018, https://www.nytimes.com/interactive/2018/10/02/us/politics/donald-trump-tax-schemes-fred-trump.html.

15. This number was exceeded in 2020, when a total of twenty-nine major candidates competed for the Democratic presidential nomination.

16. For a colorful, if unflattering, account of the 2016 campaign, see especially chapter 2 of Matt Taibbi, *Insane Clown President: Dispatches from the 2016 Circus* (New York: Random House, 2017).

17. Stephen B. Oates, *Abraham Lincoln: The Man Behind the Myths* (New York: Harper & Row, 1984).

18. For a more detailed discussion of the causes of the American Civil War, see chapter 9 of *Ages of Discord*.

19. David Brion Davis, "Slavery, Emancipation, and Progress," in *British Abolitionism and the Question of Moral Progress in History*, edited by Donald A. Yerxa (Columbia, SC: University of South Carolina Press, 2012), 18–19.

20. The specific mixture of forces that drove these declines was different, because American society greatly changed over the 150 years following the antebellum era. I defer the discussion of why relative wages declined in recent decades until chapter 3. The reasons why relative wages declined between the 1820s and 1860s are discussed in chapters 8 and 9 of *Ages of Discord*. Briefly, the decline was due to oversupply of labor resulting from massive overseas immigration plus migration from overpopulated rural areas of the Eastern Seaboard.

21. All of these trends are described and referenced in my 2016 book, *Ages of Discord*.

22. Phillips, *Wealth and Democracy*.

23. The next big increase was in 1873, from 243 to 293. See George B. Galloway, *History of the House of Representatives* (New York: Crowell, 1976).

24. Joanne B. Freeman, "When Congress Was Armed and Dangerous," *New York Times*, January 11, 2011, https://www.nytimes.com/2011/01/12/opinion/12freeman.html.

25. David M. Potter, *The Impending Crisis, 1848–1861* (New York: Harper & Row, 1976).

26. In 1820, China's economy was by far the largest on earth and accounted for 32.9 percent of the world's GDP. See Angus Maddison, *The World Economy: Historical Statistics* (Paris: OECD Publishing, 2003).

27. Georg Orlandi et al., "Structural-Demographic Analysis of the Qing Dynasty (1644–1912) Collapse in China," preprint, submitted November 2, 2022. https://osf.io/preprints/socarxiv/5awhk/.

28. Stephen R. Platt, *Autumn in the Heavenly Kingdom: China, the West, and the Epic Story of the Taiping Civil War* (New York: Vintage Books, 2012).

29. Platt, *Autumn in the Heavenly Kingdom*, 18.

30. Orlandi et al., "Structural-Demographic Analysis of the Qing Dynasty (1644–1912) Collapse in China."

31. Platt, *Autumn in the Heavenly Kingdom*, 114–16.

32. The Armed Conflict Location & Event Data Project (https://acleddata.com/) reported that twenty-five Americans died in the political unrest of 2020.

33. *MCCA Report on the 2020 Protests and Civil Unrest* (Salt Lake City: Major Cities Chiefs Association, October 2020), https://majorcitieschiefs.com/wp-content/uploads/2021/01/MCCA-Report-on-the-2020-Protest-and-Civil-Unrest.pdf.
34. Thomas Johansmeyer, "How 2020 protests changed insurance forever," World Economic Forum, February 22, 2021, https://www.weforum.org/agenda/2021/02/2020-protests-changed-insurance-forever/.

CHAPTER 2: STEPPING BACK: LESSONS OF HISTORY

1. Daniel Hoyer et al., "How long were periods of internal peace and stability in historical polities? An analysis with CrisisDB," manuscript in preparation.
2. This dictum, which I proposed in my book *War and Peace and War*, paraphrases the historian Arnold Toynbee's phrase about civilizations. See Peter Turchin, *War and Peace and War: The Rise and Fall of Empires* (New York: Plume, 2007).
3. I cover this ground in much greater detail in chapters 9 and 10 of *War and Peace and War*.
4. In the south, the noble houses of Armagnac and Foix fought over the viscounty of Béarn. In the north and east, the barons of the provinces of Picardy and Burgundy rebelled against royal taxation. Also in the north, Robert d'Artois and his aunt Mahaut struggled over the County of Artois, while in Flanders the new bourgeoisie, using the urban proletariat as shock troops, rebelled against the old urban patriciate. In the west, Brittany descended into a civil war between the Blois and Montfort factions when its duke, John III, died without direct heirs.
5. This maxim is often attributed to Mark Twain, but there is no substantive evidence that he made this remark. See Quote Investigator's research into this particular quote: https://quoteinvestigator.com/2014/01/12/history-rhymes/.
6. The one exception was Calais, which the English kept for another century, finally losing it in 1558.
7. The reason for this decline, in addition to the high mortality of nobles, was downward social mobility, as impoverished nobles lost their elite status and were forced into the commoner stratum. See chapter 4 of Peter Turchin and Sergey A. Nefedov, *Secular Cycles* (Princeton: Princeton University Press, 2009).
8. Fernand Braudel, *The Identity of France*, vol. 2, bk. 2, *People and Production* (New York: HarperCollins, 1991), 159.
9. For more, see "Anglo-French Wars," Wikimedia Foundation, last modified September 11, 2022, 19:07, https://en.wikipedia.org/wiki/Anglo-French_Wars.
10. The first cycle is from about 1200 to 1450, the second one from 1450 to 1660, and the third one from 1660 to 1770. You can read about these cycles in chapters 4 and 5 of my book *Secular Cycles*.

11. Specifically, in 1215–17, in 1263–67, and in 1321–27. See table 2.5 in *Secular Cycles*.
12. Here's a good rundown: Charlotte Ahlin, "Learn the History That Inspired the Lannisters & Impress All Your Friends," *Bustle,* December 4, 2018, https://www.bustle.com/p/the-inspiration-for-the-lannisters-from -game-of-thrones-came-from-a-number-of-fascinating-historical-figures -13222107.
13. This quote comes from Edward Hall's *Hall's Chronicle: Containing the History of England, During the Reign of Henry the Fourth, and the Succeeding Monarchs, to the End of the Reign of Henry the Eighth*, which was originally printed in London in 1809.
14. See *Secular Cycles.*
15. For more, see "Anglo-French Wars," Wikimedia Foundation, last modified September 11, 2022, 19:07, https://en.wikipedia.org/wiki/Anglo-French_Wars.
16. See chapter 7 in Peter Turchin, *Historical Dynamics: Why States Rise and Fall* (Princeton: Princeton University Press, 2003).
17. Read about the remarkable life of Ibn Khaldun and his brilliant contributions to historical sociology in chapter 4 of *War and Peace and War.*
18. Kublai and his successors (the Yuan dynasty) ruled China and Mongolia. Jagataids established an empire in Turkestan and Transoxania. Hulagu and his successors (known as Il-Khanids) ruled Persia and Mesopotamia. Finally, the Golden Horde under the Juchid dynasty extended its control over the western parts of the Great Steppe, as well as Russia.
19. For historically minded readers, here are the details. In China, the civil war between the successors of Kublai broke out in 1328. The 1350s saw numerous revolts led by native leaders, and in 1368, one of these leaders expelled the Mongols and established the Ming dynasty.

   Turkestan was unified until 1333–1334, when a nomad-led insurrection broke out against the Jagataid regime in eastern Turkestan. By 1350, the power in Transoxania had passed into the hands of local Turkic nobles. After a period of turmoil, a new dynasty was established by Timur (also known as Tamerlane in the West). Timur unified Transoxania in 1379 and conquered Iran from 1383–85. The Timurid dynasty also lasted about a century. In 1469, Persia was lost to the White Sheep Horde, while Transoxania splintered between warring branches of Timur's descendants.

   The Persia of Il-Khans underwent dissolution in 1335. After a period of civil war, it was conquered by Timur. When the Timurids lost Persia in 1469, another turbulent period followed, and eventually, by 1501, Persia was unified by a native dynasty, the Safavids.

   A similar course of events occurred in the Western Steppe. The Juchid rule ended in 1359, when the Golden Horde fell into anarchy. After a period of civil war, the Golden Horde underwent a revival under Timur Qutlugh. In 1399, Timur Qutlugh won a victory over the Lithuanians, pushing them west, and reconsolidated his dominion over Russia. In the middle of the fifteenth century, however, the revived Golden Horde began disintegrating again. The first piece to secede was the Crimean Khanate in 1443. The Khanates of Kazan and Astrakhan followed (in 1445 and 1466, respectively).

20. See Veritasium, "The Surprising Secret of Synchronization," March 31, 2021, YouTube video, 20:57, https://www.youtube.com/watch?v=t-_VPRCtiUg.

21. See Peter Turchin, "Modeling Periodic Waves of Integration in the Afro-Eurasian World-System," in *Globalization as Evolutionary Process,* edited by George Modelski, Tessaleno Devezas, and William R. Thompson (London: Routledge, 2007), 163–91.

22. The following timeline is taken from "Arab Spring," Wikimedia Foundation, last modified October 4, 2022, 05:37, https://en.wikipedia.org/wiki/Arab _Spring.

23. Attributed to Mao.

24. See Leonid Grinin and Andrey Korotayev, "The Arab Spring: Causes, Conditions, and Driving Forces," in *Handbook of Revolutions in the 21st Century: The New Waves of Revolutions, and the Causes and Effects of Disruptive Political Change,* edited by Jack A. Goldstone, Leonid Grinin, and Andrey Korotayev (Switzerland: Springer, 2022), 595–624, https://doi.org/10.1007/978-3-030 -86468-2.

25. For more, see "Revolutions of 1848," Wikimedia Foundation, last modified September 23, 2022, 10:12, https://en.wikipedia.org/wiki/Revolutions_of _1848#Events_by_country_or_region.

CHAPTER 3: "THE PEASANTS ARE REVOLTING"

1. Guy Standing, *The Precariat: The New Dangerous Class* (London: Bloomsbury, 2011).

2. As a post on Steven Pinker's website says: "Is the world really falling apart? Is the ideal of progress obsolete? In this elegant assessment of the human condition in the third millennium, cognitive scientist and public intellectual Steven Pinker urges us to step back from the gory headlines and prophecies of doom, which play to our psychological biases. Instead, follow the data: In 75 jaw-dropping graphs, Pinker shows that life, health, prosperity, safety, peace, knowledge, and happiness are on the rise, not just in the West, but worldwide. This progress is not the result of some cosmic force. It is a gift of the Enlightenment: the conviction that reason and science can enhance human flourishing." See "Enlightenment Now: The Case for Reason, Science, Humanism, and Progress," Steven Pinker, last updated on April 22, 2022, https://

stevenpinker.com/publications/enlightenment-now-case-reason-science
-humanism-and-progress.

3. Max Roser, "Extreme poverty: how far have we come, how far do we still have to go?" Our World in Data, November 22, 2021, https://ourworldindata.org/extreme-poverty-in-brief.

4. Michael J. Boskin, "The best solution for inequality? Economic growth," World Economic Forum, December 13, 2019, https://www.weforum.org/agenda/2019/12/economic-growth-is-the-answer.

5. "Historical Income Tables: Households," United States Census Bureau, last updated August 18, 2022, https://www.census.gov/data/tables/time-series/demo/income-poverty/historical-income-households.html.

6. Tonya Garcia, "CEO average pay climbed more than $1 million in 2016," *MarketWatch,* April 13, 2017, https://www.marketwatch.com/story/ceo-average-pay-climbed-more-than-1-million-in-2016-2017-04-12.

7. "State of Working America Data Library," Economic Policy Institute, accessed August 10, 2022, https://www.epi.org/data/.

8. Anne Case and Angus Deaton, *Deaths of Despair and the Future of Capitalism* (Princeton: Princeton University Press, 2020).

9. All statistics in this paragraph are from "State of Working America Data Library," Economic Policy Institute.

10. In one category—white women—wages for noncollege graduates did not decrease in absolute terms.

11. John Komlos, "Growth of Welfare and Its Distribution in the U.S., 1979–2013," *Journal of Income Distribution* 28, no. 1 (2019): 1–19, https://doi.org/10.25071/1874-6322.40399.

12. See chapter 3 in *Ages of Discord.*

13. John Komlos and Marieluise Baur, "From the Tallest to (One of) the Fattest: The Enigmatic Fate of the American Population in the 20th Century," preprint, submitted September 14, 2003, https://doi.org/10.2139/ssrn.444501.

14. See figure 11.1 and explanatory text in chapter 11 of *Ages of Discord.*

15. Robert William Fogel, *The Escape from Hunger and Premature Death, 1700–2100: Europe, America, and the Third World* (New York: Cambridge University Press, 2004).

16. See figure 3.5 in *Ages of Discord.*

17. Case and Deaton, *Deaths of Despair,* 752–60.

18. John Komlos, *Foundations of Real-World Economics,* 3rd ed. (New York: Routledge, 2023).

19. Case and Deaton, *Deaths of Despair,* figures 5.1 and 5.2.

20. Case and Deaton, *Deaths of Despair,* figure 5.1.

21. Case and Deaton, *Deaths of Despair,* figure 4.1.

22. See Komlos, *Foundations of Real-World Economics.*

23. The following account is a summary of chapter 12 in *Ages of Discord.*
24. See table 7.1 and figure 7.1, and the associated discussion in *Ages of Discord* explaining the empirical basis for this periodization.
25. Such as the conservatives in the National Association of Manufacturers. Roosevelt also had to deal with an antagonistic Supreme Court. For an analysis of different elite factions during the New Deal, see G. William Domhoff and Michael J. Webber, *Class and Power in the New Deal: Corporate Moderates, Southern Democrats, and the Liberal-Labor Coalition* (Stanford: Stanford University Press, 2011).
26. I return to this point in chapter 6, where I discuss the "Great Compression"; for more detail, see chapter 4 of *Ages of Discord.*
27. Robert D. Putnam, *Bowling Alone: The Collapse and Revival of American Community* (New York: Simon & Schuster, 2000).
28. See Kim Phillips-Fein, *Invisible Hands: The Businessmen's Crusade Against the New Deal* (New York: W. W. Norton, 2009).
29. See George J. Borjas, *We Wanted Workers: Unraveling the Immigration Narrative* (New York: W. W. Norton, 2016).
30. *Ages of Discord*, chapter 12.
31. See the discussion in the section on modeling labor oversupply and general well-being in chapter 12 of *Ages of Discord.*
32. Anna Stansbury and Lawrence Summers, "Declining Worker Power and American Economic Performance," paper presented at the BPEA Conference, March 19, 2020, https://www.brookings.edu/wp-content/uploads/2020/03/stansbury-summers-conference-draft.pdf.
33. Lawrence Mishel and Josh Bivens, "Identifying the policy levers generating wage suppression and wage inequality," Economic Policy Institute, May 13, 2021, https://www.epi.org/unequalpower/publications/wage-suppression-inequality/.
34. Noam Scheiber, "Middle-Class Pay Lost Pace. Is Washington to Blame?" *New York Times,* May 13, 2021, https://www.nytimes.com/2021/05/13/business/economy/middle-class-pay.html.
35. See Putnam, *Bowling Alone.*
36. See David G. Blanchflower and Andrew J. Oswald, "Trends in Extreme Distress in the United States, 1993–2019," *American Journal of Public Health* 110, no. 10 (2020): 1538–44, https://doi.org/10.2105/ajph.2020.305811. These authors focused on the question "Now thinking about your mental health, which includes stress, depression, and problems with emotions, for how many days during the past 30 days was your mental health not good?" and defined *extreme stress* as the proportion of respondents who gave the maximum possible answer—that is, thirty days.
37. George Ward et al., "(Un)Happiness and Voting in U.S. Presidential Elec-

tions," *Journal of Personality and Social Psychology* 120, no. 2 (2021): 370–83, https://doi.org/10.1037/pspi0000249.

38. As quoted in Case and Deaton, *Deaths of Despair*, 54–55.

39. From *The Twelve Chairs*, a very popular Soviet novel, this phrase is a parody of a saying by Karl Marx: "The emancipation of the working class must be conquered by the working class themselves."

40. Nick Hanauer, "The Pitchforks Are Coming . . . for Us Plutocrats," *Politico Magazine*, July/August 2014, https://www.politico.com/magazine/story/2014/06/the-pitchforks-are-coming-for-us-plutocrats-108014/.

CHAPTER 4: THE REVOLUTIONARY TROOPS

1. Claudia Goldin, "Enrollment in institutions of higher education, by sex, enrollment status, and type of institution: 1869–1995," table Bc523–536 in *Historical Statistics of the United States, Earliest Times to the Present: Millennial Edition*, edited by Susan B. Carter et al. (New York: Cambridge University Press, 2006), http://dx.doi.org/10.1017/ISBN-9780511132971.Bc510-736.

2. US Department of Education, Institute of Education Sciences, "Immediate College Enrollment Rate," National Center for Education Statistics, last updated May 2022, https://nces.ed.gov/programs/coe/indicator/cpa.

3. Noah Smith, "America Is Pumping Out Too Many Ph.D.s," *Bloomberg*, January 4, 2021, https://www.bloomberg.com/opinion/articles/2021-01-04/america-is-pumping-out-too-many-ph-d-s.

4. Guy Standing, "Meet the precariat, the new global class fuelling the rise of populism," World Economic Forum, November 9, 2016, https://www.weforum.org/agenda/2016/11/precariat-global-class-rise-of-populism/.

5. This discussion follows the material in *Ages of Discord* on elite overproduction in chapters 4 and 13. See, in particular, figures 4.4 and 13.4. See also "Salary Distribution Curves," NALP, accessed August 10, 2022, https://www.nalp.org/salarydistrib.

6. David Callahan, *The Cheating Culture: Why More Americans Are Doing Wrong to Get Ahead* (Boston: Mariner Books, 2004), 211.

7. Associated Press, "College bribery scandal: students sue elite schools in class action," *The Guardian*, March 14, 2019, https://www.theguardian.com/us-news/2019/mar/14/college-admisisons-scandal-fraud-lawsuit-yale-usc-stanford.

8. Jack A. Goldstone, *Revolution and Rebellion in the Early Modern World* (Berkeley: University of California Press, 1991); Turchin, *Historical Dynamics*; Andrey Korotayev et al., "A Trap at the Escape from the Trap? Demographic-Structural Factors of Political Instability in Modern Africa and West Asia," *Cliodynamics: The Journal of Quantitative History and Cultural Evolution* 2, no. 2 (2011): 276–303, https://doi.org/10.21237/c7clio22217.

9. See Goldstone, *Revolution and Rebellion*.

10. Goldstone, *Revolution and Rebellion*, 417.

11. Goldstone, *Revolution and Rebellion*, 417.

12. Goldstone, *Revolution and Rebellion*, 420.

13. Keith T. Poole and Howard Rosenthal, "The Polarization of American Politics," *The Journal of Politics* 46, no. 4 (1984): 1061–79, https://doi.org/10.2307/2131242; Keith T. Poole and Howard Rosenthal, *Congress: A Political-Economic History of Roll Call Voting* (Oxford: Oxford University Press, 2000); Nolan McCarty, Keith T. Poole, and Howard Rosenthal, *Polarized America: The Dance of Ideology and Unequal Riches* (Cambridge, MA: MIT Press, 2006).

14. See chapter 4, especially figure 4.8a, in *Ages of Discord*.

15. See also "Radical Politics," Wikimedia Foundation, last modified August 31, 2022, 17:44, https://en.wikipedia.org/wiki/Radical_politics.

16. Calculated from Pew Research Center data showing that in 2020, 61 percent of more educated voters voted for Biden and 37 percent for Trump. Among young voters (ages 18–29), 59 percent voted Democratic, and 35 percent voted Republican. Very crudely, we can estimate the proportion of both young and more educated (which approximates college students) who voted for Biden as $1 - (1 - 0.61)(1 - 0.59) = 0.84$. See Ruth Igielnik, Scott Keeter, and Hannah Hartig, "Behind Biden's 2020 Victory," Pew Research Center, June 30, 2021, https://www.pewresearch.org/politics/2021/06/30/behind-bidens-2020-victory/.

17. Gwynn Guilford and Nikhil Sonnad, "What Steve Bannon really wants," *Quartz*, February 3, 2017, https://qz.com/898134/what-steve-bannon-really-wants/.

18. Steven Greenhouse, "Bernie Sanders says Democrats are failing: 'The party has turned its back on the working class,'" *The Guardian*, January 10, 2022, https://www.theguardian.com/us-news/2022/jan/10/bernie-sanders-democrats-failing-working-class-interview.

19. Her Twitter account was reinstated in November 2022, and her official congressional account remains active.

20. My sources are *Days of Rage* and *An American Radical*: Bryan Burrough, *Days of Rage: America's Radical Underground, the FBI, and the Forgotten Age of Revolutionary Violence* (New York: Penguin Books, 2016); Susan Rosenberg, *An American Radical: Political Prisoner in My Own Country* (New York: Citadel Press, 2011).

21. She started as a follower of the anarchist Mikhail Bakunin but later converted to Marxism.

CHAPTER 5: THE RULING CLASS

1. This opinion—that America is a plutocracy—is shared by a number of influential thinkers, including Paul Krugman, Joseph Stiglitz, Kevin Phillips, and

Chrystia Freeland. I will discuss the empirical basis for this claim, stemming from the work of Martin Gilens and Benjamin Page, later in the chapter.

2. This famous quip comes from the American political scientist Charles Tilly. Our analysis of Seshat: Global History Databank, which tested all major classes of theories about the evolution of complex societies against each other, showed that warfare is the main driver of social complexity, in addition to agriculture. See Peter Turchin et al., "Disentangling the Evolutionary Drivers of Social Complexity: A Comprehensive Test of Hypotheses," *Science Advances* 8, no. 25 (2022), https://doi.org/10.1126/sciadv.abn3517. This theme is more fully explored in my forthcoming book, *The Great Holocene Transformation.*

3. You can read about this evolution in my book *Ultrasociety.* Peter Turchin, *Ultrasociety: How 10,000 Years of War Made Humans the Greatest Cooperators on Earth* (Chaplin, CT: Beresta Books, 2016).

4. Turchin et al., "Disentangling the Evolutionary Drivers of Social Complexity." This theme is more fully explored in my forthcoming book, *The Great Holocene Transformation.*

5. See also "2011 Egyptian revolution," Wikimedia Foundation, last modified October 2, 2022, 12:50, https://en.wikipedia.org/wiki/2011_Egyptian_revolution.

6. Andrey Korotayev and Julia Zinkina, "Egyptian Revolution: A Demographic Structural Analysis," *Entelequia* 13 (2011): 139–69; Andrey Korotayev and L. Isaev, "The Anatomy of the Egyptian Counter-revolution," *Mirovaya Ekonomika i Mezhdunarodnye Otnosheniya* 8 (2014): 91–100.

7. World Bank data on school enrollment: https://data.worldbank.org/indicator/SE.TER.ENRR?end=2018&locations=EG&start=1971&view=chart.

8. James Palmer, "Xi's Prosperity Gospel," China Brief, *Foreign Policy*, August 25, 2021, https://foreignpolicy.com/2021/08/25/china-xi-jinping-common-prosperity-billionaires/.

9. A detailed account can be found in chapter 9 of *Ages of Discord.*

10. Phillips, *Wealth and Democracy*, 34–36.

11. Philip H. Burch, *Elites in American History*, vol. 2, *The Civil War to the New Deal* (New York: Holmes & Meier, 1981), 47.

12. Charles A. Beard and Mary R. Beard, *The Rise of American Civilization* (New York: Macmillan, 1927), 110.

13. Gabriel Kolko provides a number of quotes: "Ignorant, unrestricted competition, carried to its logical conclusion, means death to some of the combatants and injury to all"; "Unrestricted competition had proven a deceptive mirage, and its victims were struggling on every hand to find some means of escape from the perils of their environment. In this trying situation, it was perfectly natural that the idea of rational cooperation in lieu of cutthroat competition should suggest itself." See Gabriel Kolko, *The Triumph of Conservatism: A Reinterpretation of American History, 1900–1916* (New York: Free Press, 1963), 13–14.

14. "Editorial Comment," *The Bankers' Magazine,* 1901, 497–514.

15. G. William Domhoff, *Who Rules America?*, 5th ed., *Power, Politics, and Social Change* (New York: McGraw-Hill, 2006).

16. See also E. Digby Baltzell, *Philadelphia Gentlemen: The Making of a National Upper Class* (Piscataway, NJ: Transaction Publishers, 1989); and E. Digby Baltzell, *The Protestant Establishment Revisited* (New Brunswick, NJ: Transaction Publishers, 1991).

17. The Wikipedia article provides a number of quotes: "Plutocracy," Wikimedia Foundation, last modified September 13, 2022, 19:49, https://en.wikipedia.org/wiki/Plutocracy.

18. This view is similar to the class-domination theory developed by the sociologist G. William Domhoff in a series of influential publications, including the book *Who Rules America?* (The first edition was published in 1967, and as of 2022, the book is in its eighth edition.) Like mine, Domhoff's analysis is framed within the Four Networks theory of power, or as I have explained it in chapter 1, the four sources of social power. However, as I will argue later in the book, the economic elite (or the 1 percent) rule in a coalition with the top members of the credentialed class (the 10 percent).

19. "Lobbying Data Summary," OpenSecrets, accessed August 10, 2022, https://www.opensecrets.org/federal-lobbying/summary.

20. "Industries," OpenSecrets, accessed August 10, 2022, https://www.opensecrets.org/federal-lobbying/industries.

21. Here again I follow closely Domhoff's ideas in *Who Rules America?*

22. See also "Martha Mitchell effect," Wikimedia Foundation, last modified August 4, 2022, 13:56, https://en.wikipedia.org/wiki/Martha_Mitchell_effect.

23. "Well, unfortunately . . . the judges are compromised, along with the politicians. The Communist Chinese have subverted, taken over this nation from top to bottom along with the globalists." See Banned.Video, "Oath Keeper Stewart Rhodes—'We're already at war, Trump needs to be a wartime president right now,'" BitChute, December 13, 2020, video, 0:24, https://www.bitchute.com/video/w7ut83CCvRby.

24. Trudy Ring, "Maddow: Russians May Be Controlling Our Government," *Advocate,* March 10, 2017, https://www.advocate.com/politics/2017/3/10/maddow-russians-may-be-controlling-our-government.

25. See also G. William Domhoff, "There Are No Conspiracies," Who Rules America?, March 2005, https://whorulesamerica.ucsc.edu/theory/conspiracy.html.

26. "Our Vision and Mission: Inform, Empower & Advocate," OpenSecrets, accessed August 10, 2022, https://www.opensecrets.org/about/.

27. "Power Elite Database," Who Rules America?, accessed August 10, 2022, https://whorulesamerica.ucsc.edu/power_elite/.

28. Martin Gilens and Benjamin I. Page, "Testing Theories of American Politics: Elites, Interest Groups, and Average Citizens," *Perspectives on Politics* 12, no. 3 (2014): 564–81, https://doi.org/10.1017/s1537592714001595.

29. See Michael J. Graetz and Ian Shapiro, *Death by a Thousand Cuts: The Fight over Taxing Inherited Wealth* (Princeton: Princeton University Press, 2006).

30. As usual in academia, the 2014 article by Gilens and Page was a subject of critique, summarized by Dylan Matthews in "Remember that study saying America is an oligarchy? 3 rebuttals say it's wrong," *Vox,* May 9, 2016, https:// www.vox.com/2016/5/9/11502464/gilens-page-oligarchy-study. Gilens and Page responded to these critics in a *Washington Post* article ("Critics argued with our analysis of U.S. political inequality. Here are 5 ways they're wrong," May 23, 2016, https://www.washingtonpost.com/news/monkey-cage/wp/2016 /05/23/critics-challenge-our-portrait-of-americas-political-inequality -heres-5-ways-they-are-wrong/). More recently, the arguments over technical points have given way to a series of articles in various fields agreeing with the Gilens/Page thesis and presenting additional evidence that America's politics are dominated by the extremely wealthy.

31. "Nearly three-fourths (71%) of Americans say it is 'unacceptable' for people to illegally immigrate to the U.S." See Emily Ekins and David Kemp, "E Pluribus Unum: Findings from the Cato Institute 2021 Immigration and Identity National Survey," Cato Institute, April 27, 2021, https://www.cato.org/survey -reports/e-pluribus-unum-findings-cato-institute-2021-immigration-identity -national-survey.

32. Angela Nagle, "The Left Case Against Open Borders," *American Affairs* 2, no. 4 (2018), https://americanaffairsjournal.org/2018/11/the-left-case-against -open-borders/.

33. See chapter 12 in *Ages of Discord*.

34. I want to acknowledge that the question of whether immigration depresses the wages of native workers, or not, is a very contentious issue in economics. George Borjas and his colleagues estimate that the wage elasticity of immigration is between −0.3 and −0.4. In other words, when the number of migrants increases by 10 percent, the wages of native workers decline by 3–4 percent. David Card and colleagues, in contrast, find a much smaller effect or even no effect. See Alan de Brauw, "Does Immigration Reduce Wages?," *Cato Journal,* Fall 2017, https://www.cato.org/cato-journal/fall-2017/does-immi gration-reduce-wages#. The current consensus seems to be that the truth is somewhere in between these two estimates. In other words, a 10 percent increase in immigration depresses the wages by 2 percent. The debate is highly technical, because small variations in how data are analyzed result in large changes to the size of estimated effects. Proponents of immigration often read the literature selectively to emphasize the lack of effects. One go-to article that

is often cited in support of no effect is by a coauthor of David Card, Giovanni Peri ("Do immigrant workers depress the wages of native workers?" IZA World of Labor, May 2014, https://doi.org/10.15185/izawol.42). On the basis of his review of twenty-seven empirical studies, Peri concludes that "most studies for industrialized countries have found no effect on wages, on average, and only modest effects on wage differentials between more and less educated immigrant and native workers." However, his analysis does not distinguish countries with strong labor-protecting institutions, such as Denmark, from countries with weak or absent labor-protecting institutions, such as the US. In his list of reasons "why immigrants may NOT depress natives' wages," he doesn't even include the restraining effect of labor institutions on wage decreases resulting from labor oversupply. Most of the mechanisms that he *does* list work in the long run. Thus, a onetime immigration shock might be expected to produce positive effects in five to ten years of time. But when high immigration continues for decades, the negative short-term effects become, in essence, long term. In summary, there is a lot of uncertainty about this issue, in large part because, as I emphasized in the body of the book, immigration is only one of the forces affecting wages, and probably not even the main one (see chapter 3). Offshoring of production and automation are probably more important factors. On another level, whether immigration depresses wages in reality is, perhaps, not even the main issue. Both the wealthy 1 percent and the working class believe that it does, which creates its own "social reality." And a final thought: when representatives of the ruling class in the mainstream media and in think tanks point to arcane analyses by economists (who themselves are part of the ruling class, the credentialed 10 percent), this is utterly unconvincing to the common people, who know "in their guts" that increased competition from immigrants depresses their economic well-being. The best way for the ruling class to demonstrate to the working class that immigration doesn't depress their wages is to get median wages back into the growth regime, as they were before the modern immigration wave, which will again parallel increases in GDP per capita (and worker productivity).

35. Quoted in Kitty Calavita, *U.S. Immigration Law and the Control of Labor: 1820–1924* (London: Academic Press, 1984), 49.

CHAPTER 6: WHY IS AMERICA A PLUTOCRACY?

1. The following discussion integrates insights from G. William Domhoff, Charles Tilly, and the sociologist Michael Mann.

2. On the "military revolution" of the fifteenth century, and other military revolutions before it, see my forthcoming book, *The Great Holocene Transformation*.

3. Thus, the military revolution circa 1500 is best called the gunboat revolution. See Peter Turchin, "A Theory for Formation of Large Empires," *Journal of Global History* 4, no. 2 (2009): 191–217, https://doi.org/10.1017/s174002280900312x.

4. This quote originates in Cicero's Fifth Philippic, which you can read on Project Gutenberg here: https://www.gutenberg.org/files/11080/11080-8.txt.

5. I am indebted to Nina Witoszek for these details on the origins of the Nordic model.

6. Heather Cox Richardson, *How the South Won the Civil War: Oligarchy, Democracy, and the Continuing Fight for the Soul of America* (New York: Oxford University Press, 2020).

7. Heather McGhee, *The Sum of Us: What Racism Costs Everyone and How We Can Prosper Together* (New York: One World, 2021).

8. Thomas Frank, *The People, No: A Brief History of Anti-Populism* (New York: Metropolitan Books, 2020). The parentheticals included in this quote are King's oratory interjections.

9. Patriotic Millionaires, accessed August 10, 2022, https://patrioticmillionaires.org/.

10. Details in chapter 10 of *Ages of Discord*.

11. Douglas Fraser, Resignation Letter from the Labor-Management Group, July 17, 1978, https://www.historyisaweapon.com/defcon1/fraserresign.html.

12. Domhoff and Webber, *Class and Power in the New Deal*.

13. Phillips, *Wealth and Democracy*.

14. See chapter 4 in *Ages of Discord*.

15. Thomas Piketty, *Capital in the Twenty-First Century* (Cambridge, MA: Harvard University Press, 2014).

16. Walter Scheidel, *The Great Leveler: Violence and the History of Inequality from the Stone Age to the Twenty-First Century* (Princeton: Princeton University Press, 2018).

17. For the sources of these quotes, see chapter 12 in *Ages of Discord*.

18. The Morozov family was the fifth richest in Russia around 1900.

19. Lizunov, V. S., "Origins," in *The Past Passes Before Me* [in Russian] (Orekhovo-Zuyevo: Bogorodsk-Noginsk, 2007), https://www.bogorodsk-noginsk.ru/articles/24_lizunov1.html.

CHAPTER 7: STATE BREAKDOWN

1. For a discussion of how Hussein wielded power, see *War and Peace and War*.

2. Peter Turchin, "Building nations after conflict," *Nature* 453 (2008): 986–87, https://doi.org/10.1038/453986a.

3. See also "Fall of Kabul (2021)," Wikimedia Foundation, last modified October

3, 2022, 18:20, https://en.wikipedia.org/wiki/Fall_of_Kabul_(2021)#Capture _of_Kabul.

4. For details, see *Secular Cycles.*

5. Robert C. Allen, *Farm to Factory: A Reinterpretation of the Soviet Industrial Revolution* (Princeton: Princeton University Press, 2003).

6. However, the late Soviet Union had developed its own elite overproduction—in particular, overproduction of "technical intelligentsia," or people with engineering degrees.

7. This has nothing to do with Asimov's fictional science of history.

8. Hugh Trevor-Roper, "Re-inventing Hitler," *The Sunday Times,* February 18, 1973.

9. Jack A. Goldstone et al., "A Global Model for Forecasting Political Instability," *American Journal of Political Science* 54, no. 1 (2010): 190–208, https:// doi.org/10.1111/j.1540-5907.2009.00426.x.

10. For a critique of this approach, see Zach Jones, "An Analysis of Polity IV and Its Components," http://zmjones.com/polity/.

11. Polity IV has now been replaced by the next iteration, Polity5 Project. See "The Polity Project," Center for Systemic Peace, http://www.systemicpeace .org/polityproject.html. Note, also, that they now classify countries with Polity scores between minus five and five as "anocracies."

12. Goldstone et al., "A Global Model," 196.

13. Barbara F. Walter, *How Civil Wars Start: And How to Stop Them* (New York: Crown, 2022), 127–28. See also Jonathan Haidt, "Why the Past 10 Years of American Life Have Been Uniquely Stupid," *The Atlantic,* April 11, 2022, https://www.theatlantic.com/magazine/archive/2022/05/social-media -democracy-trust-babel/629369/.

14. Lars-Erik Cederman and Nils B. Weidmann, "Predicting Armed Conflict: Time to Adjust Our Expectations?," *Science* 355, no. 6324 (2017): 474–76.

15. Zbigniew Brzezinski, *The Grand Chessboard: American Primacy and Its Geostrategic Imperatives* (New York: Basic Books, 1997), 45.

16. "Ukraine is the biggest prize": Carl Gershman, "Former Soviet states stand up to Russia. Will the U.S.?" *Washington Post,* September 26, 2013, https:// www.washingtonpost.com/opinions/former-soviet-states-stand-up-to -russia-will-the-us/2013/09/26/b5ad2be4-246a-11e3-b75d-5b7f66349852 _story.html. In June of 2022, NATO designated Russia as the "most significant and direct threat."

17. "Oligarchs be warned: we will use every tool to freeze and seize your criminal proceeds," declares US Department of Justice Deputy Attorney-General Lisa Monaco on announcing a special Klepto Capture task force. See https://www .justice.gov/opa/pr/attorney-general-merrick-b-garland-announces-launch -task-force-kleptocapture.

18. In March of 2022, Mikhail Fridman (founder of the largest private bank in Russia and worth over $10 billion) had his available money frozen by the UK's government. He told Bloomberg News that his ATM card no longer worked and he'd been limited to £2,500/month spending by the UK. After his assets were frozen, Fridman lamented, "I don't know how to live. I don't know. I really don't know." (See Stephanie Baker, "Broke Oligarch Says Sanctioned Billionaires Have No Sway Over Putin," *Bloomberg*, March 17, 2022, https://www.bloomberg.com/news/features/2022-03-17/broke-russian-oligarch-fridman-says-sanctioned-billionaires-can-t-sway-putin.) Fridman wasn't the only target. Western governments claim to have frozen or seized over $30 billion in Russian oligarchs' assets since the start of the Russia-Ukraine war. (See "Russian Elites, Proxies, and Oligarchs Task Force Joint Statement," US Department of the Treasury, June 29, 2022, https://home.treasury.gov/news/press-releases/jy0839.)

19. Victoria Nuland, "Remarks" (speech), US-Ukraine Foundation Conference, Washington, DC, December 13, 2013, https://2009-2017.state.gov/p/eur/rls/rm/2013/dec/218804.htm.

20. "Ukraine crisis: Transcript of leaked Nuland-Pyatt call," BBC News, February 7, 2014, https://www.bbc.com/news/world-europe-26079957.

21. Christian Neef, "Yanukovych's Fall: The Power of Ukraine's Billionaires," *Der Spiegel*, February 25, 2014, https://www.spiegel.de/international/europe/how-oligarchs-in-ukraine-prepared-for-the-fall-of-yanukovych-a-955328.html.

22. Christian Neef, "Yanukovych's Fall: The Power of Ukraine's Billionaires."

23. Aaron Maté, "By using Ukraine to fight Russia, the US provoked Putin's war," *Aaron Mate* (Substack blog), March 5, 2022, https://mate.substack.com/p/by-using-ukraine-to-fight-russia.

24. Lally Weymouth, "Interview with Ukrainian presidential candidate Petro Poroshenko," *Washington Post*, April 25, 2014, https://www.washingtonpost.com/opinions/interview-with-ukrainian-presidential-candidate-petro-poroshenko/2014/04/25/74c73a48-cbbd-11e3-93eb-6c0037dde2ad_story.html.

25. See Shaun Walker, "Azov fighters are Ukraine's greatest weapon and may be its greatest threat," *The Guardian*, September 10, 2014, https://www.theguardian.com/world/2014/sep/10/azov-far-right-fighters-ukraine-neo-nazis; and Andrew E. Kramer, "Islamic Battalions, Stocked with Chechens, Aid Ukraine in War with Rebels," *New York Times,* July 7, 2015, https://www.nytimes.com/2015/07/08/world/europe/islamic-battalions-stocked-with-chechens-aid-ukraine-in-war-with-rebels.html.

26. Maté, "By using Ukraine to fight Russia, the US provoked Putin's war."

27. For example, Akhmetov lost the jewel of his business empire, the Azovstal Iron and Steel Works, which was destroyed during the siege of Mariupol, while Firtash lost the Azot chemical plant in Severodonetsk.

28. Casey Michel, "Who Is Ihor Kolomoisky?" *The Spectator,* March 13, 2022, https://www.spectator.co.uk/article/who-is-ihor-kolomoisky/; David Clark, "Will Zelenskyy target all Ukrainian oligarchs equally?" *UkraineAlert* (blog), Atlantic Council, July 10, 2021, https://www.atlanticcouncil.org/blogs/ukrainealert/will-zelenskyy-target-all-ukrainian-oligarchs-equally/; see also Maté, "By using Ukraine to fight Russia, the US provoked Putin's war."

CHAPTER 8: HISTORIES OF THE NEAR FUTURE

1. Peter Turchin et al., "A History of Possible Futures: Multipath Forecasting of Social Breakdown, Recovery, and Resilience," *Cliodynamics: The Journal of Quantitative History and Cultural Evolution* 9, no. 2 (2018): 124–39, https://doi.org/10.21237/c7clio9242078.

2. Peter Turchin, "Multipath Forecasting: The Aftermath of the 2020 American Crisis," preprint, submitted April 4, 2021, https://osf.io/preprints/socarxiv/f37jy/.

3. Note that "exposed" here includes interactions via social media. Unlike a biological epidemic, a radicalization epidemic does not require physical contact.

4. See Bruce D. Malamud, Gleb Morein, and Donald L. Turcotte, "Forest Fires: An Example of Self-Organized Critical Behavior," *Science* 281, no. 5384 (1998): 1840–42, https://doi.org/10.1126/science.281.5384.1840; and R. Silva et al., "Nonextensive models for earthquakes," *Physical Review E* 73, no. 2 (2006): 1–5, https://doi.org/10.1103/physreve.73.026102.

5. Here, to keep the model simple, I focus on only the two main drivers of instability: immiseration and elite overproduction. As we saw in chapter 2, additional structural forces of instability are state weakness (failing fiscal health and weakened legitimacy of the state) and geopolitical factors. These forces can be included in the model, but at the expense of making it more complex.

6. You can see the trajectories predicted by the model in Turchin, "Multipath Forecasting: The Aftermath of the 2020 American Crisis."

7. G. William Domhoff, *Who Rules America?*, 8th ed., *The Corporate Rich, White Nationalist Republicans, and Inclusionary Democrats in the 2020s* (London: Routledge, 2022), 105.

8. Domhoff, *Who Rules America?*, 106.

9. Parker Thayer, "Living Room Pundit's Guide to Soros District Attorneys," Capital Research Center, January 18, 2022, https://capitalresearch.org/article/living-room-pundits-guide-to-soros-district-attorneys/.

10. Jeremy B. White, "4 wealthy donors fuel overhaul of California's criminal justice system," *Politico,* July 17, 2021, https://www.politico.com/states/california/story/2021/07/17/four-wealthy-donors-fuel-overhaul-of-californias-criminal-justice-system-1388261.

11. Mark Mizruchi, *The Fracturing of the American Corporate Elite* (Cambridge, MA: Harvard University Press, 2013), 286.

12. For a critique of Mizruchi's thesis, see also "Is the Corporate Elite Fractured, or Is There Continuing Corporate Dominance? Two Contrasting Views" by G. William Domhoff in *Class, Race and Corporate Power* 3, no. 1 (2015), https://doi.org/10.25148/CRCP.3.1.16092135.

13. Stephen Marche, "The next US civil war is already here—we just refuse to see it," *The Guardian*, January 4, 2022, https://www.theguardian.com/world/2022/jan/04/next-us-civil-war-already-here-we-refuse-to-see-it.

14. Southern Poverty Law Center, *The Year in Hate and Extremism 2019* (Montgomery, AL: Southern Poverty Law Center, 2020), https://www.splcenter.org/sites/default/files/yih_2020_final.pdf; and Southern Poverty Law Center, *The Year in Hate and Extremism 2021* (Montgomery, AL: Southern Poverty Law Center, 2022), https://www.splcenter.org/sites/default/files/splc-2021-year-in-hate-extremism-report.pdf.

15. Nicholas Bogel-Burroughs, Shaila Dewan, and Kathleen Gray, "F.B.I. Says Michigan Anti-Government Group Plotted to Kidnap Gov. Gretchen Whitmer," *New York Times*, April 13, 2021, https://www.nytimes.com/2020/10/08/us/gretchen-whitmer-michigan-militia.html.

16. Ryan Lucas, "Oath Keepers face seditious conspiracy charges. DOJ has mixed record with such cases," NPR, February 1, 2022, https://www.npr.org/2022/02/01/1076349762/oath-keepers-charged-capitol-riot-seditious-conspiracy.

17. Ezra Klein, "Bernie Sanders: The Vox Conversation," *Vox*, July 28, 2015, https://www.vox.com/2015/7/28/9014491/bernie-sanders-vox-conversation.

18. David Weigel, "Bernie Sanders criticizes 'open borders' at Hispanic Chamber of Commerce," *Washington Post*, July 30, 2015, https://www.washingtonpost.com/news/post-politics/wp/2015/07/30/bernie-sanders-criticizes-open-borders-at-hispanic-chamber-of-commerce/.

19. Also, they tend not to be very effective as social media influencers. In an analysis of social media, *Politico* and the Institute for Strategic Dialogue found that despite cries of censorship, "GOP-friendly voices far outweigh liberals in driving conversations" online. See Mark Scott, "Despite cries of censorship, conservatives dominate social media," *Politico*, October 26, 2020, https://www.politico.com/news/2020/10/26/censorship-conservatives-social-media-432643.

20. Robert E. Scott, "We can reshore manufacturing jobs, but Trump hasn't done it," Economic Policy Institute, August 10, 2020, https://www.epi.org/publication/reshoring-manufacturing-jobs/.

21. Ronald Radosh, "Steve Bannon, Trump's Top Guy, Told Me He Was 'a Leninist,'" *Daily Beast,* August 22, 2016, https://www.thedailybeast.com/steve-bannon-trumps-top-guy-told-me-he-was-a-leninist.

22. Benjamin R. Teitelbaum, *War for Eternity: Inside Bannon's Far-Right Circle of Global Power Brokers* (New York: Dey Street Books, 2020).

23. Guilford and Sonnad, "What Steve Bannon really wants."

24. Guilford and Sonnad, "What Steve Bannon really wants."

25. So far. Who knows what 2024 will bring . . .

26. At least as of the time of this writing. Given that the majority of Republicans subscribe to the view that the 2020 election was stolen from Trump, the battle continues.

27. In the long run, a scientific discipline, combining formal models with Big Data and advanced by a community of researchers, will always beat any individual, no matter how brilliant they are. At the same time, I will be the first one to admit that cliodynamics is a very young discipline, and we are only starting to perceive the outlines of the elephant.

28. Nicholas Confessore, "How Tucker Carlson Stoked White Fear to Conquer Cable," *New York Times*, April 30, 2022, https://www.nytimes.com/2022/04/30/us/tucker-carlson-gop-republican-party.html.

29. The first article in the series mentions Carlson's book in passing, dismissing it as "his Fox-era jeremiad about America's selfish elites."

30. Here are some representative quotes:

    "Dishonest propagandist"—Jon Stewart (Dominick Mastrangelo, "Jon Stewart rips 'dishonest propagandist' Tucker Carlson for Putin comments," *The Hill*, March 3, 2022.)

    "Dull racist"—*The New Republic* (Matt Ford, "Tucker Carlson Is Deadly Boring," *The New Republic*, April 29, 2021.)

    "Traitor"—Cheri Jacobus (@CheriJacobus, "Tucker Carlson is the Trump/Putin 'link' and he's now finishing the job of pulling it all together," Twitter, February 22, 2022, 10:08 p.m.)

    "He's a very talented demagogue"—Bill Kristol (Michael Kranish, "How Tucker Carlson became the voice of White grievance," *Washington Post*, July 14, 2021.)

    "Foreign asset"—Ana Navarro (Dominick Mastrangelo, "Panel on 'The View' calls for DOJ to probe Tucker Carlson over Putin rhetoric," *The Hill*, March 14, 2022.)

31. Dominick Mastrangelo, "Jon Stewart rips 'dishonest propagandist' Tucker Carlson for Putin comments," *The Hill*, March 3, 2022, https://thehill.com/homenews/media/596764-jon-stewart-rips-dishonest-propagandist-tucker-carlson-for-putin-comments.

32. It is remarkable how many counter-elites in America have law degrees from Yale: from left-wingers like Chesa Boudin to right-wingers like Stewart Rhodes, the leader of the Oath Keepers.

33. Jason Zengerle, "The Rise of the Tucker Carlson Politician," *New York Times Magazine*, March 22, 2022, https://www.nytimes.com/2022/03/22/magazine/tucker-carlson-politician.html.

34. Niall Stanage, "Cruz, Rubio ramp up criticisms of big business," *The Hill*, May 3, 2021, https://thehill.com/homenews/campaign/551318-exclusive-cruz-rubio-ramp-up-criticisms-of-big-business/.

35. Niall Stanage, "Cruz, Rubio ramp up criticisms of big business."

CHAPTER 9: THE WEALTH PUMP AND THE FUTURE OF DEMOCRACY

1. Daniel Hoyer et al., "Flattening the Curve: Learning the lessons of world history to mitigate societal crises," preprint, submitted on January 2, 2022, https://doi.org/10.31235/osf.io/hyj48.

2. John E. Archer, *Social Unrest and Popular Protest in England, 1780–1840* (New York: Cambridge University Press, 2000), 89.

3. Edward Royle, *Revolutionary Britannia? Reflections on the Threat of Revolution in Britain, 1789–1848* (Manchester, UK: Manchester University Press, 2000), 171.

4. The three Anglo-Dutch wars of the seventeenth century for sea supremacy resulted in English defeat. The conflict was ended when, in 1688, the Dutch ruler, William III of Orange, invaded England and made himself king. (This conquest was later "spun" as the Glorious Revolution.) Russia similarly suffered from invasions by more powerful neighbors. For example, Polish troops occupied Moscow's Kremlin during the Time of Troubles.

5. Here I summarize a more detailed description in chapter 9 of *Secular Cycles*.

6. Pugachev's Rebellion (1773–1775) was an uprising of peasants and Cossacks led by Yemelyan Pugachev, who claimed to be the tsar Peter III (who in reality had been assassinated in a palace coup). Pugachev's principal goal was to abolish serfdom.

7. Turchin and Nefedov, *Secular Cycles*, chapter 9.

8. Here are a few of the most important reforms: relaxation of censorship of the media, judicial reform, military modernization, local self-government, education reforms, reform of the Russian Orthodox Church, and economic modernization.

9. More precisely, it is an index of the authorities' efforts to suppress extremism.

10. Turchin and Nefedov, *Secular Cycles*, chapter 9.

11. In most cases, of course, ruling classes don't rise to the challenge, which is why the great majority of cases in CrisisDB end with a revolution or a bloody civil war.

12. That is, peasants were required to work for their lords without compensation a certain number of days per week.

13. Turchin and Nefedov, *Secular Cycles*, chapter 9.

14. Turchin and Nefedov, *Secular Cycles*, chapter 9.

15. Daniel Hoyer et al., "Flattening the Curve: Learning the lessons of world history to mitigate societal crises."

16. See chapter 8 in *Ultrasociety*.

17. See figure 2 in Oscar Ortmans et al., "Modeling Social Pressures Toward Political Instability in the United Kingdom after 1960: A Demographic Structural Analysis," *Cliodynamics: The Journal of Quantitative History and Cultural Evolution* 8, no. 2 (2017), https://doi.org/10.21237/c7clio8237313.

18. Note that here I am concerned not with global inequality, in which the important factor is declining between-country inequality, but with trends in *within-country* inequality. This is one of the important indicators that a wealth pump is operating (or not, if inequality is subsiding).

19. Christina Boll et al., "Overeducation—New Evidence for 25 European Countries," HWWI Research Paper No. 173, Hamburg Institute of International Economics, Hamburg, Germany, 2016, https://www.econstor.eu/bitstream/10419/130613/1/857142143.pdf.

20. Sarah Babb and Alexander Kentikelenis, "People have long predicted the collapse of the Washington Consensus. It keeps reappearing under new guises," *Washington Post*, April 16, 2021, https://www.washingtonpost.com/politics/2021/04/16/people-have-long-predicted-collapse-washington-consensus-it-keeps-reappearing-under-new-guises/.

21. Amory Gethin, Clara Martínez-Toledano, and Thomas Piketty, "How politics became a contest dominated by two kinds of elite," *The Guardian*, August 5, 2021, https://www.theguardian.com/commentisfree/2021/aug/05/around-the-world-the-disadvantaged-have-been-left-behind-by-politicians-of-all-hues.

22. "World Inequality Database," World Inequality Database, accessed August 10, 2022, https://wid.world/.

23. At the same time, the bottom half of earners (slightly) increased their share, so this appears to be genuine income compression, if not huge.

CHAPTER A1: A NEW SCIENCE OF HISTORY

1. This section is a lightly adapted and rearranged passage from Michael Flynn's book *In the Country of the Blind*.

2. Adapted from Michael Flynn, *In the Country of the Blind* (New York: Tor Books, 2001).

3. For those interested in details, see my books *Quantitative Analysis of Movement* and *Complex Population Dynamics*.

4. I discuss the influence of Leo Tolstoy on cliodynamics in *War and Peace and War*.

5. James Gleick, *Chaos: Making a New Science* (New York: Viking Press, 1987).

6. Arnold Toynbee made this remark in response to critique from his colleagues: "History is not just one damn thing after another."

7. Peter Turchin, "Psychohistory and Cliodynamics," *Cliodynamica* (blog), September 3, 2012, https://peterturchin.com/cliodynamica/psychohistory-and -cliodynamics/.

8. James Gleick, *Chaos: Making a New Science*.

9. William C. Davis, *A Concise History of the Civil War* (Fort Washington, PA: Eastern National, 2007), http://npshistory.com/publications/civil_war_series /1/sec1.htm.

10. Peter Turchin et al., "War, space, and the evolution of Old World complex societies," *Proceedings of the National Academy of Sciences* 110, no. 41 (2013): 16384–89, https://doi.org/10.1073/pnas.1308825110.

11. See *Ultrasociety*.

12. See "American Civil War," GWonline, accessed August 10, 2022, https:// gwonline.unc.edu/node/11653; and Guy Gugliotta, "New Estimate Raises Civil War Death Toll," *New York Times*, April 2, 2012, https://www.nytimes.com /2012/04/03/science/civil-war-toll-up-by-20-percent-in-new-estimate.html.

13. *War and Peace and War*, chapter 10.

14. See Hammad Sheikh, Ángel Gómez, and Scott Atran, "Empirical Evidence for the Devoted Actor Model," *Current Anthropology* 57, no. S13 (2016), https://doi.org/10.1086/686221; Nafees Hamid et al., "Neuroimaging 'will to fight' for sacred values: an empirical case study with supporters of an Al Qaeda associate," *Royal Society Open Science* 6, no. 6 (2019), https://doi.org /10.1098/rsos.181585; and Elaine Reese and Harvey Whitehouse, "The Development of Identity Fusion," *Perspectives on Psychological Science* 16, no. 6 (2021): 1398–1411, https://doi.org/10.1177/1745691620968761.

15. Thomas Carlyle, *On Heroes, Hero-Worship, and the Heroic in History* (London: James Fraser, 1841). Read for free here: https://www.gutenberg.org/files/1091 /1091-h/1091-h.htm.

16. William James, "Great Men, Great Thoughts, and the Environment," *Atlantic Monthly*, October, 1880, https://www.theatlantic.com/magazine/archive/1880 /10/great-men-great-thoughts-and-the-environment/632282/.

17. See Karl R. Popper, *The Poverty of Historicism* (London: Routledge, 1957).

18. Conway Zirkle, "The role of Liberty Hyde Bailey and Hugo de Vries in the rediscovery of Mendelism," *Journal of the History of Biology* 1, no. 2 (1968): 205–18, https://www.jstor.org/stable/4330495.

19. Jack A. Goldstone, "Demographic Structural Theory: 25 Years On," *Cliodynamics: The Journal of Quantitative History and Cultural Evolution* 8, no. 2 (2017), https://doi.org/10.21237/c7clio8237450.

20. Goldstone, "Demographic Structural Theory: 25 Years On."

CHAPTER A2: A HISTORICAL MACROSCOPE

1. Centaurians don't have genders as we understand them. Instead, each individual passes through life stages that could be approximately referred to as female and male.

2. Centaurians enjoy life spans of 250–300 Terran years.

3. "Seshat: Global History Databank," http://seshatdatabank.info/, accessed August 10, 2022.

4. The actual saying is "Genius is 1 percent *inspiration* and 99 percent *perspiration.*"

5. See also "Domesday Book," Wikimedia Foundation, last modified September 25, 2022, 17:34, https://en.wikipedia.org/wiki/Domesday_Book.

6. Haihui Zhang, "What Are Chinese Local Gazetteers?" University of Pittsburgh, last updated April 28, 2021, https://pitt.libguides.com/chinese_local_gazetteers.

7. For example: Jed O. Kaplan et al., "Holocene carbon emissions as a result of anthropogenic land cover change," *The Holocene* 21, no. 5 (2010): 775–91, https://doi.org/10.1177/0959683610386983.

8. *The Sopranos*, season 5, episode 10, "Cold Cuts," created by David Chase, aired May 9, 2004, on HBO, https://www.hbo.com/the-sopranos/season-5/10-cold-cuts.

9. David Reich, *Who We Are and How We Got Here: Ancient DNA and the New Science of the Human Past* (New York: Pantheon Books, 2018).

10. Richard H. Steckel, "Heights and human welfare: Recent developments and new directions," *Explorations in Economic History* 46, no. 1 (2009): 1–23, https://doi.org/10.1016/j.eeh.2008.12.001.

11. "A single death is a tragedy, a million deaths is a statistic" is the actual quote, widely but apparently inaccurately attributed to Stalin.

12. This is an actual record from the baptismal register of St. Stephen's Church in Norwich, England. See "Parish register," Wikimedia Foundation, last modified December 31, 2021, 07:25, https://en.wikipedia.org/wiki/Parish_register.

13. If you are interested in learning about my answer to this Big Question, read my popular book *Ultrasociety: How 10,000 Years of War Made Humans the Greatest Cooperators on Earth* (2016) and a more technical book, *The Great Holocene Transformation*, to be published in 2023.

14. Guy D. Middleton, "The show must go on: Collapse, resilience, and transformation in 21st-century archaeology," *Reviews in Anthropology* 46, no. 2–3 (2017): 78–105, https://doi.org/10.1080/00938157.2017.1343025.

BIBLIOGRAPHY

Ahlin, Charlotte. "Learn the History That Inspired the Lannisters & Impress All Your Friends." *Bustle,* December 4, 2018. https://www.bustle.com/p/the -inspiration-for-the-lannisters-from-game-of-thrones-came-from-a-number -of-fascinating-historical-figures-13222107.

Allen, Robert C. *Farm to Factory: A Reinterpretation of the Soviet Industrial Revolution.* Princeton: Princeton University Press, 2003.

Archer, John E. *Social Unrest and Popular Protest in England, 1780–1840.* New York: Cambridge University Press, 2000.

Associated Press. "College bribery scandal: students sue elite schools in class action." *The Guardian,* March 15, 2019. https://www.theguardian.com/us -news/2019/mar/14/college-admisisons-scandal-fraud-lawsuit-yale-usc -stanford.

Babb, Sarah, and Alexander Kentikelenis. "People have long predicted the collapse of the Washington Consensus. It keeps reappearing under new guises." *Washington Post,* April 16, 2021. https://www.washingtonpost.com/politics/2021 /04/16/people-have-long-predicted-collapse-washington-consensus-it-keeps -reappearing-under-new-guises/.

Baker, Stephanie. "Broke Oligarch Says Sanctioned Billionaires Have No Sway Over Putin." *Bloomberg,* March 17, 2022. https://www.bloomberg.com/news /features/2022-03-17/broke-russian-oligarch-fridman-says-sanctioned -billionaires-can-t-sway-putin.

Baltzell, E. Digby. *Philadelphia Gentlemen: The Making of a National Upper Class.* Piscataway, NJ: Transaction Publishers, 1989.

Baltzell, E. Digby. *The Protestant Establishment Revisited.* New Brunswick, NJ: Transaction Publishers, 1991.

Banned.Video. "Oath Keeper Stewart Rhodes—'We're already at war, Trump needs to be a wartime president right now.'" BitChute, December 13, 2020. Video, 0:24. https://www.bitchute.com/video/w7ut83CCvRby.

Barstow, David, Susanne Craig, and Russ Buettner. "Trump Engaged in Suspect Tax Schemes as He Reaped Riches from His Father." *New York Times*, October 2, 2018. https://www.nytimes.com/interactive/2018/10/02/us/politics/donald -trump-tax-schemes-fred-trump.html.

BBC. "Ukraine crisis: Transcript of leaked Nuland-Pyatt call." BBC News, February 7, 2014. https://www.bbc.com/news/world-europe-26079957.

Blanchflower, David G., and Andrew J. Oswald. "Trends in Extreme Distress in the United States, 1993–2019." *American Journal of Public Health* 110, no. 10 (2020): 1538–44. https://doi.org/10.2105/ajph.2020.305811.

Bogel-Burroughs, Nicholas, Shaila Dewan, and Kathleen Gray. "F.B.I. Says Michigan Anti-Government Group Plotted to Kidnap Gov. Gretchen Whitmer." *New York Times*, April 13, 2021. https://www.nytimes.com/2020/10/08/us /gretchen-whitmer-michigan-militia.html.

Boll, Christina, Julian Leppin, Anja Rossen, and Andre Wolf. "Overeducation— New Evidence for 25 European Countries." HWWI Research Paper No. 173, Hamburg Institute of International Economics, Hamburg, Germany, 2016. https://www.econstor.eu/bitstream/10419/130613/1/857142143.pdf.

Borjas, George J. *We Wanted Workers: Unraveling the Immigration Narrative.* New York: W. W. Norton, 2016.

Boskin, Michael J. "The best solution for inequality? Economic growth." World Economic Forum, December 13, 2019, https://www.weforum.org/agenda/2019 /12/economic-growth-is-the-answer.

Braudel, Fernand. *The Identity of France.* Vol. 2, bk. 2, *People and Production.* New York: HarperCollins, 1991.

Brzezinski, Zbigniew. *The Grand Chessboard: American Primacy and Its Geostrategic Imperatives.* New York: Basic Books, 1997.

Burrough, Bryan. *Days of Rage: America's Radical Underground, the FBI, and the Forgotten Age of Revolutionary Violence.* New York: Penguin Books, 2016.

Case, Anne, and Angus Deaton. *Deaths of Despair and the Future of Capitalism.* Princeton: Princeton University Press, 2020.

Chase, David, creator. *The Sopranos.* Season 5, episode 10, "Cold Cuts." Aired May 9, 2004, on HBO. https://www.hbo.com/the-sopranos/season-5/10-cold-cuts.

Clark, David. "Will Zelenskyy target all Ukrainian oligarchs equally?" *UkraineAlert* (blog), Atlantic Council, July 10, 2021. https://www.atlanticcouncil.org/blogs /ukrainealert/will-zelenskyy-target-all-ukrainian-oligarchs-equally/.

Confessore, Nicholas. "How Tucker Carlson Stoked White Fear to Conquer Cable." *New York Times*, April 30, 2022. https://www.nytimes.com/2022/04 /30/us/tucker-carlson-gop-republican-party.html.

Crockett, Zachary. "Donald Trump is the only US president ever with no political or military experience." *Vox,* January 23, 2017. https://www.vox.com/policy-and -politics/2016/11/11/13587532/donald-trump-no-experience.

Davis, David Brion. "Slavery, Emancipation, and Progress." In *British Abolitionism and the Question of Moral Progress in History*, edited by Donald A. Yerxa. Columbia, SC: University of South Carolina Press, 2012, 18–19.

Davis, William C. *A Concise History of the Civil War*. Fort Washington, PA: Eastern National, 2007. http://npshistory.com/publications/civil_war_series /1/sec1.htm.

Domhoff, G. William. "Power Elite Database." Who Rules America? Accessed August 10, 2022. https://whorulesamerica.ucsc.edu/power_elite/.

Domhoff, G. William. *Who Rules America?*, 5th ed., *Power, Politics, and Social Change.* New York: McGraw-Hill, 2006.

Domhoff, G. William, and Michael J. Webber. *Class and Power in the New Deal: Corporate Moderates, Southern Democrats, and the Liberal-Labor Coalition.* Redwood City: Stanford University Press, 2011.

Douglas, Karen M., Robbie M. Sutton, Mitchell J. Callan, Rael J. Dawtry, and Annelie J. Harvey. "Someone Is Pulling the Strings: Hypersensitive Agency Detection and Belief in Conspiracy Theories." *Thinking & Reasoning* 22, no. 1 (2016): 57–77. https://doi.org/10.1080/13546783.2015.1051586.

DQYDJ. "Average, Median, Top 1%, and all United States Net Worth Percentiles." DQYDJ. Accessed August 10, 2022. https://dqydj.com/average-median-top-net -worth-percentiles/.

Dupuy, Trevor N. *Understanding War: History and Theory of Combat*. St. Paul: Paragon House, 1987.

Ekins, Emily, and David Kemp. "E Pluribus Unum: Findings from the Cato Institute 2021 Immigration and Identity National Survey." Cato Institute. April 27, 2021. https://www.cato.org/survey-reports/e-pluribus-unum-findings-cato-institute -2021-immigration-identity-national-survey.

Federal Reserve Economic Data. "Federal Net Outlays as Percent of Gross Domestic Product." Economic Research, Federal Reserve Bank of St. Louis. Last modified April 1, 2022. https://fred.stlouisfed.org/series/FYONGDA188S.

Fogel, Robert William. *The Escape from Hunger and Premature Death, 1700–2100: Europe, America, and the Third World*. New York: Cambridge University Press, 2004.

Frank, Thomas. *The People, No: A Brief History of Anti-Populism*. New York: Metropolitan Books, 2020.

Frank, Thomas. *What's the Matter with Kansas? How Conservatives Won the Heart of America*. New York: Picador, 2005.

Fraser, Douglas. Resignation Letter from the Labor-Management Group, July 17, 1978. https://www.historyisaweapon.com/defcon1/fraserresign.html.

Freeman, Joanne B. "When Congress Was Armed and Dangerous." *New York Times*, January 11, 2011. https://www.nytimes.com/2011/01/12/opinion/12freeman.html.

Garcia, Tonya. "CEO average pay climbed more than $1 million in 2016." *MarketWatch*, April 13, 2017. https://www.marketwatch.com/story/ceo-average-pay-climbed-more-than-1-million-in-2016-2017-04-12.

Gethin, Amory, Clara Martínez-Toledano, and Thomas Piketty. "How politics became a contest dominated by two kinds of elite." *The Guardian*, August 5, 2021. https://www.theguardian.com/commentisfree/2021/aug/05/around-the-world-the-disadvantaged-have-been-left-behind-by-politicians-of-all-hues.

Ghani, Ashraf, and Clare Lockhart. *Fixing Failed States: A Framework for Rebuilding a Fractured World*. New York: Oxford University Press, 2008.

Gilens, Martin, and Benjamin I. Page. "Testing Theories of American Politics: Elites, Interest Groups, and Average Citizens." *Perspectives on Politics* 12, no. 3 (2014): 564–81. https://doi.org/10.1017/s1537592714001595.

Gleick, James. *Chaos: Making a New Science*. New York: Viking Press, 1987.

Goldin, Claudia. "Enrollment in institutions of higher education, by sex, enrollment status, and type of institution: 1869–1995." Table Bc523-536 in *Historical Statistics of the United States, Earliest Times to the Present: Millennial Edition*, edited by Susan B. Carter, Scott Sigmund Gartner, Michael R. Haines, Alan L. Olmstead, Richard Sutch, and Gavin Wright. New York: Cambridge University Press, 2006. http://dx.doi.org/10.1017/ISBN-9780511132971.Bc510-736.

Goldstone, Jack A. "Demographic Structural Theory: 25 Years On." *Cliodynamics: The Journal of Quantitative History and Cultural Evolution* 8, no. 2 (2017): 85–112. https://doi.org/10.21237/c7clio8237450.

Goldstone, Jack A. *Revolution and Rebellion in the Early Modern World*. Berkeley: University of California Press, 1991.

Goldstone, Jack A., Robert H. Bates, David L. Epstein, Ted Robert Gurr, Michael B. Lustik, Monty G. Marshall, Jay Ulfelder, and Mark Woodward. "A Global Model for Forecasting Political Instability." *American Journal of Political Science* 54, no. 1 (2010): 190–208. https://doi.org/10.1111/j.1540-5907.2009.00426.x.

Graetz, Michael J., and Ian Shapiro. *Death by a Thousand Cuts: The Fight over Taxing Inherited Wealth*. Princeton: Princeton University Press, 2006.

Greenhouse, Steven. "Bernie Sanders says Democrats are failing: 'The party has turned its back on the working class.'" *The Guardian*, January, 10 2022. https://

www.theguardian.com/us-news/2022/jan/10/bernie-sanders-democrats-failing -working-class-interview.

Grinin, Leonid, and Andrey Korotayev. "The Arab Spring: Causes, Conditions, and Driving Forces." In *Handbook of Revolutions in the 21st Century: The New Waves of Revolutions, and the Causes and Effects of Disruptive Political Change,* edited by Jack A. Goldstone, Leonid Grinin, and Andrey Korotayev. Switzerland: Springer, 2022, 595–624. https://doi.org/10.1007/978-3-030 -86468-2.

Gugliotta, Guy. "New Estimate Raises Civil War Death Toll." *New York Times,* April 2, 2012. https://www.nytimes.com/2012/04/03/science/civil-war-toll-up -by-20-percent-in-new-estimate.html.

Guilford, Gwynn, and Nikhil Sonnad. "What Steve Bannon Really Wants." *Quartz,* February 3, 2017. https://qz.com/898134/what-steve-bannon-really-wants/.

GWonline. "American Civil War." GWonline. Accessed August 10, 2022. https:// gwonline.unc.edu/node/11653.

Haidt, Jonathan. "Why the Past 10 Years of American Life Have Been Uniquely Stupid." *The Atlantic,* April 11, 2022. https://www.theatlantic.com/magazine /archive/2022/05/social-media-democracy-trust-babel/629369/.

Hanauer, Nick. "The Pitchforks Are Coming . . . For Us Plutocrats." *Politico Magazine,* July/August 2014. https://www.politico.com/magazine/story/2014/06/the -pitchforks-are-coming-for-us-plutocrats-108014/.

Igielnik, Ruth, Scott Keeter, and Hannah Hartig. "Behind Biden's 2020 Victory." Pew Research Center, June 30, 2021. https://www.pewresearch.org/politics/2021 /06/30/behind-bidens-2020-victory/.

Johansmeyer, Thomas. "How 2020 protests changed insurance forever." World Economic Forum. February 22, 2021. https://www.weforum.org/agenda/2021 /02/2020-protests-changed-insurance-forever/.

Kaplan, Jed O., Kristen M. Krumhardt, Erle C. Ellis, William F. Ruddiman, Carsten Lemmen, and Kees Klein Goldewijk. "Holocene Carbon Emissions as a Result of Anthropogenic Land Cover Change." *The Holocene* 21, no. 5 (2010): 775–91. https://doi.org/10.1177/0959683610386983.

Kolko, Gabriel. *The Triumph of Conservatism: A Reinterpretation of American History, 1900–1916.* New York: Free Press, 1963.

Komlos, John. *Foundations of Real-World Economics.* 3rd ed. New York: Routledge, 2023.

Komlos, John. "Growth of Welfare and Its Distribution in the U.S., 1979–2013." *Journal of Income Distribution* 28, no. 1 (2019): 1–19. https://doi.org/10.25071 /1874-6322.40399.

Komlos, John, and Marieluise Baur. "From the Tallest to (One of) the Fattest: The Enigmatic Fate of the American Population in the 20th Century." Preprint, submitted September 14, 2003. https://doi.org/10.2139/ssrn.444501.

Korotayev, Andrey, and Julia Zinkina. "Egyptian Revolution: A Demographic Structural Analysis." *Entelequia* 13 (2011): 139–69.

Korotayev, Andrey, and L. Isaev. "The Anatomy of the Egyptian Counter-revolution." *Mirovaya Ekonomika i Mezhdunarodnye Otnosheniya* 8 (2014): 91–100.

Korotayev, Andrey, Julia Zinkina, Svetlana Kobzeva, Justislav Bozhevolnov, Daria Khaltourina, Artemy Malkov, and Sergey Malkov. "A Trap at the Escape from the Trap? Demographic-Structural Factors of Political Instability in Modern Africa and West Asia." *Cliodynamics: The Journal of Quantitative History and Cultural Evolution* 2, no. 2 (2011): 276–303. https://doi.org/10.21237/c7clio22217.

Kramer, Andrew E. "Islamic Battalions, Stocked with Chechens, Aid Ukraine in War with Rebels." *New York Times,* July 7, 2015. https://www.nytimes.com /2015/07/08/world/europe/islamic-battalions-stocked-with-chechens-aid -ukraine-in-war-with-rebels.html.

Krugman, Paul. *The Conscience of a Liberal.* New York: W. W. Norton, 2007.

Lizunov, V. S. "Origins." In *The Past Passes Before Me* [in Russian]. Orekhovo-Zuyevo: Bogorodsk-Noginsk, 2007. https://www.bogorodsk-noginsk.ru/articles /24_lizunov1.html.

Major Cities Chiefs Association. *MCCA Report on the 2020 Protests and Civil Unrest.* Salt Lake City, UT: Major Cities Chiefs Association, October 2020. https:// majorcitieschiefs.com/wp-content/uploads/2021/01/MCCA-Report-on-the -2020-Protest-and-Civil-Unrest.pdf.

Mann, Michael. *The Sources of Social Power: A History of Power from the Beginning to A.D. 1760.* Cambridge, UK: Cambridge University Press, 1986.

Malamud, Bruce D., Gleb Morein, and Donald L. Turcotte. "Forest Fires: An Example of Self-Organized Critical Behavior." *Science* 281, no. 5384 (1998): 1840–42. https://doi.org/10.1126/science.281.5384.1840.

Marche, Stephen. "The next US civil war is already here—we just refuse to see it." *The Guardian,* January 4, 2022. https://www.theguardian.com/world/2022/jan /04/next-us-civil-war-already-here-we-refuse-to-see-it.

Mastrangelo, Dominick. "Jon Stewart rips 'dishonest propagandist' Tucker Carlson for Putin comments." *The Hill,* March 3, 2022. https://thehill.com/homenews /media/596764-jon-stewart-rips-dishonest-propagandist-tucker-carlson-for -putin-comments.

Maté, Aaron. "By using Ukraine to fight Russia, the US provoked Putin's war." *Aaron Mate* (Substack blog), March 5, 2022. https://mate.substack.com/p/by -using-ukraine-to-fight-russia.

McCarty, Nolan, Keith T. Poole, and Howard Rosenthal. *Polarized America: The Dance of Ideology and Unequal Riches.* Cambridge, MA: MIT Press, 2006.

McGhee, Heather. *The Sum of Us: What Racism Costs Everyone and How We Can Prosper Together.* New York: One World, 2021.

Michel, Casey. "Who Is Ihor Kolomoisky?" *The Spectator,* March 13, 2022. https://www.spectator.co.uk/article/who-is-ihor-kolomoisky-.

Middleton, Guy D. "The show must go on: Collapse, resilience, and transformation in 21st-century archaeology." *Reviews in Anthropology* 46, no. 2–3 (2017): 78–105. https://doi.org/10.1080/00938157.2017.1343025.

Mishel, Lawrence, and Josh Bivens. "Identifying the policy levers generating wage suppression and wage inequality." Economic Policy Institute, May 13, 2021. https://www.epi.org/unequalpower/publications/wage-suppression-inequality/.

Mizruchi, Mark. *The Fracturing of the American Corporate Elite.* Cambridge, MA: Harvard University Press, 2013.

Nagle, Angela. "The Left Case Against Open Borders." *American Affairs,* 2, no. 4 (2018). https://americanaffairsjournal.org/2018/11/the-left-case-against-open-borders/.

Neef, Christian. "Yanukovych's Fall: The Power of Ukraine's Billionaires." *Der Spiegel,* February 25, 2014. https://www.spiegel.de/international/europe/how-oligarchs-in-ukraine-prepared-for-the-fall-of-yanukovych-a-955328.html.

Oates, Stephen B. *Abraham Lincoln: The Man Behind the Myths.* New York: Harper & Row, 1984.

OpenSecrets. "Lobbying Data Summary." OpenSecrets. Accessed August 10, 2022. https://www.opensecrets.org/federal-lobbying/summary.

OpenSecrets. "Election Trends." OpenSecrets. Accessed August 10, 2022. https://www.opensecrets.org/elections-overview/election-trends.

OpenSecrets. "Industries." OpenSecrets. Accessed August 10, 2022. https://www.opensecrets.org/federal-lobbying/industries.

OpenSecrets. "Our Vision and Mission: Inform, Empower & Advocate." OpenSecrets. Accessed August 10, 2022. https://www.opensecrets.org/about/.

Orlandi, Georg, Daniel Hoyer, Zhao Hongjun, James S. Bennett, Majid Benam, Kathryn Kohn, and Peter Turchin. "Structural-Demographic Analysis of the Qing Dynasty (1644–1912) Collapse in China." Preprint, submitted November 2, 2022. https://osf.io/preprints/socarxiv/5awhk/.

Ortmans, Oscar, Elisabetta Mazzeo, Kira Meshcherina, and Andrey Korotayev. "Modeling Social Pressures Toward Political Instability in the United Kingdom After 1960: A Demographic Structural Analysis." *Cliodynamics: The Journal of Quantitative History and Cultural Evolution* 8, no. 2 (2017): 113–58. https://doi.org/10.21237/c7clio8237313.

Palmer, James. "Xi's Prosperity Gospel." China Brief, *Foreign Policy,* August 25, 2021. https://foreignpolicy.com/2021/08/25/china-xi-jinping-common-prosperity-billionaires/.

Patriotic Millionaires. Accessed August 10, 2022. https://patrioticmillionaires.org/.

Phillips, Kevin. *Wealth and Democracy: A Political History of the American Rich.* New York: Broadway Books, 2002.

Phillips-Fein, Kim. *Invisible Hands: The Businessmen's Crusade Against the New Deal.* New York: W. W. Norton, 2009.

Piketty, Thomas. *Capital in the Twenty-First Century.* Cambridge, MA: Harvard University Press, 2014.

Platt, Stephen R. *Autumn in the Heavenly Kingdom: China, the West, and the Epic Story of the Taiping Civil War.* New York: Vintage Books, 2012.

Poole, Keith T., and Howard Rosenthal. *Congress: A Political-Economic History of Roll Call Voting.* Oxford: Oxford University Press, 2000.

Poole, Keith T., and Howard Rosenthal. "The Polarization of American Politics." *The Journal of Politics* 46, no. 4 (1984): 1061–79. https://doi.org/10.2307/2131242.

Popper, Karl R. *The Poverty of Historicism.* London: Routledge, 1957.

Potter, David M. *The Impending Crisis, 1848–1861.* New York: Harper & Row, 1976.

Putnam, Robert D. *Bowling Alone: The Collapse and Revival of American Community.* New York: Simon & Schuster, 2000.

Radosh, Ronald. "Steve Bannon, Trump's Top Guy, Told Me He Was 'a Leninist.'" *Daily Beast,* August 22, 2016. https://www.thedailybeast.com/steve-bannon-trumps-top-guy-told-me-he-was-a-leninist.

Reich, David. *Who We Are and How We Got Here: Ancient DNA and the New Science of the Human Past.* New York: Pantheon Books, 2018.

Ring, Trudy. "Maddow: Russians May Be Controlling Our Government." *Advocate,* March 10, 2017. https://www.advocate.com/politics/2017/3/10/maddow-russians-may-be-controlling-our-government.

Robinson, Andrew. "Did Einstein really say that?" *Nature* 557 (2018): 30. doi: https://doi.org/10.1038/d41586-018-05004-4.

Rosenberg, Susan. *An American Radical: Political Prisoner in My Own Country.* New York: Citadel Press, 2011.

Roser, Max. "Extreme poverty: how far have we come, how far do we still have to go?" Our World in Data. Accessed November 22, 2021. https://ourworldindata.org/extreme-poverty-in-brief.

Royle, Edward. *Revolutionary Britannia? Reflections on the Threat of Revolution in Britain, 1789–1848.* Manchester, UK: Manchester University Press, 2000.

Sauter, Michael B., Grant Suneson, and Samuel Stebbins. "The Net Worth of the American Presidents: Washington to Trump." *24/7 Wall St.,* March 2, 2020. https://247wallst.com/special-report/2020/03/02/the-net-worth-of-the-american-presidents-washington-to-trump-3/.

Scheiber, Noam. "Middle-Class Pay Lost Pace. Is Washington to Blame?" *New York Times,* May 13, 2021. https://www.nytimes.com/2021/05/13/business/economy/middle-class-pay.html.

Scheidel, Walter. *The Great Leveler: Violence and the History of Inequality from the Stone Age to the Twenty-First Century.* Princeton: Princeton University Press, 2018.

Scott, Mark. "Despite cries of censorship, conservatives dominate social media." *Politico,* October 26, 2020. https://www.politico.com/news/2020/10/26/censor ship-conservatives-social-media-432643.

Scott, Robert E. "We can reshore manufacturing jobs, but Trump hasn't done it." Economic Policy Institute, August 10, 2020. https://www.epi.org/publication /reshoring-manufacturing-jobs/.

Seshat: Global History Databank. Accessed August 10, 2022. http://seshatdatabank .info/.

Silva, R., G. S. França, C. S. Vilar, and J. S. Alcaniz. "Nonextensive models for earthquakes." *Physical Review E* 73, no. 2 (2006): 1–5. https://doi.org/10.1103 /physreve.73.026102.

Smith, Noah. "America Is Pumping Out Too Many Ph.D.s." *Bloomberg,* January 4, 2021. https://www.bloomberg.com/opinion/articles/2021-01-04/america-is -pumping-out-too-many-ph-d-s.

Southern Poverty Law Center. *The Year in Hate and Extremism 2019.* Montgomery, AL: Southern Poverty Law Center, 2020. https://www.splcenter.org/sites/default /files/yih_2020_final.pdf.

Southern Poverty Law Center. *The Year in Hate and Extremism 2021.* Montgomery, AL: Southern Poverty Law Center, 2022. https://www.splcenter.org/sites/default /files/splc-2021-year-in-hate-extremism-report.pdf.

Stanage, Niall. "Cruz, Rubio ramp up criticisms of big business." *The Hill,* May 3, 2021. https://thehill.com/homenews/campaign/551318-exclusive-cruz-rubio -ramp-up-criticisms-of-big-business/.

Standing, Guy. "Meet the precariat, the new global class fuelling the rise of popu-lism." World Economic Forum. November 9, 2016. https://www.weforum.org /agenda/2016/11/precariat-global-class-rise-of-populism/.

Standing, Guy. *The Precariat: The New Dangerous Class.* London: Bloomsbury, 2011.

Stansbury, Anna, and Lawrence Summers. "Declining Worker Power and Ameri-can Economic Performance." Paper presented at the BPEA Conference, March 19, 2020. https://www.brookings.edu/wp-content/uploads/2020/03/stansbury -summers-conference-draft.pdf.

Steckel, Richard H. "Heights and human welfare: Recent developments and new directions." *Explorations in Economic History* 46, no. 1 (2009): 1–23. https://doi .org/10.1016/j.eeh.2008.12.001.

Stiglitz, Joseph E. *The Price of Inequality: How Today's Divided Society Endangers Our Future.* New York: W. W. Norton, 2012.

Storey, R. L. *The End of the House of Lancaster.* New York: Stein and Day, 1967.

Taylor, Jennifer. "Here's How Much Every Living US President Is Worth: Where Does Biden Rank?" GOBankingRates. May 30, 2022. https://www.gobank ingrates.com/net-worth/politicians/heres-how-much-every-living-us -president-is-worth/.

Teitelbaum, Benjamin R. *War for Eternity: Inside Bannon's Far-Right Circle of Global Power Brokers.* New York: Dey Street Books, 2020.

Thayer, Parker. "Living Room Pundit's Guide to Soros District Attorneys," Capital Research Center. January 18, 2022. https://capitalresearch.org/article/living-room-pundits-guide-to-soros-district-attorneys/.

Trevor-Roper, Hugh. "Re-inventing Hitler." *The Sunday Times,* February 18, 1973.

Turchin, Peter. *Ages of Discord: A Structural-Demographic Analysis of American History.* Chaplin, CT: Beresta Books, 2016.

Turchin, Peter. "Building nations after conflict." *Nature* 453 (2008): 986–87. https://doi.org/10.1038/453986a.

Turchin, Peter. "Modeling Periodic Waves of Integration in the Afro-Eurasian World-System." In *Globalization as Evolutionary Process,* edited by George Modelski, Tessaleno Devezas, and William R. Thompson. London: Routledge, 2007, 163–91.

Turchin, Peter. "A Theory for Formation of Large Empires." *Journal of Global History* 4, no. 2 (2009): 191–217. https://doi.org/10.1017/s174002280900312x.

Turchin, Peter, Harvey Whitehouse, Sergey Gavrilets, Daniel Hoyer, Pieter François, James S. Bennett, Kevin C. Feeney, et al. "Disentangling the Evolutionary Drivers of Social Complexity: A Comprehensive Test of Hypotheses." *Science Advances* 8, no. 25 (2022). https://doi.org/10.1126/sciadv.abn3517.

Turchin, Peter, Nina Witoszek, Stefan Thurner, David Garcia, Roger Griffin, Daniel Hoyer, Atle Midttun, James Bennett, Knut Myrum Næss, and Sergey Gavrilets. "A History of Possible Futures: Multipath Forecasting of Social Breakdown, Recovery, and Resilience." *Cliodynamics: The Journal of Quantitative History and Cultural Evolution* 9, no. 2 (2018): 124–39. https://doi.org/10.21237/c7clio9242078.

United States Census Bureau. "Historical Income Tables: Households." United States Census Bureau. Last updated August 18, 2022. https://www.census.gov/data/tables/time-series/demo/income-poverty/historical-income-households.html.

US Department of Education, Institute of Education Sciences. "Immediate College Enrollment Rate." National Center for Education Statistics. Last updated May 2022. https://nces.ed.gov/programs/coe/indicator/cpa.

Veritasium. "The Surprising Secret of Synchronization." March 31, 2021. YouTube video, 20:57. https://www.youtube.com/watch?v=t-_VPRCtiUg.

Walker, Shaun. "Azov fighters are Ukraine's greatest weapon and may be its greatest threat." *The Guardian,* September 10, 2014. https://www.theguardian.com/world/2014/sep/10/azov-far-right-fighters-ukraine-neo-nazis.

Walter, Barbara F. *How Civil Wars Start: And How to Stop Them.* New York: Crown, 2022.

Ward, George, Jan-Emmanuel De Neve, Lyle H. Ungar, and Johannes C. Eichstaedt. "(Un)Happiness and Voting in U.S. Presidential Elections." *Journal of Personality and Social Psychology* 120, no. 2 (2021): 370–83. https://doi.org/10.1037/pspi0000249.

Weigel, David. "Bernie Sanders criticizes 'open borders' at Hispanic Chamber of Commerce." *Washington Post,* July 30, 2015. https://www.washingtonpost.com/news/post-politics/wp/2015/07/30/bernie-sanders-criticizes-open-borders-at-hispanic-chamber-of-commerce/.

Weymouth, Lally. "Interview with Ukrainian presidential candidate Petro Poroshenko." *Washington Post,* April 25, 2014. https://www.washingtonpost.com/opinions/interview-with-ukrainian-presidential-candidate-petro-poroshenko/2014/04/25/74c73a48-cbbd-11e3-93eb-6c0037dde2ad_story.html.

White, Jeremy B. "4 wealthy donors fuel overhaul of California's criminal justice system." *Politico,* July 17, 2021. https://www.politico.com/states/california/story/2021/07/17/four-wealthy-donors-fuel-overhaul-of-californias-criminal-justice-system-1388261.

Wolff, Edward N. "Household Wealth Trends in the United States, 1962 to 2019: Median Wealth Rebounds . . . but Not Enough." NBER Working Paper No. 28383, National Bureau of Economic Research, Cambridge, MA, January 2021. https://www.nber.org/system/files/working_papers/w28383/w28383.pdf.

Zengerle, Jason. "The Rise of the Tucker Carlson Politician." *New York Times Magazine,* March 22, 2022, https://www.nytimes.com/2022/03/22/magazine/tucker-carlson-politician.html.

Zhang, Haihui. "What Are Chinese Local Gazetteers?" University of Pittsburgh. Last updated April 28, 2021. https://pitt.libguides.com/chinese_local_gazetteers.

Zirkle, Conway. "The Role of Liberty Hyde Bailey and Hugo de Vries in the Rediscovery of Mendelism." *Journal of the History of Biology* 1, no. 2 (1968): 205–18. https://www.jstor.org/stable/4330495.

INDEX